THE SAMUEL & ALTHEA STROUM LECTURES
IN JEWISH STUDIES

THE SAMUEL & ALTHEA STROUM LECTURES
IN JEWISH STUDIES

Judaism
and Hellenism
in Antiquity

Conflict or Confluence?

Lee I. Levine

University of Washington Press
SEATTLE *&* LONDON

Library of Congress Cataloging-in-Publication Data

Levine, Lee I.
Judaism and Hellenism in antiquity : conflict or confluence? / Lee I. Levine
p.   cm. — (The Samuel & Althea Stroum lectures in Jewish studies)
Includes bibliographical references and index.
ISBN 0-295-97682-9 (alk. paper)
1. Judaism—Relations—Greek.   2. Jews—Civilization—Greek
influences.   3. Judaism—History—Post-exilic period, 586 B.C.–210 A.D.
4. Greece—Religion.   5. Synagogues—History.   6. Hellenism
I. Title.   II. Series: Samuel and Althea Stroum lectures in Jewish studies.
BM536.G7L49   1998
296'.09'014—dc21   97-46205
CIP

The Samuel & Althea Stroum Lectures in Jewish Studies

Samuel Stroum, businessman, community leader, and philanthropist, by a major gift to the Jewish Federation of Greater Seattle, established the Samuel and Althea Stroum Philanthropic Fund.

In recognition of Mr. and Mrs. Stroum's deep interest in Jewish history and culture, the Board of Directors of the Jewish Federation of Greater Seattle, in cooperation with the Jewish Studies Program of the Henry M. Jackson School of International Studies at the University of Washington, established an annual lectureship at the University of Washington known as the Samuel and Althea Stroum Lectureship in Jewish Studies. This lectureship makes it possible to bring to the area outstanding scholars and interpreters of Jewish thought, thus promoting a deeper understanding of Jewish history, religion, and culture. Such understanding can lead to an enhanced appreciation of the Jewish contributions to the historical and cultural traditions that have shaped the American nation.

The terms of the gift also provide for the publication from time to time of the lectures or other appropriate materials resulting from or related to the lectures.

To my parents-in-law,
Anne and Irving Karp

Contents

Preface

JUDAISM'S ENCOUNTER WITH HELLENISM IN THE ANCIENT world has fascinated scholars for generations. These two ostensibly different cultures clashed on occasion, yet in most instances contacts of Jews and Judaism with the Hellenistic-Roman world proved immensely fructifying and creative. Some Jews may have been intimidated by this culture, but many found it attractive, stimulating, and even indispensable. Jewish exposure to Greek wisdom is dramatically reflected in an account told by Aristotle about a Jew he met in Asia Minor (as reported by Clearchus of Soli):

> Now this man, who was entertained by a large circle of friends and was on his way from the interior to the coast, not only spoke Greek, but had the soul of a Greek. During my stay in Asia, he visited the same places as I did, and came to converse with me and some other scholars, to test our learning. But as one who had been intimate with many cultivated persons, it was rather he who imparted to us something of his own. (Josephus, *Against Apion* 1.180-81)

The story assumes that some Jews, at least, were well acquainted with Greek philosophical terms and issues, and Aristotle's admiration was indeed remarkable.

The Jewish encounter with Greco-Roman culture was both extensive and intensive. All Jewish communities, in Palestine and throughout the Diaspora, were affected, as was every area of Jewish life. The intensive contact following Alexander's conquest gained even more momentum under the Hasmoneans and Hero d. Even with the destruction of Jerusalem and the Temple, and defeat at the hands of the Roman armies on three occasions within a period of 65 years (between 70 and 135 C.E.), this process continued right up to the end of late antiquity. Because the phenomenon was so ubiquitous, the evidence in this regard is extensive. A myriad of sources—literary, epigraphical, and archeological—attests to this influence in one form or another, and to a greater or lesser degree.

The subject of the impact of Hellenism on Jewish society has always been close to my academic interests. Influenced by the oral and written teachings of my mentors, Saul Lieberman, Salo Baron, Elias Bickerman, Morton Smith, and, most significantly, Gerson Cohen, I have pursued the subject throughout my academic career, teaching about this issue and often referring to it in my writings.

The Samuel and Althea Stroum lecture series offered an opportunity to address the phenomenon of the influence and impact of Greco-Roman culture on the Jews of antiquity in a more concerted manner. For this I am most appreciative.

Given the magnitude and complexity of this phenomenon, it is impossible to do justice to the topic in any single volume. Yet, the issue is too important not to try and offer an overview, even within the purview of this modest volume. In order to avoid casting the net too widely, I have chosen to focus on three topics, which are diverse in nature yet span the entire Greco-Roman and Byzantine eras: the city of Jerusalem at the end of the Second Temple period, rabbinic culture, and the ancient synagogue. These topics involve the use of a wide range of sources that have come down to us from antiquity, such as Josephus, the New Testament, and Philo, as well as archeology (including artistic and epigraphical remains) and rabbinic literature.

I wish to thank a number of colleagues who were kind enough to read all or parts of this manuscript; their comments were most enlightening and helpful: Professors Joseph Geiger, David Golinkin,

Eric Gruen, Uriel Rappaport, and Daniel Schwartz. Needless to say, I bear full responsibility for the substance and form of what follows.

My thanks to Naomi Pascal, Julidta Tarver, and Patricia Draher of the University of Washington Press for their help in facilitating this publication, to the Jewish Studies Program of the University of Washington for funding the preparation of the manuscript for publication, and to Ḥani Davis for accomplishing this last task with skill and professionalism.

I am grateful to Professor Hillel Kieval for his kind invitation to offer these lectures at the University of Washington in Seattle as part of the Samuel and Althea Stroum Lectures of 1994. The warm reception of the members of the Jewish Studies Program made that week an unforgettable one for my wife, Mira, and me. A very special thanks in this regard is due Dorothy Becker, administrator of the Jewish Studies Program, for her care and concern before, during, and after the lecture series. There could be no better representative of Seattle hospitality at its best.

March 1998
Jerusalem

JUDAISM AND HELLENISM IN ANTIQUITY

CHAPTER I

Hellenism and the
Jewish World of Antiquity

ONE OF THE MOST ENGAGING AND PRODUCTIVE AREAS OF research in the modern study of Jewish history in antiquity is the issue of Hellenization. In attempting to legitimize the scientific study of Jewish topics, nineteenth-century scholars often highlighted phenomena common to Jews and their surrounding society.[1] Only in the twentieth century, however, has this field become central to the concerns of both Jewish and Christian scholars.

A number of factors—some academic, others of a quite different nature—come into play in bringing this subject to the fore. Prominent in the latter category is the Jewish experience in the modern era. Given an open cosmopolitan setting in the Western world, Jews have been able to navigate relatively freely and unencumbered. This freedom affects where they live, and has socioeconomic, political, and cultural implications as well. Jews have not only become integrated into the wider society, but they have also brought many elements of the outside world into their homes, organizations, schools, and synagogues. Not surprisingly, then, the involvement of Jews in the outside world and the profound influences that this

---

1. G. D. Cohen, *Studies in the Variety of Rabbinic Cultures* (New York: Jewish Publication Society, 1991), pp. 299–324; I. Schorsch, "Ideology and History," in H. Graetz, *The Structure of Jewish History and Other Essays*, ed. I. Schorsch (New York: Jewish Theological Seminary, 1975), pp. 1–62. See also A. Momigliano, "J. G. Droysen between Greeks and Jews," *History and Theory* 9 (1970): 139–53 (reprinted in A. Momigliano, *Essays in Ancient and Modern Historiography* [Oxford: Blackwell, 1977], pp. 307–23).

contact has had upon them have stimulated scholars to investigate the Greco-Roman (and medieval Spanish) experience, which in many ways is analogous to the Jewish situation today.

Moreover, many Jewish scholars were especially interested in exploring this realm owing to their own religious biases. For those of more liberal persuasion the implications of discovering outside influences are clear. Indication of such contacts and their salutary effects on the Jews serves to strengthen the hand of these scholars in contemporary debates. Indeed, arguing for religious change in light of new developments in the modern world gains a measure of legitimacy if one can demonstrate that similar dynamics were operative in both the Second Temple and rabbinic periods. It is thus not coincidental that research in this area has often emanated from those associated in some way with the Reform and Conservative movements, such as L. Zunz, A. Geiger, L. Herzfeld, K. Kohler, I. Elbogen, I. Davidson, L. Finkelstein, S. W. Baron, G. Cohen, B. Cohen, S. J. D. Cohen, and others.[2]

2. L. Zunz, *Die Namen der Juden: Eine Geschichtliche Untersuchung* (Leipzig: L. Fort, 1837); idem, *Literaturgeschichte der syngogalen Poesie* (Berlin: Gerschel, 1865); A. Geiger, *Urschrift und Übersetzungen der Bibel in ihrer Abhängigkeit von der innern Entwicklung des Judenthums* (Breslau: Hainauer, 1857); M. Meyer, "Abraham Geiger's Historical Judaism," in *New Perspectives on Abraham Geiger: An HUC-JIR Symposium* (Cincinnati: Hebrew Union College Press, 1975), pp. 3–16. On L. Herzfeld, see S. Baron, *History and Jewish Historians: Essays and Addresses* (Philadelphia: Jewish Publication Society, 1964), pp. 322–43; K. Kohler, "Über die Ursprunge und Grundformen der synagogalen Liturgie," *MGWJ* 37 (1893): 441–51, 489–97; I. Elbogen, *Jewish Liturgy: A Comprehensive History* (Philadelphia: Jewish Publication Society, 1993); I. Davidson, *Otzar Hashira Vehapiyyut* (4 vols.; New York: Jewish Theological Seminary, 1924–33); L. Finkelstein, "Maccabean Documents in the Passover Haggadah," *HTR* 30 (1943): 1–38; Baron, *History and Jewish Historians*, pp. 23–42; idem, *A Social and Religious History of the Jews* (18 vols.; New York: Columbia University Press, 1952–83); G. D. Cohen, "The Blessing of Assimilation," in *Great Jewish Speeches throughout History*, ed. S. Forman (North Vale, NJ: Jason Aronson, 1994), pp. 183–91; S. J. D. Cohen, "The Origins of the Matrilineal Principle in Rabbinic Law," *AJS Review* 10 (1985): 19–53. See also S. Heschel, "Abraham Geiger on the Origins of Christianity: The Political Strategies of *Wissenschaft*

On an academic level, the nature and extent of such outside influences are continuously being highlighted by the ongoing discovery of ancient materials. Ancient texts often point to the commonality between biblical practices and those of the surrounding cultures, and to the apparent influences of the latter on the former. The discoveries of Nuzi, Mari, Ugarit, and Ebla are cases in point for the biblical period, and the many documents that have surfaced over this last century relating to Greco-Roman Egypt and elsewhere tell the same story for later antiquity.[3] A number of studies have dealt with Hellenism specifically and the Roman East generally, further highlighting this widespread cultural influence in various parts of the region.[4]

Of no less importance is the steady stream of archeological discoveries brought to light over the last century which not only have added to our knowledge of antiquity but, more specifically, have had a considerable impact on the study of Hellenization. Throughout antiquity the material culture of the Jews was heavily indebted to, and in many cases totally dependent on, that of the regnant contemporary culture. The Jews never boasted an architectural or artistic tradition of their own (save, perhaps, a limited cluster of symbols that evolved only in late antiquity). In scores of excavations at Jewish sites, evidence for the impact of contem-

---

des Judentums in an Era of Acculturation," in *Jewish Assimilation, Acculturation and Accommodation: Past Traditions, Current Issues and Future Prospects,* ed. M. Mor (Lanham, Nebr.: University Press of America, 1992), pp. 110–26.

3. See, for example, N. Sarna, *Understanding Genesis* (New York: Jewish Theological Seminary, 1966), pp. 4–23, 39–59, 86–92, 102–3, 127–29; V. Tcherikover, A. Fuks, and M. Stern, *CPJ.*

4. See, for example, P. Grimal et al., *Hellenism and the Rise of Rome* (London: Weidenfeld and Nicolson, 1968); F. Millar, "The Phoenician Cities: A Case-Study of Hellenisation," in *Proceedings of the Cambridge Philological Society* 209 (1983): 55–68; A. Kuhrt and S. Sherwin-White, eds., *Hellenism in the East* (London: Duckworth, 1987); G. W. Bowersock, *Hellenism in Late Antiquity* (Cambridge: Cambridge University Press, 1990); F. Millar, *The Roman East, 31 BC–AD 337* (Cambridge: Harvard University Press, 1993).

porary civilization is discernible at every turn, from architecture and art to small finds and epigraphical remains. Thus, archeological data continuously enhance our awareness of the extent of Hellenization, while serving to open new avenues of investigation and research.[5]

THE ISSUE OF "HELLENISM" AND "HELLENIZATION" IN MODERN RESEARCH

Two studies on Hellenization and the Jews in the Greco-Roman period, conducted in the 1930s and 1940s, constituted major contributions in their own right and have also had a profound influence on subsequent research. Two scholars, living on separate continents and investigating very different historical contexts on the basis of entirely different sources, published within five years of each other what proved to be pioneering studies in the field. E. Bickerman's monograph *Der Gott der Makkabäer* (1937; English trans. *The God of the Maccabees*, 1979), with its revolutionary interpretation of the causes of Antiochus IV's persecutions in 167 B.C.E., focused on the Seleucid context of this period of Jewish history and the key role of Jewish Hellenizers in promoting these events. In subsequent years, Bickerman published a series of seminal studies elucidating the wider context of events and documents relating to Jewish history in the Hellenistic era. His other two books on the subject, *From Ezra to the Last of the Maccabees* (1962) and his posthumous *The Jews in the Greek Age* (1988), further elaborate on the extensive influence of Hellenism on the Jews in the period between the conquest of Alexander and the Maccabean uprising.

---

5. Convenient summaries of archeological excavations and finds may be found in *NEAEHL*; R. Hachlili, *Ancient Jewish Art and Archaeology in the Land of Israel* (Leiden: Brill, 1988). See also E. Meyers and J. Strange, *Archaeology, the Rabbis and Early Christianity* (Nashville: Abingdon, 1981).

Bickerman, one of the foremost scholars of ancient history in the twentieth century, approached Jewish history with an unmatched command of Greco-Roman sources as well as a profound understanding of classical society and culture.

The other seminal work, appearing in 1942, was S. Lieberman's *Greek in Jewish Palestine*. Here, for the first time, in a series of incisive and wide-ranging studies by one who was later recognized as the foremost talmudic scholar of the century, was an exposition of the extent to which the rabbis knew Greek and were familiar with Greek culture. A companion volume, *Hellenism in Jewish Palestine*, appeared eight years later. True enough, the existence of well over three thousand Greek and Latin loanwords in rabbinic literature had already been noted for decades, since the appearance of S. Krauss's monumental *Griechische und Lateinische Lehnwörter im Talmud, Midrasch und Targum* (1899). Lieberman, however, went beyond the use of Greek and Latin words and phrases to demonstrate just how extensive this familiarity was—embracing rabbinic knowledge of pagan customs, administrative organization, legal terminology, and the natural sciences. The timing of Lieberman's first publication was influenced by the discovery of the Bet She'arim necropolis in the southwestern Galilee in the late 1930s. Having been in constant contact with the site's excavator, B. Mazar, Lieberman learned of the high degree of Hellenization at this major Jewish necropolis that has come to be identified with R. Judah the Prince, editor of the Mishnah, as well as with later Patriarchs and several rabbinic figures. How, it was asked, could one explain such widespread Hellenization in a supposedly rabbinic cemetery? Such a correlation, according to Lieberman, should not be surprising, for indeed many rabbis were well versed in contemporary Greco-Roman culture.

The studies of Bickerman and Lieberman signaled a surge of investigations over the ensuing decades, all relating to Hellenistic contacts and influences on the Jews and Judaism.[6] E. R. Good-enough, having devoted many years to compiling data regarding Jewish art in this period, presented the material in a fully documented and accessible fashion in his multivolume work *Jewish Symbols in the Greco-Roman Period* (1953–68). In fact, Good-enough is to be credited with having a major hand in creating the field of ancient Jewish art history, which hitherto had been largely unknown. However, as Goodenough emphasized on a number of occasions, his collection of Jewish art was not assembled for its own sake but served as a stepping stone for a grand theory regarding the meaning of these Jewish symbols and the nature of Judaism at this time. His claim was that Jewish art is the most important evidence for understanding popular Judaism in antiquity, and that the most fundamental beliefs of the Jews revolved around the ideas of mysticism and salvation—ideas that he claimed were common themes in popular Greco-Roman religions of the time. Thus, Jewish art forms, and the religious beliefs reflected therein, can only be understood within their Greco-Roman setting. While Goodenough's suggested reconstruction of popular mystical religion among Jews was severely criticized by both Jewish and non-Jewish scholars, his notions regarding the extensive Hellenization of Jewish art and its nonrabbinic provenance gained much acceptance in subsequent years.[7]

6. Mention should be made of H. A. Wolfson's two-volume monumental study, *Philo: Foundations of Religious Philosophy in Judaism, Christianity, and Islam* (Cambridge: Harvard University Press, 1948). As majestic as this study was, and despite its revolutionary thesis regarding our understanding of the Greek and Jewish worlds of Philo, Wolfson's work had a limited impact on other fields of ancient Jewish studies. This was undoubtedly due to the fact that Philonic research was all too often viewed as sui generis and not reflective of what was going on in most Jewish circles of antiquity.

7. For a comprehensive and insightful summary of the reactions to Good-enough's magnum opus, see M. Smith, "Goodenough's 'Jewish Symbols' in Retrospect," *JBL* 86 (1967): 53–68.

During the fifteen years in which Goodenough's volumes were published, other scholars were addressing the issue of Hellenism from various perspectives. M. Smith's popular article entitled "Palestinian Judaism in the First Century" (1956) made a brief but trenchant statement regarding the impact of Hellenism before 70 C.E. on Jewish society in general and on the Pharisees in particular. A year later, S. Stein's article on the relationship of the Passover seder and *Haggadah* to Greco-Roman symposia pointed to the remarkable parallels between these two religious and social frameworks,[8] and B. Cohen's two-volume *Jewish and Roman Law: A Comparative Study* (1966) suggested many points of contact between these two legal corpora (see below, chapter III).

In the 1960s, a number of Israeli scholars further highlighted a wide variety of Hellenistic influences on Jewish civilization in antiquity. A. Schalit's *King Herod* (1960, Hebrew) and V. Tcherikover's *Hellenistic Civilization and the Jews* (1931, Hebrew; rev. ed. in English, 1961) addressed the Hellenistic and Roman contexts as vital to understanding the historical developments in Palestine during the last three centuries B.C.E. In particular, Schalit stressed the political and cultural setting under Augustus necessary to gain a full appreciation of Herod and his policies. In describing Hellenistic and Hasmonean Palestine, Tcherikover took pains to point out the broad political and socioeconomic setting that influenced much of Jewish history during these centuries. Moreover, he devoted the last half of his book to the Jews of Egypt, pointing out the ways this large Diaspora community adjusted to its surroundings— politically, socially, economically, and culturally. Tcherikover had already addressed some of these issues in his prolegomenon to *Cor-*

8. Idem, "Palestinian Judaism in the First Century," in *Israel: Its Role in Civilization*, ed. M. Davis (New York: Jewish Theological Seminary, 1956), pp. 67–81; S. Stein, "The Influence of Symposia Literature on the Literary Form of the Pesah Haggadah," *JJS* 8 (1957): 13–44.

pus Papyrorum Judaicarum in 1957 (with A. Fuks and M. Stern, 3 vols., 1957–64). Likewise, in the early 1960s, Y. Gutman examined Jewish authors of Hellenistic Egypt and the impact of Greek culture on their writings. In an entirely different area, G. Scholem's monograph *Jewish Gnosticism, Merkavah Mysticism and Talmudic Tradition* (1960) served to further demonstrate the impact of foreign cultures—this time gnostic circles—on Jewish mysticism of the first centuries c.e. Finally, in 1966, M. Margalioth published his reconstruction of *Sepher Ha-Razim*, a fourth-century Jewish handbook of practical magic that was heavily indebted to popular pagan (later Christian) traditions and practices ubiquitous throughout the ambient Roman-Byzantine world.

At about this time Christian scholars became actively involved in the question of the Hellenization of Jewish society. The motivation for their studies differed from one person to another, but common to all was the desire to elucidate as fully as possible the world of Jesus and the early Jewish-Christian church in Jerusalem and Judaea. There was also the realization that the old dichotomy between Palestinian and Diaspora Judaism, with only the latter seen as profoundly Hellenized, was fast becoming obsolete. It had become evident that Palestinian Judaism itself was significantly Hellenized. Thus, if one wished to delineate the sources of Hellenistic influence on the early church, and particularly on Paul and other New Testament authors, one would have to consider Jerusalem, Judaea, and the Galilee and not only Alexandria, Antioch, Asia Minor, or Rome.

J. Sevenster's book *Do You Know Greek? How Much Greek Could the First Jewish Christians Have Known?* (1968) made a strong case for the knowledge of Greek among early Christians, including Jesus. The implications of such a thesis are far-reaching, for if indeed Jesus knew and spoke Greek, then the possibility that some of the gospel traditions have preserved his actual sayings would be that much greater. Sevenster's study was followed in 1970 by Fitzmyer's article on the languages of first-century c.e. Palestine which clearly and persuasively demonstrated the dominance of the two linguae francae of the time, Aramaic and Greek.[9] In the following year, M. Smith published *Palestinian Parties and Politics That Shaped the Old Testament*, which spanned much of the first millennium B.C.E., from the First Temple to the Hellenistic periods. Among the studies therein, Smith devoted a chapter to Hellenization, in which he treated in detail the contributions of the Persian and Greek worlds to the development of Palestine in the pre-Alexandrian era. The roots of later Hellenization were to be found in this meeting of cultures as far back as the Persian period, the sixth to fourth centuries B.C.E.

A landmark study, published in German in 1969 and appearing in English translation in 1974, was Hengel's two-volume *Judaism and Hellenism: Studies in Their Encounter in Palestine during the Early Hellenistic Period*. Hengel claimed that Jews and Judaism had already encountered significant Hellenistic influence in the third century B.C.E. and that many Jewish groups had quickly absorbed and adapted themselves to the regnant cultural patterns of the Hellenistic world. He sought parallels to explain a wide range of developments within Jewish society in the 150 years between the death of Alexander the Great and the Maccabean revolt. Not only did Hengel claim to find Hellenistic elements in the Jewish books and sects of this era (e.g., Ben Sira, the Ḥasidim, the Dead Sea sect), but he canvassed Palestinian archeological and pagan evidence in order to paint as comprehensive a picture as possible of the cultural transformation in the region as a whole. Hengel also adopted Bickerman's thesis regarding the Hellenizers' role in instigating the persecutions of Antiochus IV in 167 B.C.E., carrying the theory a step further by attributing to these Jews a zealotry which advocated abrogation, or at least the radical curtailment, of the authority of

---

9. J. Fitzmyer, "Languages of Palestine in the First Century A.D.," *CBQ* 32 (1970): 501–31.

the Law within Jewish society. Hengel subsequently followed this monumental study with a number of monographs that treated the question of Hellenization in the later Second Temple period,[10] the most significant being *The "Hellenization" of Judaea in the First Century after Christ* (1989).

Throughout the past few decades more focused studies have appeared, exploring specific aspects of Hellenization in greater depth. H. Fischel's work opened up new vistas of research vis-à-vis the ties between rabbinic midrash and the larger Greco-Roman world, as had D. Daube's studies on rabbinic hermeneutical rules several decades earlier.[11] Other studies, to mention but a representative sample, dealt with a range of topics: Hellenistic Jewish, especially apocalyptic, literature (J. J. Collins), Hellenistic Judaism (L. L. Grabbe), Philo (H. A. Wolfson, A. Mendelson), Ben Sira (J. T. Sanders), Qumran (D. Winston, S. Shaked, M. Hengel, D. Mendels), Pharisees (E. Bickerman, M. Geller), epigraphy (B. Lifshitz), Josephus' Greek milieu (T. Rajak), Josephus' use of Greek models and values in describing biblical figures (L. Feldman), Jewish nationalism (D. Mendels), Pharisaic-rabbinic schools and their teachings in light of parallel developments in Greek philosophical schools (J. Goldin, S. J. D. Cohen, S. Mason, P. Alexander), ha-

10. For example, *The Son of God: The Origin of Christology and the History of Jewish-Hellenistic Religion* (Philadelphia: Fortress, 1976); *Jews, Greeks and Barbarians* (Philadelphia: Fortress, 1980); "The Interpretation of Judaism and Hellenism in the Pre-Maccabean Period," in *The Cambridge History of Judaism* 2, ed. W. D. Davies and L. Finkelstein (Cambridge: Cambridge University Press, 1989), pp. 167–228; *The Johannine Question* (London: SCM Press, 1989), pp. 109–35; *The Pre-Christian Paul* (London: SCM Press, 1991), pp. 54–62.

11. H. Fischel, "Story and History: Observations on Greco-Roman Rhetoric and Pharisaism," *American Oriental Society, Middle West Branch* (1968): 59–88; idem, "Studies in Cynicism and the Ancient Near East: The Transformation of a 'Chria,'" in *Religions in Antiquity: Essays in Memory of Erwin Ramsdell Goodenough*, ed. J. Neusner (Leiden: Brill, 1968), pp. 372–411; idem, *Rabbinic Literature and Greco-Roman Philosophy* (Leiden: Brill, 1973); D. Daube, "Rabbinic Methods and Interpretation and Hellenistic Rhetoric," *HUCA* 22 (1949): 239–64; idem, "Alexandrian Methods of Interpretation and the Rabbis," in *Festschrift Hans Lewald* (Basel: Helbing & Lichtenhahn, 1953), pp. 27–44.

lakhah (B. Cohen, S. J. D. Cohen), and late antique Palestine (M. Avi-Yonah).[12] Recent articles by U. Rappaport and T. Rajak have treated the general phenomenon of Hellenism under the Hasmoneans with considerable insight and refinement.[13]

As might have been anticipated, this emphasis in scholarly literature during recent decades has not gone unanswered. The pen-

12. J. J. Collins, *Between Athens and Jerusalem* (New York: Crossroad, 1983); idem, "Jewish Apocalyptic against Its Hellenistic Environment," *BASOR* 220 (1975): 27–36; L. L. Grabbe, "Hellenistic Judaism," in *Judaism in Late Antiquity: Part Two, Historical Syntheses*, ed. J. Neusner (Leiden: Brill, 1995), pp. 53–83; Wolfson, *Philo*; A. Mendelson, *Secular Education in Philo of Alexandria* (Cincinnati: Hebrew Union College Press, 1982); J. T. Sanders, *Ben Sira and Demotic Wisdom* (Chico: Scholars, 1983). On Qumran, see below, chapter III, n. 15; E. Bickerman, "La chaîne de la tradition pharisienne," *RB* 49 (1952): 44–54; M. Geller, "New Sources for the Origin of the Rabbinic Ketubah," *HUCA* 49 (1978): 227–45; B. Lifshitz, "Greek and Hellenism among the Jews of Eretz Israel," *Eshkolot* 5 (1967): 20–28 (Hebrew); idem, *Donateurs et fondateurs dans les synagogues juives* (Paris: Gabalda, 1967); T. Rajak, *Josephus: The Historian and His Society* (Philadelphia: Fortress, 1984); L. Feldman, *Jew and Gentile in the Ancient World: Attitudes and Interactions from Alexander to Justinian* (Princeton: Princeton University Press, 1993), pp. 594–96 (bibliography); D. Mendels, *The Rise and Fall of Jewish Nationalism* (New York: Doubleday, 1992); J. Goldin, *Studies in Midrash and Related Literature* (Philadelphia: Jewish Publication Society, 1988), pp. 57–76; S. J. D. Cohen, "Patriarchs and Scholarchs," *PAAJR* 48 (1981): 57–85; S. Mason, "Greco-Roman, Jewish, and Christian Philosophies," in *Approaches to Ancient Judaism* new series 4, ed. J. Neusner (Atlanta: Scholars, 1993), pp. 1–28; P. Alexander, "Quid Athenis et Hierosolymis? Rabbinic Midrash and Hermeneutics in the Graeco-Roman World," in *A Tribute to Geza Vermes: Essays on Jewish and Christian Literature*, ed. P. R. Davies and R. T. White (Sheffield: Sheffield Academic Press, 1990), pp. 101–24; B. Cohen, *Jewish and Roman Law: A Comparative Study* (New York: Jewish Theological Seminary, 1966); S. J. D. Cohen, "Origins"; M. Avi-Yonah, *The Jews of Palestine: A Political History from the Bar Kokhba War to the Arab Conquest* (New York: Schocken, 1976), pp. 71–76.

13. U. Rappaport, "On the Hellenization of the Hasmoneans," *Tarbiz* 60 (1991): 477–503 (Hebrew); idem, "Hellenization of the Hasmoneans," in *Jewish Assimilation, Acculturation and Accommodation: Past Traditions, Current Issues and Future Prospects*, ed. M. Mor (Lanham, Nebr.: University Press of America, 1992), pp. 1–13; T. Rajak, "The Hasmoneans and the Uses of Hellenism," in *A Tribute to Geza Vermes: Essays on Jewish and Christian Literature*, ed. P. R. Davies and R. T. White (Sheffield: Sheffield Academic Press, 1990), pp. 261–80.

dulum was bound to swing in the opposite direction, both for academic and, at times, nonacademic reasons. As early as 1961, S. Sandmel sounded a methodological clarion call, warning of the dangers of parallelomania; similar phenomena might not necessarily be a consequence of direct influence. In a number of instances, a response if not a rebuttal to one of the above-noted works was immediate. G. Alon responded critically to many of Lieberman's examples; E. E. Urbach, A. D. Nock, and others to Goodenough's thesis; L. Feldman, F. Millar, M. Stern, and M. D. Herr to Hengel's magnum opus; and, after some time, I. Gruenwald, D. Halperin, E. Schweid, M. Idel, and J. Dan to Scholem's thesis.[14] At times the authors debated whether there was any Hellenistic influence whatsoever in a given area. Another issue was to determine the extent of this Hellenization; how cogent were the arguments in favor of extensive exposure to and adoption of Greek ways? In a series of ar-

14. Response to Lieberman: G. Alon, *Studies in Jewish History* (Tel Aviv: Hakibbutz Hameuchad, 1958), 2, pp. 248–77 (Hebrew); responses to Goodenough: E. E. Urbach, "The Rabbinical Laws of Idolatry in the Second and Third Centuries in the Light of Archaeological and Historical Facts," *IEJ* 9 (1959): 149–65, 229–45; A. D. Nock, *Essays on Religion and the Ancient World*, 2 (Oxford: Clarendon, 1972), pp. 877–918; for other responses to Goodenough, see studies cited by M. Smith, "Goodenough's 'Jewish Symbols'"; responses to Hengel: L. Feldman, "Hengel's 'Judaism and Hellenism' in Retrospect," *JBL* 96 (1977): 371–82; idem, "How Much Hellenism in Jewish Palestine?" *HUCA* 57 (1987): 83–111; idem, *Jew and Gentile*, pp. 3–83; F. Millar, "The Background to the Maccabean Revolution: Reflections on Martin Hengel's 'Judaism and Hellenism,'" *JJS* 29 (1978): 1–21; M. Stern, *Studies in Jewish History: The Second Temple Period* (Jerusalem: Yad Ben-Zvi, 1991), pp. 3–21 (Hebrew); M. D. Herr, "Hellenism and Judaism in Eretz Israel," *Eshkolot* new series 2–3 (1977–78): 20–27 (Hebrew); responses to Scholem: I. Gruenwald, *Apocalyptic and Merkavah Mysticism* (Leiden: Brill, 1980); D. Halperin, *The Faces of the Chariot: Early Jewish Responses to Ezekiel's Vision* (Tübingen: Mohr, 1988); E. Schweid, *Judaism and Mysticism According to Gershom Scholem: A Critical Analysis and Programmatic Discussion* (Atlanta: Scholars, 1985); M. Idel, *Kabbalah: New Perspectives* (New Haven: Yale University Press, 1988), pp. 30–32; J. Dan, *The Ancient Jewish Mysticism* (Tel Aviv: Ministry of Defense, 1989) (Hebrew); idem, "Jewish Gnosticism," *JSQ* 2 (1995): 309–28.

ticles and in the volume *Alien Wisdom: The Limits of Hellenization*
(1975), A. Momigliano offered a judicious treatment of the nature
of Hellenization and the extent of its influence both in the Diaspora
and Judaea.

The ensuing exchanges among scholars have helped to further
refine the arguments of each side, and certain claims have been re-
formulated in response to criticism. For example, Lieberman appears to have adopted a more cautious stance about the nature and
degree of Hellenistic influence on the rabbis in his article "How
Much Greek in Jewish Palestine?" (1963) and in the introduction to
the Hebrew translation of his two books (1963).[15] Likewise, Goodenough in volume XII (1965) responded to critiques of his first
eleven volumes by backtracking on certain claims and moderating
(some would say thus undermining) several aspects of his overall
theory. Finally, over the last several decades, other studies have attempted to minimize the extent of Greek or Roman influence
claimed by earlier authors. B. Bokser's monograph on the Passover
seder and W. S. Towner's article on rabbinic hermeneutical rules, as
well as those of B. S. Jackson and R. Katzoff on the relationship between Jewish and Roman law, are cases in point.[16]

15. S. Lieberman, "How Much Greek in Jewish Palestine?" in *Biblical and Other Studies*, ed. A. Altmann (Cambridge: Harvard University Press, 1963), pp. 123–41; idem, *Greek and Hellenism in Jewish Palestine*, 2d ed. (Jerusalem: Bialik, 1984), pp. xi–xiii (Hebrew).

16. B. Bokser, *The Origins of the Seder: The Passover Rite and Early Rabbinic Judaism* (Berkeley: University of California Press, 1984); W. S. Towner, "Her-meneutical Systems of Hillel and the Tannaim: A Fresh Look," *HUCA* 53 (1982): 101–35; B. S. Jackson, "On the Problem of Roman Influence on the Ha-lakah and Normative Self-Definition in Judaism," in *Jewish and Christian Self-Definition 2: Aspects of Judaism in the Graeco-Roman Period*, ed. E. P. Sanders et al. (Philadelphia: Fortress, 1981), pp. 157–203; R. Katzoff, "Sperber's Dictio-nary of Greek and Latin Legal Terms in Rabbinic Literature: A Review-Essay," *JSJ* 20 (1989): 194–206.

On the influence of Christian literature, art, and archeology on Jewish life in later antiquity, see below, chapters III and IV.

WHAT IS MEANT BY "HELLENISM" AND "HELLENIZATION"?

The terms "Hellenism" and "Hellenization" are often used interchangeably to indicate the ways in which Greek culture affected the Orient. Attempts to distinguish between the two have resulted in many different variations. For example, the following distinctions have been suggested: Hellenism refers to native Greek culture; Hellenization describes Greek culture abroad.[17] Hellenism is the distinctively classical Greek cultural ambience; Hellenization points to the larger cultural vortex of the Hellenistic age, which included Eastern as well as Western components. Hellenism describes the conscious process of adopting Greek ways and the internalization of whatever political, social, and symbolic implications may accrue to such a deliberate process; Hellenization is the broader inculcation of a culture, often on a subconscious level. Hellenism describes an overall cultural setting; Hellenization is the ongoing process of cultural symbiosis.[18] Given these broad definitions, at times overlapping and at times contradicting one another, I shall opt for the last of these distinctions, treating these terms as two aspects of the same phenomenon; Hellenism thus refers to the cultural milieu (largely

17. On the other hand, a distinction sometimes offered would refer the term "Hellenic" to classical Greek culture, and the terms "Hellenism," "Hellenistic," and "Hellenization" to the post-Alexander period.

18. For several attempts to define these terms, see M. Hengel, *Judaism and Hellenism: Studies in Their Encounter in Palestine during the Early Hellenistic Period* (Philadelphia: Fortress, 1974), 1, pp. 1–3; Bowersock, *Hellenism*, pp. xi, 1–13; Rajak, "Hasmoneans," pp. 261–67; J. Goldstein, "Jewish Acceptance and Rejection of Hellenism," in *Jewish and Christian Self-Definition* 2: *Aspects of Judaism in the Graeco-Roman Period*, ed. E. P. Sanders et al. (Philadelphia: Fortress, 1981), pp. 64–69. See also Rappaport, "Hellenization of the Hasmoneans," pp. 1–2; and the earlier comments of H. Bengtson, *History of Greece: From the Beginnings of the Byzantine Era*, trans. and updated by E. F. Bloedow (Ottawa: University of Ottawa Press, 1988), pp. 280–91; Grimal et al., *Hellenism and the Rise of Rome*, pp. 1–20. For an in-depth analysis of the term "Hellenism" in modern research, see R. Bichler, *"Hellenismus": Geschichte und Problematik eines Epochenbegriffs* (Darmstadt: Wissenschaftliche Buchgesellschaft, 1983).

Greek) of the Hellenistic, Roman, and—to a somewhat more lim-ited extent—Byzantine periods, while Hellenization describes the process of adoption and adaptation of this culture on a local level. I prefer being as inclusive as possible with regard to the phenom-ena discussed, thus allowing for the widest possible variety of ex-pressions and the greatest number of distinctions. If, in the end, some ambiguity remains as to what, indeed, falls into these cate-gories and what does not, so be it; in fact, it may not be so different from the way the ancients themselves viewed these matters. The reasoning behind this decision and some of its implications will be spelled out below.

Discussion of Hellenism and Hellenization over the last several generations has been both fascinating and instructive. For decades, scholars have worked, consciously or not, from two assumptions. The first is that Hellenism involved Greek ideas and practices that reached the East either directly from Greece itself or, more likely, via one of several major Hellenistic urban centers, such as Alexan-dria or Antioch. Thus, the search for classical Greek institutions or Greek philosophical ideas was often regarded as the true litmus test of Hellenistic influence.[19] R. Harrison, for example, has formulated this view thusly: "Hellenization is usually understood as the process through which post-classical Greek civilization promoted itself and assimilated peoples with an eye toward the unification of the known world into a single nation sharing a common culture."[20]

A second assumption is that Hellenism was a given phenome-non, to be either affirmed or denied; it either existed or did not ex-ist within a society. Judaea was considered either Hellenized or not, with very few more subtle distinctions being made. Thus, in the de-bate that was vigorously pursued throughout the 1970s and 1980s

19. S. Sandmel, "Parallelomania," *JBL* 81 (1962): 1–13; Feldman, "How Much Hellenism?" pp. 106–8.
20. R. Harrison, "Hellenization in Syria-Palestine: The Case of Judea in the Third Century BCE," *BA* 57 (1994): 98–108.

over the question of Hellenization in pre-Hasmonean Palestine, several clearly demarcated opinions emerged. On the one side were those who advocated a significant degree of outside influence (inter alios, E. Bickerman, M. Hengel, and J. Goldstein); on the other were those who minimized such influence on Jewish society (V. Tcherikover, followed by S. Sandmel, F. Millar, L. Feldman, M. Stern, and M. D. Herr).[21] According to this latter view, whatever influence existed was confined to a small elite within Jewish society.

Let us examine in turn each of the above two assumptions. In defining Hellenism or Hellenization, it is important to realize that this phenomenon should not be regarded only as the extent to which "classical" Greek culture, i.e., religion, literature, or philosophy, reached the East. Rather, consideration should be given to all aspects of society—economic, social, political, and material, no less than the religious and cultural. Indications that religious, literary, and philosophical influences were absorbed would certainly suggest an advanced degree of Hellenization, but such instances are relatively rare, while evidence of influence in other areas of life is much more common.

Moreover, Hellenization constituted more than simply the dissemination of Greek social mores, language, and institutions throughout the East; it cannot be measured only by the extent to which the peoples and cultures of this region were drawn to this one regnant culture. What took place was as much a process of se-

21. All of these authors have been noted above. See also S. Sandmel, "Hellenism and Judaism," in *Great Confrontations in Jewish History*, ed. S. M. Wagner and A. D. Breck (Denver: University of Denver Press, 1977), pp. 21–38.

Regarding the extent of Hellenization in third- and fourth-century Palestine, a similar debate took place a generation ago as a result of the Bet She'arim excavations. Alon adopted a minimalist position, claiming that only Jews in Hellenistic urban centers were really Hellenized; Lifshitz took a maximalist stance, claiming that the Greek in Bet She'arim is reflective of all Palestinian Jewry; Lieberman held a middle-of-the-road position. See Alon, *Studies* 2, pp. 248–77; Lifshitz, "Greek and Hellenism," pp. 20–28; S. Lieberman, *Greek in Jewish Palestine* (New York: Jewish Theological Seminary, 1942), pp. 91–92.

lection, adoption, and adaptation as it was of conquest and subjugation. Moreover, without denying the dominant role of Greek civilization, we should recognize that Hellenization was far more complex than merely the impact of the West on the East. The story of Alexander the Great and his soldiers marrying Persian women and adopting assorted Persian customs is indicative of the very profound processes coalescing in the wake of the Greek conquest of the East. In this encounter, the East left its mark as well, whether it be of the Egyptian, Syrian, Iranian, Babylonian, or Jewish variety.

Indeed, the Hellenistic world was the scene of a veritable potpourri of cultural forces, a marketplace of ideas and fashions from which one could choose. In this light, therefore, Hellenization is not merely the impact of Greek culture on a non-Greek world, but rather the interplay of a wide range of cultural forces on an *oikumene* (the civilized world as then known) defined in large part—but not exclusively—by the Greek conquests of the fourth and third centuries B.C.E.[22]

The influences affecting Judaea in the Hellenistic period might have been directly linked with the Greek world, as evidenced by Jewish claims of ties forged with Sparta, Judaea's treaties with Rome, or the Rhodian-stamped wine-jar handles found in Jerusalem. More often, however, such influences were not direct, but came through—and sometimes directly from—nearby centers, such as Alexandria, Antioch, Damascus, or the coastal cities of Phoenicia and Palestine. Such influences filtered through each Hellenistic center according to the dominant styles and ambience of each locale, and were often moderated or nuanced by assorted Eastern traditions.[23]

22. For such an instance of Eastern patterns penetrating the Hellenistic-Roman world, see S. J. Lieberman, "A Mesopotamian Background for the So-called *Aggadic* 'Measures' of Biblical Hermeneutics," *HUCA* 58 (1987): 157–225.

23. M. Smith, *Palestinian Parties and Politics That Shaped the Old Testament* (New York: Columbia University Press, 1971), pp. 75–79.

A striking example of the penetration of wide-ranging Eastern influences (and not only those of Greek origin) into the least expected area of Jewish life is Qumran. The Dead Sea documents reveal a sect whose ideology and practices were heavily influenced by the larger Hellenistic world. Among the sect's fundamental beliefs and practices—determinism, dualism, the solar calendar, communal property, angelology, celibacy, the desire to create a utopia, and many organizational patterns—most have little, if any, roots in earlier Jewish tradition. However, they are well attested in the Hellenistic and Eastern worlds of the third and second centuries B.C.E. Clearly, despite a conscious effort to isolate itself from both Jewish and non-Jewish societies, this sect was heavily influenced by ideas from the wider Hellenistic world to which it presumably had been exposed in its formative stages. How and when this contact took place is unclear, although various suggestions have been advanced. Nevertheless, the fact that such a complex process was at work is undeniable.[24]

Turning to the second of the assumptions noted above—namely, that too often one speaks of an overall Hellenistic influence with few distinctions being made—this, too, has undergone significant refinement over the last decade or so. First and foremost is the realization that the penetration of Greek culture into the Orient was uneven. Elements of Greek culture were to be found in the Near East even before Alexander, including Athenian coins, statuettes, and decorations on household objects. In the Hellenistic period, Greek language, business practices, and various forms of technol-

24. See chapter III, n. 15; H. Stegemann, *Die Entstehung der Qumrangemeinde* (Bonn: Rheinische Friedrich-Wilhelms-Universität, 1971); J. Murphy-O'Connor, "The Essenes and Their History," *RB* 81 (1974): 215–44; idem, "Demetrius I and the Teacher of Righteousness," *RB* 83 (1976): 400–420; F. D. Weinert, "A Note on 4Q159 and a New Theory of Essene Origins," *RQ* 9 (1977): 223–30; J. H. Charlesworth, "The Origin and Subsequent History of the Authors of the Dead Sea Scrolls: Four Transitional Phases among the Qumran Essenes," *RQ* 10 (1980): 213–33.

ogy and material culture quickly made their mark on Eastern societies. Moreover, contact between Greeks and peoples of the East, from professional ties to social contacts and even marriage, became more intensive at this time. Conversely, elements of Greek civic and institutional life were considerably slower in leaving their mark. Cities founded *de novo* and settled by Greek colonists or soldiers almost always enjoyed the full rights of Greek civic life. Many of them boasted the institutions associated with a Greek city—the theater, *gymnasium*, and agora. However, not always did native cities-turned-*poleis* have such amenities, and their introduction depended on the population's wishes and the king's agreement. Palmyra, for example, boasted a *bouleuterion* (council hall) but no theater; Petra had the latter but not the former.

Alexandria aside, little is known about the writing of belles lettres and philosophy in the East, although there are many instances of people from the East traveling to Athens and Rome and making their mark there. The cultural and intellectual influence of the West on the East was largely expressed in the shaping of local traditions around Greek models; in this Egyptian Jewry took the lead. For example, the *Letter of Aristeas* followed a number of Greek literary conventions (e.g., romantic and symposia literature); 2 Maccabees and Josephus, Hellenistic historiographical models; Ben Sira, Hellenistic wisdom literature; and Philo the Elder and Theodotus, Greek poetry. Thus, in surveying all these literary genres, it is clear that the impact of Greek and other foreign elements was unbalanced, and this must be borne in mind when judging the degree of Hellenistic influence on the Jews.[25]

Having recognized the existence of outside influences and their uneven impact, it is necessary to make additional assessments and

25. E. Bickerman and M. Smith, *The Ancient History of Western Civilization* (New York: Harper and Row, 1979), pp. 142–45; E. Bickerman, *The Jews in the Greek Age* (Cambridge: Harvard University Press, 1988), pp. 298–305; Hengel, *Judaism and Hellenism* 1, pp. 60–61.

distinctions in an attempt to capture the complexity of the Hellenization process. First is the degree of influence in any one particular area. Are we speaking of heavy impact, whereby large doses of Hellenistic culture were absorbed into Jewish society or parts thereof, thus creating varieties of syncretism? Hengel's priestly Hellenizers are a case in point. Or perhaps what took place was a kind of synthesis or symbiosis, whereby outside influences were comfortably integrated into a framework without any revolutionary upheavals, as was the case with the Hasmoneans and other moderate Hellenizers, according to Bickerman. Finally, many influences were clearly external and remained quite superficial, in essence merely lending a Greek label to an already existent phenomenon in Jewish society. For example, Tcherikover imagined the Jerusalem *polis* to have functioned in this way (see below, chapter II). Nevertheless, it should be clear that all three types of contact might occur simultaneously, not only within different strata of society but also with regard to different people within the same stratum. Some Jews were undoubtedly more receptive to foreign models than others. Thus, it would be quite arbitrary and misleading to define the encounter of the Greek and Jewish worlds in terms of only one of the above options.[26]

Moreover, to fully appreciate the complexity of the Hellenization process, other distinctions must be made as well. For example, the material culture was influenced to a different degree than were other kinds of cultural expression, social mores, and political institutions, while religious beliefs and practices were affected to yet a different degree. Clearly, distinctions also have to be made as to the degree of receptivity in each area, as well as from region to region and from class to class. Thus, since the Jewish people never had a unique material culture of their own, contemporary culture largely

26. See A. Segal, *Rebecca's Children: Judaism and Christianity in the Roman World* (Cambridge: Harvard University Press, 1986), pp. 22–28.

determined how they built their homes, city walls, streets, and public buildings (including the two Jerusalem Temples and, later on, their synagogues), what sorts of decorations they used, how they made their eating utensils, what clothes they wore, and how they buried their dead. From era to era, the Jews would adopt the regnant styles and fashions of the time. However, at the other end of the spectrum, Jewish religious beliefs and practices were always assumed to have been different, unique, and steadfast, and thus one might well expect more resistance to acculturation.

These two realms specifically—the material and the religious—have often been invoked as two very different spheres in relation to the issue at hand; influence has been much more readily granted in the former but often denied in the latter. The physical and material dimensions have on occasion been compared to the shell, and the religious and cultural domains likened to the kernel.[27] While there may be some justification for such a dichotomy, it is far from absolute and can only be granted if we are discussing the degree of influence on each. If the physical realm was almost always indebted to outside models, such dependence was clearly not the case in the spiritual realm. The difference, however, is one of degree only, as will become evident below.

A further distinction in assessing the extent of Hellenistic influence on Jewish society concerns the particular class affected. Clearly,

27. See, for example, Meyers and Strange, *Archaeology, Rabbis and Early Christianity*, p. 93; Sandmel, "Hellenism and Judaism," pp. 32–34, has the following to say:

> In my view, Palestinian Judaism is unquestionably a by-product of the hellenistic age. Unquestionably it absorbed Greek vocabulary and exhibits echoes of Greek rhetoric and philosophy. But in my understanding, what is more characteristic of Palestinian Judaism is its rejection of the hellenistic civilization in terms of genuine substance. . . . But hellenistic thought and hellenistic thought-patterns as matters of substance made no inroads. Genuine syncretism, if it occurred, was restricted to what must be denominated as minor fringe groups. Rabbinic Judaism resisted all but surface hellenization.

one cannot assume the same measure of openness to foreign influences (i.e., acculturation) in the lower classes as in the upper, wealthy strata of society. The upper classes could more easily afford to travel (owing to political, diplomatic, or business affairs), acquire cosmopolitan tastes and material goods, and build more lavishly than others. Thus, the desire to emulate Greco-Roman mores (and the means to do so) was far more pronounced among the upper than the lower social strata. The extent of Hellenistic-Roman influence within this class is vividly demonstrated in the remains of the upper city of Herodian Jerusalem (see below, chapter II).

Another distinction—the difference between city and village—should also be borne in mind when assessing the extent of Hellenization. An urban center, almost by definition, is a meeting place for diverse peoples and ideas, and the opportunities for contact and influence, whether sought after or not, were far greater there than in a more isolated and insulated village. Thus, we should expect many more instances of outside influence at urban sites than in rural settings, and indeed this pattern is easily discernible in the case of Jerusalem and the ancient synagogue (see below, chapters II and IV).

The degree of Hellenization, in ancient Palestine at least, was also influenced by the particular location within the country. Jewish communities in the Hellenized cities of Palestine such as Bet Shean (Scythopolis) or in coastal cities such as Caesarea, Ascalon, and Jaffa were deeply acculturated. The situation in the latter was probably similar in many respects to that of Diaspora communities, which were intensively immersed in Greco-Roman life. As a result, Greek language and institutions were most prominent within these Palestinian urban centers, and the Jews' adaptation to their surroundings there was far more pronounced than in the rest of the country. At the other end of the spectrum, the more geographically isolated regions were far less Hellenized, as, for example, the Upper

Galilee, the Golan, and southern Judaea. As ironic as it may seem, Jerusalem seems to have been the most Hellenized Jewish urban center in Roman Palestine, although Tiberias and Sepphoris also exhibited a high degree of acculturation. Smaller cities or towns such as Jericho, Adoraim in Idumaea, and Gamla were affected, but to a far lesser extent.

Hellenization in the Diaspora has always been justifiably recognized as extensive. This phenomenon is especially well documented vis-à-vis the major center of Jewish life in the Diaspora in the Second Temple period, Alexandria. While a book such as 3 Maccabees reflects deep suspicion and hostility to the surrounding world, such works appear to have been in the distinct minority. The cultural achievement of Alexandrian Jewry involved the creation of drama, historiography, poetry, and philosophy in a Greek mold while drawing from the biblical narrative. Already in the second century B.C.E., Aristobulus claimed that Greek civilization had its source in Jewish tradition, as Greek philosophers such as Pythagoras, Plato, and Aristotle had drawn their inspiration from the Hebrew Bible. The quintessential expression of this Alexandrian Jewish thrust was, of course, the first-century philosopher Philo, who deftly combined the biblical narrative and Middle Platonist thought in expositing biblical narratives and themes. As D. Winston has noted: ". . . much in Philo's thought represents a highly successful fusion of Judaism and Hellenism, a virtual restructuring of biblical thought through the categories of Greek philosophy." [28]

While the extent of Hellenization of Alexandrian Jewry can rarely be matched in contemporary Palestine, the issue boils down to the difference in degree and intensity of this phenomenon. There is no denying that many Jews of Palestine were significantly

28. D. Winston, "Iranian Components in the Bible, Apocrypha and Qumran," *History of Religion* 5 (1966): 3.

Hellenized. It has become widely recognized today that the dichotomy, which finds expression in many earlier histories of the period between a "Jewish" or "Pharisaic-rabbinic" Palestine on the one hand and a Hellenized Diaspora on the other, is no longer tenable,[29] and Palestinian Judaism can be regarded as Hellenistic Judaism as well.[30] Among Jews in Palestine and the Diaspora, there was a range of responses to Hellenistic influences rather than a sharp dichotomy, a diversity rather than a polarity.[31]

Finally, a paramount consideration, no less important than any of the above, is the chronological distinction. The degree of Hellenization was clearly of a different order in the first to fourth centuries c.e. than in the third to first centuries b.c.e. Generally speaking, as time went on, Hellenistic-Roman influence steadily increased.[32] This claim holds true despite the radical shift between sources of the Hellenistic and early Roman periods and those of later antiquity. While Josephus, Philo, the New Testament, the Dead Sea scrolls, and apocryphal-pseudepigraphical literature dominate earlier centuries, rabbinic literature together with epigraphical and synagogue remains are central to late antiquity. Despite this difference in sources, the process of Hellenization continued unabated. What once was restricted to certain aspects of society, specific classes, or particular geographical regions now spread in ever wider circles over time. Whether it was a matter of increased familiarity

29. For contrasting views on Hellenization in Palestine and the Diaspora, see Sandmel, "Hellenism and Judaism," pp. 23–38; Hengel, *Judaism and Hellenism* 1, pp. 104–6.

30. See also idem, *"Hellenization" of Judaea*, p. 53.

31. C. C. Hill, *Hellenists and Hebrews: Reappraising Division within the Earliest Church* (Minneapolis: Fortress, 1992), pp. 1–2.

32. This reality is evident in Palestine (see chapter IV). See also ibid., pp. 53–54. However, in certain places, such as Egypt, it appears that the Jewish community of late antiquity became more insulated, using more Hebrew language and Hebrew names than before. This is clearly the result of the severe political, social, and economic setbacks it suffered in the first centuries c.e. See Tcherikover et al., *CPJ* 1, pp. 93–111.

and comfort or a reduced fear of foreign or pagan elements, these influences often became more ensconced in the fabric of society as time went on.

When one is dealing with literary or historical phenomena that clearly attempt to reassert Jewish interests or values, there is at times a tendency to label these as a Jewish reaction to Hellenism. In some cases this may be true, but the issues also may have been more complex. In fact, reactions to Hellenism may have been shared by other Eastern peoples as well. Thus, in a sense, such reactions were in essence just another form of Hellenization. It can be argued that not only did the wider Hellenistic world provide the means of expression for these aspirations, but that Jews were now doing what others were doing, and in much the same way. What is different in such cases, of course, is that patterns of expression and behavior were now being shaped by the conquered peoples and cultures, and not by the conquerors. The Hasmonean aspirations for sovereignty, the development of apocalyptic literature, and the crystallization of the institution of conversion have all been viewed as instances of the reassertion of Jewish identity, both collective and individual. These developments have often been explained as a Jewish response to an ever-threatening Hellenism and as expressions of Jewish primacy over the surrounding pagan world. Such an assertion is undoubtedly correct. Yet, when viewed contextually—in terms of similar phenomena in the Hellenistic East—such developments parallel behavior common to other peoples as well. In some instances, the Jews may have adopted such responses from the surrounding world; in others, they may have responded independently, though in a similar way, to other peoples in comparable circumstances. In any case, whether indirectly or directly, we have here instances in which the conditions and context of the larger Hellenistic *oikumene* are crucial in understanding Jewish political and religious responses.

A conceptual mistake made frequently in the past equates Hel-

lenization and assimilation. To assume a degree of Hellenization
has often been construed as the Jews' loss of national or religious
identity in favor of something else. Such a phenomenon, well
known in later Jewish history and especially in modern times, was
rare in antiquity, at least according to the sources at our disposal.
There are very few cases of Jews abandoning their ethnic and religious identity in order to integrate into the larger Greco-Roman
society. Whether the disappearance of many Jewish communities
in later antiquity was due to assimilation, migration, persecution,
or some other calamity is difficult to assess. In addressing the issue
of Hellenization below, we will be dealing with various forms of
acculturation, i.e., the adoption of foreign ideas, mores, and institutions and their adaptation in one form or another to a Jewish setting.[33] As noted, this process affected practically all circles of Jewish
society—sometimes more, sometimes less. It is well-nigh impossible to find any one group, whether political, social, or religious,
that was not influenced in some measure by outside factors.

This is where scholarly discussion stands today. No one can deny
such influences; the challenge is to formulate more subtle distinctions, determining how much, in which areas, and at what pace
these changes took place. Only when we abandon sweeping generalizations and begin addressing these distinctions will we have a
better grasp of the process in its entirety.

It must be borne in mind, however, that while progress will assuredly be made, there are and always will be serious limitations to
the degree of definition and exactitude that can be achieved in this
realm. While this caveat is true with regard to almost every area in
the history of antiquity, it is especially relevant to the subject at
hand. We have limited sources at our disposal, though it must be
admitted that those concerning the Jews are relatively rich in comparison with those of other Oriental peoples. Perspective is crucial

33. G. D. Cohen, "Blessing."

in assessing a historical phenomenon, and the lack of extensive comparative material is a serious liability. Limited perspective renders provisional any judgment regarding the Jews.

As noted at the outset, fueling this discussion are a number of factors that goad scholars to further research. The contemporary world, with its seductions and attractions, demonstrates just how irresistible such influences can be for all peoples who come into contact with them. The phenomenon of Americanization throughout much of contemporary society is a striking case in point. Moreover, the ongoing flow of archeological data continually reaffirms the integration and reliance of Jewish society on outside models and influences. All this is compounded by the natural desire of scholars to account for the origins of various phenomena; when earlier Jewish tradition cannot adequately explain them, the natural inclination is to look elsewhere, and this is where the factor of Hellenization comes into play.

Finally, ancient sources themselves testify to the impact of Greco-Roman culture on the lives of conquered nations.[34] Josephus, in considering the names of cities, regions, and peoples, as well as political institutions, has the following to say about the pervasiveness of Hellenistic influence:

> Of the nations some still preserve the names which were given them by their founders, some have changed them, while yet others have modified them to make them more intelligible to their neighbors. It is the Greeks who are responsible for this change of nomenclature; for when in after ages they rose to power, they appropriated even the glories of the past, embellishing the nations with names which they could understand and imposing on them forms of government, as though they were descended from themselves. (*Antiquities* 1.121)

---

34. See in this regard the comments of M. Goodman, "Jewish Attitudes to Greek Culture in the Period of the Second Temple," in *Jewish Education and Learning*, ed. G. Abramson and T. Parfitt (Chur, Switzerland: Harwood Academic Publishers, 1994), pp. 167–74.

Other Jewish sources attest to the impact of Hellenization within the Jewish context. Philo, whose efforts, as noted, were directed toward demonstrating the total harmony between Jewish and Greek concepts and values, speaks of the synagogue in classic Greek terms: ". . . the Jews every seventh day occupy themselves with the philosophy of their fathers, dedicating that time to the acquiring of knowledge and the study of the truths of nature. For what are our places of prayer throughout the cities but schools of prudence and courage and temperance and justice . . . ?" (*On Moses* 2.216)

A number of rabbis as well approved of the incorporation of certain elements of Greek culture into Jewish frameworks in their comments on Genesis 9:27: "May God enlarge Japheth. And he shall dwell in the tents of Shem." The third-century R. Yoḥanan interpreted the words of Rabban Simeon ben Gamaliel as follows: "May the words of Japheth (i.e., the Greeks) dwell in the tents of Shem (i.e., the Jews)," and according to R. Ḥiyya bar Abba, "May the beauty of Japheth (i.e., the Greek language) dwell in the tents of Shem" (*b. Megillah* 9b). In a more specific vein, Bar Qappara interpreted this same verse as follows: "May the words of the Torah be recited in the language of Japheth in the tents of Shem" (i.e., in the synagogues, *j. Megillah* 1.11.71b; *Genesis Rabbah* 36:8).

An important caveat is in order here. While our study is devoted to the impact of Hellenism on Jewish life in antiquity, this dimension in no way exhausts the phenomenon of Jewish creativity—cultural or otherwise—throughout this era. Side by side with the absorption of outside influences, unique Jewish modes of expression and behavior were continually surfacing. At times such developments served as a counterpoint or balance to Hellenistic culture; at times they evolved independently. Outside influences were always being filtered, shaped, and selected by the Jewish body politic, or parts thereof, according to its norms and standards. Moreover, as noted above, in not a few instances Hellenistic models served to enhance particularistic developments. In this respect, G. W. Bowersock proposed a useful formulation when he noted that through its wide range of cultural expression in art, language, and thought, Hellenism offered the East "an extraordinary flexible medium of both cultural and religious expression. It was a medium not necessarily antithetical to local and indigenous traditions. On the contrary, it provided a new and more eloquent way of giving voice to them." [35]

Thus, while each chapter in this volume will examine the nature and extent of Hellenistic influence, each will also attempt to point out the non-Hellenistic dimensions as well, so as to afford a more comprehensive and balanced picture of the dynamics at play.

We will focus on the Hellenistic influences in three important dimensions of Jewish life in antiquity: the city of Jerusalem in the late Second Temple period, Pharisaic-rabbinic culture, and the ancient synagogue. These three topics, of course, in no way exhaust the subject, but they do allow us to focus on three very different frameworks in Jewish life and creativity—the Jewish city par excellence, the religious tradition about which we are best informed and which eventually became normative in Jewish life, and the institution that was central to every Jewish community in antiquity. Examination of such diverse frameworks will afford us an idea of the extent and variety of such influences and of the dynamic interplay between foreign notions and Jewish society and tradition as then constituted.

One final word regarding the title chosen for this volume. I have called it *Judaism and Hellenism in Antiquity* despite the fact that several aspects of rabbinic culture can be dated to the Byzantine period (post-324 C.E.) and are to be understood in terms of the later, Christian, orbit. To an even greater degree, developments within the ancient synagogue are often best understood in terms of their

---

35. Bowersock, *Hellenism*, p. 7. See also E. M. Meyers, "The Challenge of Hellenism for Early Judaism and Christianity," *BA* 55 (1992): 84–91.

immediate Byzantine context. Nevertheless, the title was chosen not merely because the overwhelming majority of data presented in this volume relates to the earlier, pre-fourth-century Common Era. Of more importance is the fact that many of the cultural elements which found expression under Byzantine rule originated in the Roman period and were later adopted by both Christians and Jews. Thus, the term "late antiquity" has come to emphasize, inter alia, the cultural continuum of the first seven centuries of the Common Era.[36] Not only was Hellenism not alien to the Byzantine context; it indeed flourished throughout that society, as recent studies have argued justifiably and persuasively: "Under Constantinople's aegis, the Imperial Hellenism, decidedly Greek in form and outlook, replaced the old Graeco-Roman culture as the dominant way of life in the Roman East."[37] Finally, the use of the terms "Judaism" and "Hellenism" in the title raises a plethora of associations relating to cultural interaction, which is precisely what we shall explore in what follows.

36. See, for example, P. Brown, *The World of Late Antiquity* (London: Harcourt Brace and Jovanovich, 1971), pp. 7–21; F. M. Clover and R. S. Humphreys, "Towards a Definition of Late Antiquity," in *Tradition and Innovation in Late Antiquity*, ed. F. M. Clover and R. S. Humphreys (Madison: University of Wisconsin Press, 1989), pp. 10–11.

37. Ibid., p. 10; see also Bowersock, *Hellenism*, pp. xi–xii; M. L. W. Laistner, *Christianity and Pagan Culture in the Later Roman Empire* (Ithaca: Cornell University Press, 1951); A. Cameron, *The Mediterranean World in Late Antiquity* (London: Routledge, 1993), pp. 182–86; idem, *The Later Roman Empire AD 284–430* (Cambridge: Harvard University Press, 1993), pp. 151–69.

CHAPTER II

Second Temple Jerusalem

THE JEWISH DIMENSION

By the Hasmonean and Herodian periods, Jerusalem had been under Jewish hegemony/autonomy for almost one thousand years. The city is usually regarded as a quintessentially Jewish one. Undoubtedly it was. The issue, however, is to determine the nature of this Jewishness and what it included.

In the course of the First and Second Temple periods, Jerusalem had evolved into the central and sacred site of the Jewish people. This status was not created overnight but was the result of an ongoing process spanning many centuries. The first stage in this evolution was David's decision to conquer the city and transform it into his political and religious capital. Under the Davidic dynasty numerous associations tying Jerusalem to earlier traditions and future hopes were created (e.g., Genesis 14:18–20): psalms extolling the city were composed and historical accounts were preserved, eventually finding expression in the books of Psalms, Samuel, Kings, and later in Chronicles.[1]

---

1. Y. Zakovitch, "Biblical Traditions Regarding the Sanctification of Jerusalem," in *Jerusalem in the First Temple Period*, ed. D. Amit and R. Gonen (Jerusalem: Yad Ben-Zvi, 1991), pp. 12–22 (Hebrew); and generally J. Bright, *A History of Israel* (Philadelphia: Westminster, 1959), pp. 161–319; B. Mazar, "Jerusalem in Biblical Times," in *The Jerusalem Cathedra* 2, ed. L. I. Levine (Jerusalem: Yad Ben-Zvi, 1982), pp. 1–24. See also the bibliographies of R. P. Goldschmidt, "Jerusalem in First Temple Times," ibid., pp. 328–51; J. D. Purvis, *Jerusalem the Holy City* (Metuchen, NJ: Scarecrow, 1988), 1, pp. 93–155.

Jerusalem's status increased immeasurably following the destruction of the northern kingdom in 722 B.C.E. As a result of this catas-
trophe, Jerusalem remained the sole political and religious center
of the people of Israel. Its miraculous escape from the Assyrian
siege in 701, as well as its dramatic expansion under Hezekiah at
this time, raised the city's prestige to new heights. Isaiah's prophecy
regarding the universal scope of Jerusalem's influence and its role
as a seat of judgment and teaching for all peoples is striking and
goes to the heart of this enhanced status (Isaiah 2:2–4).[2]

The pinnacle of Jerusalem's development in the First Temple period came with Josiah's decision in 622 B.C.E. to centralize the Jewish sacrificial cult in the city. Beforehand, it had been permissible to
offer sacrifices to the God of Israel anywhere in the country; now,
only those sacrifices brought to the Jerusalem Temple were recognized as legitimate and sanctioned.[3]

The centrality of the city became even more pronounced in the
ensuing Second Temple period (536 B.C.E.–70 C.E.). The books of
Chronicles emphasize God's choice of Jerusalem by relating that
a fire descended from heaven onto the altar built there by David
(1 Chronicles 21:26; cf. 2 Samuel 24:25) and by explicitly identifying Moriah of the *'Aqedah* story with the Temple Mount
(2 Chronicles 3:1). Cyrus' recognition of the city by virtue of its
holy Temple was to be repeated later on by Hellenistic and Roman
rulers. Antiochus III's edict on behalf of Jerusalem upon its capture
in 200 B.C.E. is clear testimony of this status (*Antiquities* 12.138–44).
Moreover, the transformation of the city into the capital of a sub-

2. M. Broshi, "The Expansion of Jerusalem in the Reigns of Hezekiah and
Manasseh," *IEJ* 24 (1974): 21–26. Cf. also R. Wilson, "The City in the Old
Testament," in *Civitas: Religious Interpretations of the City*, ed. P. S. Hawkins
(Atlanta: Scholars, 1986), pp. 9–13.
3. M. Weinfeld, "From Tribe to Kingdom," in *Jerusalem in the First Temple
Period*, ed. D. Amit and R. Gonen (Jerusalem: Yad Ben-Zvi, 1991), pp. 23–39
(Hebrew); A. Rofé, "Jerusalem: The City Chosen by God," ibid., pp. 51–62
(Hebrew).

stantial political kingdom, first in the days of the Hasmoneans and later under Herod, further imbued Jerusalem with a rank and importance heretofore unmatched. During the Second Temple period (see fig. 1), the city grew fifteen-fold in size (from approximately 30 to 450 acres) and similarly in population (from approximately 5,000–6,000 to 60,000–80,000).[4]

Side by side with these political developments in the Second Temple period, and perhaps as a reflection of them, new religious practices crystallized, all of which emphasized Jerusalem's centrality and importance. One such custom was the second tithe (either the produce itself or its monetary equivalent), which was brought four times every seven years for use in the city. Other requirements included the bringing of the first fruits annually (*bikkurim*) and the fruit of a sapling in its fourth year (*'orlah*), paying an annual tax of a half sheqel, and making pilgrimage to the city, the frequency of which usually depended on geographical proximity.[5]

Parallel to this enhanced political, physical, and halakhic status, Jerusalem also enjoyed a heightened religious-ideological prominence. Isaiah, as noted, had already envisioned the city as a spiritual focus for all nations (2:1–4), and in the aftermath of the destruction, Ezekiel describes the city as the center of the world and its name as "the Lord is there" (5:5, 48:35), while 2 Chronicles refers to the Lord as "the God of Jerusalem" (32:19). Second Isaiah

---

4. On the population of Jerusalem in antiquity, see J. Jeremias, "Die Einwohnerzahl Jerusalems zur Zeit Jesu," *ZDPV* 66 (1943): 24–31; A. Byatt, "Josephus and Population Numbers in First Century Palestine," *PEQ* 105 (1973): 51–60; J. Wilkinson, "Ancient Jerusalem: Its Water Supply and Population," *PEQ* 106 (1974): 33–51; M. Broshi, "Estimating the Population of Ancient Jerusalem," *BAR* 4/2 (1978): 10–15; W. Reinhardt, "The Population Size of Jerusalem and the Numerical Growth of the Jerusalem Church," in *The Book of Acts in Its First Century Setting 4: The Book of Acts in Its Palestinian Setting*, ed. R. Bauckham (Grand Rapids: Eerdmans, 1995), pp. 237–65.

5. S. Safrai, "Religion in Everyday Life," in *The Jewish People in the First Century*, ed. S. Safrai and M. Stern (Philadelphia: Fortress, 1976), 2, pp. 817–23; idem, "The Temple," ibid., pp. 898–906.

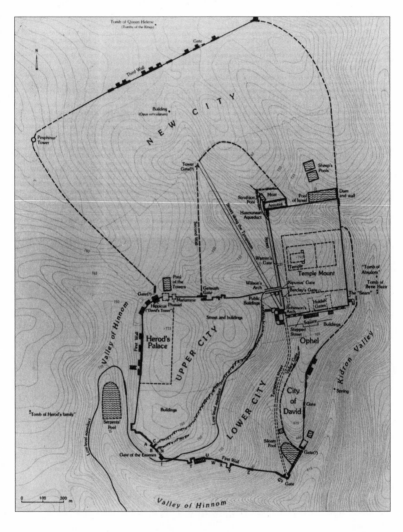

Fig. 1. Jerusalem at the end of the Second Temple period.

(48:2, 52:1) and Nehemiah (11:1) extend the category of holiness beyond the Temple itself (Isaiah 27:13; Jeremiah 31:22) to include all of Jerusalem, while Zechariah takes this one step further and includes all of Judaea as well (2:14–17). Centuries later, these ideas are elaborated in the *Letter of Aristeas* (83), Jubilees (8:17–19), as well as by Josephus (*War* 3.52) and Philo (*Embassy* 37.281). During the Hellenistic and Roman eras, the twin concepts of an eschatological and heavenly Jerusalem made their appearance (Enoch 85–90), becoming even more prominent in the generation following the destruction of the Second Temple (4 Ezra; 2 Baruch; cf. also Revelation 21–22; Hebrews 12).

Thus, by the Hellenistic-Roman period Jerusalem had become the Jewish city par excellence. Its uniqueness attracted the attention of Hellenistic writers, who admiringly described its isolation, uniqueness, and special laws. Hecataeus of Abdera, for example, portrayed the Jews as settled around the Temple and diligently following the laws of Moses under the tutelage of priests, whose otherworldliness was striking to this Greek visitor.[6]

Jerusalem's Pre-Herodian Hellenistic Dimension

Yet, throughout all these centuries of expanding religious activity, Jerusalem was not impervious to outside influences. Such influences were discernible in the city's material culture, in the literary genres produced there, and in its social and religious practices. In the Persian and early Hellenistic periods, for example, the coins of the administrative district of Yehud reflect significant influence of outside mints, such as those of the Palestinian coastal cities and Asia Minor. The very minting of coins, of course, indicates the

6. M. Stern, *Greek and Latin Authors on Jews and Judaism* (Jerusalem: Israel Academy of Sciences and Humanities, 1980), 2, pp. 20–44; A. Momigliano, *Alien Wisdom: The Limits of Hellenization* (Cambridge: Cambridge University Press, 1975), pp. 74–96.

adoption of a foreign norm. Of far greater significance, however, is the fact that the depictions on these coins are almost always imitations of symbols from surrounding cultures, including the use of figural representations—the Athenian owl, the Ptolemaic eagle, various human figures, including Ptolemy and his wife, Berenike, an unidentified warrior, a Persian king, a winged deity, perhaps several high priests (Yadua, Yoḥanan), and a local governor.[7]

What had been of peripheral significance before Alexander became much more central after his conquest; major changes in the Hellenistic period altered the face of the city dramatically. The impact of Hellenism on the Near East in general, and on Judaea and Jerusalem in particular, was considerable. From almost the very beginning of this era, we find signs of Jerusalem's participation in the life of the wider Hellenistic world, as in its diplomatic relations with Sparta which developed in the third and second centuries B.C.E., or in its use of imported Rhodian wine, as attested by the hundreds of stamped amphora handles dating from the mid-third to mid-second centuries B.C.E. Several books written or edited in the third century B.C.E., such as Ecclesiastes (Qohelet) and the Song of Songs, appear to reflect either Hellenistic genres (in the case of the latter) or Hellenistic ideas resulting in the questioning of traditional values (in the case of the former).[8] In addition, a number of

7. Y. Meshorer, *Ancient Jewish Coinage* (Dix Hills, NY: Amphora Books, 1982), 2, pp. 13–34; D. Barag, "A Silver Coin of Yohanan the High Priest and the Coinage of Judea in the Fourth Century B.C.," *INJ* 9 (1986–87): 4–21; idem, "A Coin of Bagoas with a Representation of God on a Winged-Wheel," *Qadmoniot* 25, 99–100 (1992): 97–99 (Hebrew). For a more general overview of the Greek influence in Judaea before the conquest of Alexander the Great, see M. Smith, *Palestinian Parties and Politics*, pp. 57–81.

8. Sparta: 1 Maccabees 12:1–23; Rhodian jar handles: D. Ariel, *Excavations at the City of David 1978–1985* (Qedem 30; Jerusalem: Hebrew University, 1990), pp. 13–25; Ecclesiastes: E. Bickerman, *Four Strange Books of the Bible* (New York: Schocken, 1967), pp. 139–67; R. Gordis, *Koheleth: The Man and His Word* (New York: Bloch, 1955), pp. 63–68; Hengel, *Judaism and Hellenism* 1, pp. 115–30; Song of Songs: M. Rozlaar, "The Song of Songs in Light of Hellenistic Erotic Poetry," *Eshkolot* 1 (1954): 33–48 (Hebrew); and more cautiously Y. Zakovitch,

books appear to have been written in opposition to certain Hellenizing tendencies, for example, Ben Sira and Jubilees, although even they exhibit certain outside influences.

The pièce de résistance of Judaean Hellenization, and the most dramatic of all these developments, occurred in 175 B.C.E., when the high priest Jason converted Jerusalem into a Greek *polis* replete with *gymnasium* and *ephebeion* (2 Maccabees 4). Whether this step represents the culmination of a 150-year process of Hellenization within Jerusalem in general, or whether it was only the initiative of a small coterie of Jerusalem priests with no wider ramifications, has been debated for decades.[9] The answer most probably lies somewhere between these two polar positions. In any event, Jason's move constituted a bold step in the city's adaptation to the wider world, a process which would be interrupted—but only temporarily—by the persecutions of Antiochus IV and the resultant Maccabean revolt.

A further stage in the Hellenization process took place in the ensuing period. The motivation of the Hasmonean revolt has often been misunderstood. It has been contended that this revolt came in protest to the process of Hellenization in Judaea, but this was patently not the case. The Maccabees revolted in response to the persecutions imposed by the king and, according to Bickerman and

---

The Song of Songs: Introduction and Commentary (Tel Aviv: Am Oved, 1992), pp. 17–20 (Hebrew).

9. The lines of argument regarding the extent of Hellenistic influence in pre-Hasmonean Jerusalem have been drawn rather sharply between what we might term the maximalists and minimalists. Among those ascribing to the former position are E. Bickerman, *The God of the Maccabees* (Leiden: Brill, 1979), pp. 76–92; idem, *From Ezra to the Last of the Maccabees* (New York: Schocken, 1962), pp. 93–111; Hengel, *Judaism and Hellenism* 1, pp. 267–309; J. Goldstein, *1 Maccabees* (Anchor Bible 41; New York: Doubleday, 1976), pp. 104–60; idem, *2 Maccabees* (Anchor Bible 41A; New York: Doubleday, 1984), pp. 84–112. Adherents of the minimalist position include V. Tcherikover, *Hellenistic Civilization and the Jews* (Philadelphia: Jewish Publication Society, 1961), pp. 117–203; Feldman, "Hengel's 'Judaism and Hellenism,'" pp. 371–82; Millar, "Background to the Maccabean Revolution," pp. 1–21.

others at least, at the instigation of radical Jewish Hellenizers. The fact is that the Hasmoneans themselves quickly adopted Hellenistic mores; they instituted holidays celebrating military victories (Nicanor Day on the 13th of Adar), as did the Greeks, and signed treaties with Rome and forged close alliances with the upper strata of Jerusalem society. The latter's Hellenized proclivities—like those of the Hasmoneans themselves (see below)—are attested by names such as Alexander, Diodorus, Apollonius, Eupolemus, Antiochus, Numenius, Jason, Antipater, and Aeneas.[10]

In the subsequent Hasmonean period (141–63 B.C.E.), evidence of Hellenization within Jerusalem becomes much more frequent. The document in 1 Maccabees 14 recording the public appointment of Simon as leader (or chief—*hêgoumenon*), high priest, and *strategos* is written in a style strikingly reminiscent of documents from the Hellenistic world. The structure of this declaration, the extensive arguments invoked to justify and explain such appointments, the use of purple robes and gold ornaments by the Hasmonean ruler, the dating of an era commencing with Simon's appointment, and, finally, recording the text of this document on bronze tablets and placing them in a prominent place in the Temple area and in the (Temple?) treasury are all elements borrowed directly from well-known Hellenistic practices.

---

10. See, for example, 1 Maccabees 8:17; 12:16; 14:22, 24; Josephus, *Antiquities* 13.260; 14.146. To this list one should add the proto-Pharisee Antigonus of Socho (*m. Avot* 1:3) and the Sadducee Diogenes (*Antiquities* 14.411). As noted in chapter I, several excellent overall treatments of the Hasmoneans and Hellenism include Rappaport, "On the Hellenization of the Hasmoneans," pp. 477–503; his briefer English treatment in *Jewish Assimilation*, pp. 1–13; and Rajak, "Hasmoneans," pp. 261–80.

Mention should be made of an earlier Jewish ambassador, from about 180 B.C.E., who bore the name John or Yoḥanan (2 Maccabees 4:11). It is significant that this Hebrew name appears early on (in this case before the Hellenizers' reforms), as did the Hasmonean Hebrew names at the outset of their political activity. Later on, as we have seen, Greek names became more ubiquitous for both groups.

Beginning with the second generation, the Hasmoneans began adopting Greek names in addition to their Hebrew ones: John Hyrcanus I (134–104 B.C.E.), Aristobulus I (104–103 B.C.E.), Alexander Jannaeus (103–76 B.C.E.), Salome Alexandra (76–67 B.C.E.), Aristobulus II (67–63 B.C.E.), Hyrcanus II (63–40 B.C.E.), and, finally, Antigonus (40–37 B.C.E.). Hellenization in the Hasmonean court is likewise reflected by the hiring of foreign mercenaries and, more poignantly, by the assumption of royalty by Aristobulus and Alexander Jannaeus. Even more telling in this regard is the sole rule of a queen, Salome Alexandra, whose smooth and unchallenged succession was undoubtedly facilitated by contemporary Ptolemaic practice.

Several burial monuments and graves discovered in Jerusalem from this period likewise reflect significant appropriation of Hellenistic forms. The two principal remains of such funerary monuments are the priestly Bnei Ḥezir tomb from the Qidron Valley to the east of the city, and Jason's tomb (fig. 2; also probably belonging to a priestly family) to the west, in what is known today as the Reḥavia neighborhood. Both were built in typical Hellenistic fashion, the former with its facade in classic Doric style (columns, pilasters, and frieze), the latter with its single Doric column and pyramid-type monument. Both tombs feature *kukhim*, or *loculi* (rectangular niches cut perpendicularly in the wall for primary burials), a funerary arrangement that reached Judaea from Alexandria and Palestine's southern coastal region, i.e., Marisa. The tomb of Jason displays scenes of merchant vessels and warships, a gazelle, and menorah graffiti (the latter appearing in Jewish art perhaps for the first time). Both of these tombs feature a variety of inscriptions: Hebrew in the Bnei Ḥezir tomb and Greek and Aramaic in Jason's tomb.[11]

11. L. Y. Rahmani, "Jason's Tomb," *IEJ* 17 (1967): 61–100; N. Avigad, *Early Tombs in the Kidron Valley* (Jerusalem: Bialik, 1954), pp. 37–78 (Hebrew); *NEAEHL* 2, pp. 750–51.

Fig. 2. Jason's tomb, Hasmonean period.

The coins minted by the Hasmoneans are a fascinating example of cultural synthesis, as Hellenistic and Jewish traditions meet on these tiny bronze coins. Similar to earlier mintage, such coins were issued for economic and political purposes, reflecting the current practice of both established kingdoms as well as of newly founded political entities seeking recognition and legitimacy. While only inscriptions in ancient Hebrew script (the First Temple precursor of the square Aramaic script introduced into Jewish society in the Persian period) appear on the coinage of Hyrcanus I and Aristobulus I, Greek inscriptions begin to appear regularly from the time of Alexander Jannaeus onward. These inscriptions bear the Greek

Fig. 3. Hasmonean coin from the time of Alexander Jannaeus (103–76 B.C.E.). Left: wheel or star, inscribed "Jonathan the king"; right: anchor.

name of the ruler as well as his Greek title, *basileus* (king); the Hebrew inscriptions, by contrast, bear the ruler's Hebrew name (Yehoḥanan, Judah, Jonathan, Mattathias) as well as the title "high priest" or "king" (fig. 3). On occasion, these bilingual inscriptions appear on either side of the same coin.[12]

The Hasmonean rulers appear to have lived comfortably within the Hellenistic and Jewish worlds, and this is the message they wished to convey to their people via their coins, one of the most public vehicles at their disposal. Similarly, Phoenician coins from this period exhibited native symbols together with Phoenician and Greek legends. Thus, the Hasmonean numismatic evidence is significant on two counts: it reflects the vision and policy of those who

12. Meshorer, *Coinage* 2, pp. 35–159.

ruled, while the message contained therein was aimed at the population at large for whom these coins were made.

The symbols appearing on these coins were, with rare exception, borrowed from the surrounding Hellenistic world: anchors, cornucopiae, a wheel or star design, and floral representations. However, in this regard the Hasmonean rulers introduced one very unusual dimension. No images whatsoever of living beings, either animal or human, appear on any of their coins. In fact, these coins are the first clear evidence we have of a major change in attitude and practice vis-à-vis figural representation. Jews throughout the First and Second Temple periods had no compunctions about using figural representations even in the most sacred of places, e.g., the cherubs over the holy ark or the oxen supporting the large basin in front of the Temple (Exodus 25:18–20; 1 Kings 7:44). As of the second century B.C.E., however, there was a dramatic shift in Jewish practice, seen first on Hasmonean coins, which was to continue for some three hundred years until the later second century C.E. With but very few exceptions, figural art was deliberately and almost universally eschewed by Jews throughout Judaea and the Diaspora. Not only did the Hasmonean rulers, for all their Hellenization, adhere to this practice, but they themselves may well have been the initiators of this striking change in behavior.[13]

13. That this aniconic policy became a recognized characteristic of the Jews is clearly attested by Tacitus (*Histories* 5.5.4). The reason for this change has been understood as a reaction to the aggressive policies of Antiochus IV or to the Hellenization process in general, and particularly to the introduction of pagan worship into the Jerusalem Temple. However, it has also been suggested that the policy derived from the Sadducees' stringency in their interpretation of the second commandment, or from the Eastern cultural artistic tradition introduced into Palestine by Jews who had returned from their Babylonian exile. For views on this subject, see B. Cohen, "Art in Jewish Law," *Judaism* 3 (1954): 167; M. Avi-Yonah, *Oriental Art in Roman Palestine* (Rome: University of Rome Press, 1961), pp. 13–27; M. Smith, "Goodenough's 'Jewish Symbols,'" p. 60; N. Avigad, *Beth She'arim* (New Brunswick, NJ: Rutgers University Press, 1976)

Thus, the artistic and epigraphical components of the coins minted in Jerusalem under Hasmonean auspices reveal a fascinating combination of Jewish and Hellenistic elements, reflecting the desire of the Hasmoneans to straddle and integrate both worlds. This thrust is reflected in the archeological finds from the Hasmonean palaces at Jericho as well. Side by side with the large swimming pool and the Doric-style pavilion in the most sophisticated Hellenistic aristocratic taste, we find a series of ritual baths (*miqva'ot*), reflecting the Hasmoneans' priestly obligation to maintain their ritual purity.

Other evidence from Hasmonean society, though limited, likewise points toward Jewish and Hellenistic symbiosis. Even a book as hostile to the Jewish Hellenizers and their reforms as 2 Maccabees—written toward the end of the second century B.C.E.—reflects a certain ambivalence. The book was the first to use the terms "Judaism" (2:21; 8:1; 14:38) and "Hellenism" (4:13) as contrasting values and opposing cultural forces. Yet 2 Maccabees itself was written in Greek, was patterned in the tradition of Greek "pathetic" historiography, and borrowed Greek literary motifs in its narratives. At about the same time, the additions to the Greek translation of the book of Esther used the finest of Greek linguistic and stylistic techniques, while focusing on particularistic values and emphasizing the chasm between Greek and Jew (i.e., between Haman and Mordecai). It is explicitly stated that this translation was carried out in Jerusalem around the turn of the first century B.C.E.

Thus, far from stifling Hellenistic influence, Hasmonean rule was actually catalytic. To maintain diplomatic relations, support a bureaucracy, and develop a military force, Greek language and

---

3, pp. 277–78; G. Blidstein, "The Tannaim and Plastic Art: Problems and Prospects," in *Perspectives in Jewish Learning* 5, ed. B. L. Sherwin (Chicago: Spertus College of Judaica Press, 1973), pp. 22–23.

ways had to be learned. As Bickerman has aptly remarked with regard to Hellenistic native rulers who took over in the wake of the Seleucid collapse: "Cosmopolitanism was the price of independence." [14]

HERODIAN JERUSALEM AND THE PROCESS OF HELLENIZATION

With the Roman conquest of the East and the subsequent ascension of Herod as king of Judaea in 37 B.C.E., a new era opened for Jerusalem that was marked by a far greater intensity of contact with and integration into the surrounding culture. The reasons for this significant change are threefold. First and foremost was Rome's establishment of an empire whose borders embraced the entire *oikumene*. With control of these areas firmly secured, Rome could justifiably boast of a new era referred to as the *Pax Romana*, an era which allowed for freedom and security of movement. Internal boundaries essentially disappeared, and the flow of traffic, be it commercial, social, religious, or cultural, now became commonplace. As a result, Jerusalem was linked more firmly than ever to a network of urban centers in the Roman East (see fig. 4).[15]

A second factor in Jerusalem's increased international posture relates to Herod himself. As a client king, Herod's most basic policy was to integrate his kingdom as much as possible into the warp and weft of the Roman world. By his great agility and sagacity he was able to maintain and strengthen political connections time and again in the course of his career.[16] Herod's political loyalty was

14. Bickerman, *Jews in the Greek Age*, p. 302.

15. Millar, *The Roman East*, pp. 1–23.

16. A. Schalit, *King Herod* (Jerusalem: Bialik, 1960), pp. 240–73 (Hebrew); M. Stern, *The Kingdom of Herod* (Tel Aviv: Ministry of Defense, 1992), pp. 25–46 (Hebrew); L. I. Levine, "Herod, the King and His Era," in *King Herod and His Era*, ed. M. Naor (Jerusalem: Yad Ben-Zvi, 1985), pp. 2–10 (Hebrew); Meshorer, *Coinage* 2, pp. 5–30.

*Fig. 4. Overview of Jerusalem from the northeast. The Temple Mount
and the Antonia fortress are visible in the foreground
(model, Holyland Hotel).*

matched by his fascination with the readily accessible cultural and
social world of his time, both in its Hellenistic and Roman versions.
Nicolaus of Damascus, Herod's close advisor and teacher, takes
note of Herod's enthusiasm for philosophy, rhetoric, and history.[17]

17. M. Stern, *Greek and Latin Authors* 1, pp. 248–50:
   Herod again having given up his enthusiasm for philosophy, as it commonly happens with people in authority because of the abundance of goods
that distract them, was eager again for rhetoric and pressed Nicolaus to
practise rhetoric together with him, and they practised rhetoric together.
Again, he was seized by love of history, Nicolaus praising the subject and
saying that it was proper for a statesman, and useful also for a king, to know
the works and achievements of the former generations. And Herod, becoming eager to study this subject, also influenced Nicolaus to busy himself
with history. He applied himself vigorously to that undertaking, collecting
material for the whole of history, and working incomparably harder than
other people, completed the project after a long toil. He used to say that
if Eurystheus had suggested this task to Heracles, he would have very

His personal commitment in this regard was reinforced by the people of his court, many of whom were non-Jewish, but all of whom bore either Greek or Latin names, a clear indication of their cultural proclivities. Josephus mentions, for example, a wine steward in Herod's court, and this piece of information meshes well with the large number of imported amphorae found on Masada that once contained a rich selection of Italian wines.[18] Herod's coins bore only Greek inscriptions, including his royal title, together with a repertoire of contemporary symbols (e.g., tripod, diadem, wreath, and eagle).[19]

Not only were Herod and his court attracted to the social ambience and material culture offered by Roman society; so, too, were the wealthy priestly and nonpriestly classes of Herod's Jerusalem. Excavations in the city's Jewish quarter after 1967 offer remarkable evidence of the extent to which this stratum of Jerusalem society imported and adopted the regnant artistic styles and material

---

much worn him out. Then Herod, when sailing to Rome to meet Caesar, took Nicolaus with him on the same ship, and they discussed philosophy together.

18. H. M. Cotton and J. Geiger, *Masada 2: The Yigael Yadin Excavations 1963–1965, Final Reports: The Latin and Greek Documents* (Jerusalem: Israel Exploration Society and The Hebrew University, 1989), pp. 133–77, 219–21.

19. Meshorer, *Coinage* 2, pp. 22–30. On the uniquely Roman components of Herod's behavior and practices, see J. Geiger, "Herod and Rome: New Aspects," in *The Jews in the Hellenistic-Roman World: Studies in Memory of Menahem Stern*, ed. I. Gafni, A. Oppenheimer, and D. Schwartz (Jerusalem: Z. Shazar Center, 1996), pp. 133–45 (Hebrew). The Roman/Italian influence on a wide range of phenomena in the material culture of Herodian Palestine is reviewed in a recent volume of studies, K. Fittschen and G. Foerster, eds., *Judaea and the Greco-Roman World in the Time of Herod in the Light of Archaeological Evidence* (Göttingen: Vandenhoeck and Ruprecht, 1996). The following topics are covered with respect to Roman influence: Herodian palaces, Herodian architecture of Masada, wall decorations, scroll ornamentations, and imported amphorae. On the influence of Roman army structure and organization on Herod, see I. Schatzman, *The Armies of the Hasmoneans and Herod: From Hellenistic to Roman Framework* (Tübingen: Mohr, 1991), pp. 198–216.

Fig. 5. Reconstruction of a reception hall in a large mansion discovered in the Upper City of Herodian Jerusalem.

goods from the surrounding world. Among the most relevant finds in this regard are mosaic floors featuring geometric and floral designs, frescoes similar to those found at Pompeii featuring architectural designs, colored panels, imitation marble, stucco used in imitation of ashlar blocks or architectural and floral motifs (see fig. 5), a glass decanter from Sidon (see fig. 6), imported western and eastern terra sigillata, fine or thin-walled ware, Pompeian red ware, Italian amphorae, and perfume bottles. Herodian society, in the quantity and quality of its imported wares—including the remains from Jericho and Herod's desert fortresses as well as Jerusalem—is strikingly different from its Hasmonean predecessor. Whereas Hasmonean society had relied, for the most part, on local

Fig. 6. Above: *glass decanter found in the Upper City;* below: *drawing of reconstruction with the Greek inscription "Ennion made [this]."*

ware, Herod and his upper classes used foreign-made ceramics to a much greater degree. Thus, from this aspect as well, the wealthy residential neighborhoods of the Upper City of Jerusalem and elsewhere were well ensconced in the wider Greco-Roman material culture.[20]

A third factor that had considerable influence on the cultural milieu of Herodian Jerusalem was the dramatically expanding Jewish Diaspora. With the exception of Egypt, not a great deal is known about Jewish communities outside of Judaea in the pre-Roman period. However, beginning with Roman expansion in the East and the documentation provided by Philo, Josephus, and the New Testament, we become increasingly aware of the remarkable number of Diaspora communities then in existence. These communities are characterized by their extensive geographic distribution no less than by their social and political integration into the surrounding society, though that integration was not always without its tensions and frictions.[21] Moreover, it is safe to say that, with rare exception, the communities of the Roman Diaspora were thoroughly acculturated in terms of language, names, official titles, and institutional forms.

Herod actively encouraged the involvement of Diaspora Jewry in the life of Jerusalem. He himself took the initiative by bringing a number of priestly families to Jerusalem from Egypt and Babylonia. His purpose was to replace the Hasmonean dynasty with priests who—given their places of origin—would be more beholden to him and more attuned to the needs and expectations

20. N. Avigad, *Discovering Jerusalem* (Jerusalem: Shikmona, 1980), pp. 81–202.

21. E. Schürer, *The History of the Jewish People in the Age of Jesus Christ (175 B.C.–A.D. 135)* (rev. ed.; Edinburgh: T. & T. Clark, 1973–87), 3, pp. 1–176; M. Stern, "The Jewish Diaspora," in *The Jewish People in the First Century*, ed. S. Safrai and M. Stern (Philadelphia: Fortress, 1974), 1, pp. 117–83.

of life under Roman rule.[22] Moreover, Herod's rebuilding of the Jerusalem Temple on a monumental scale served not only as a source of inspiration for Jews everywhere but also as an inducement and attraction for many to visit the city, often on the pilgrimage festivals. The multitudes streaming to the city in the course of the year were in no small degree composed of Jews from far-flung Diaspora communities. One has only to read Acts 2:9–11 to gain some notion of the extent of their dispersion; therein appears a list of places whose languages could be heard on the streets of the city during a festival: Parthia, Media, Elam, Mesopotamia, Cappadocia, Pontus, Asia, Phrygia, Pamphylia, Egypt, Cyrene, Rome, Crete, and Arabia (see fig. 7). Taken together with Philo's remarkable list, the geographical diffusion of the Jewish people appears to have been stunning.[23] Thus, representing a microcosm of the entire Roman world, the pilgrims who gathered in Jerusalem brought within its walls a wide range of cultures that could help balance any inclination toward isolation that may have existed among some native Jerusalemites.

---

22. Idem, "Social and Political Realignments in Herodian Judaea," in *The Jerusalem Cathedra* 2, ed. L. I. Levine, pp. 40–62; A. Kasher, "Herod and Diaspora Jewry," in *Studies on the Jewish Diaspora in the Hellenistic and Roman Periods*, ed. B. Isaac and A. Oppenheimer (Tel Aviv: Ramot, 1996), pp. 13–22 (Hebrew).

23. Philo (*Embassy* 281–82) describes the dispersion as follows:

As for the holy city, I must say what befits me to say. While she, as I have said, is my native city she is also the mother city not of one country Judaea but of most of the others in virtue of the colonies sent out at diverse times to the neighbouring lands Egypt, Phoenicia, the part of Syria called the Hollow and the rest as well and the lands lying far apart, Pamphylia, Cilicia, most of Asia up to Bithynia and the corners of Pontus, similarly also into Europe, Thessaly, Boeotia, Macedonia, Aetolia, Attica, Argos, Corinth and most of the best parts of Peloponnese. And not only are the mainlands full of Jewish colonies but also the most highly esteemed of the islands Euboea, Cyprus, Crete. I say nothing of the countries beyond the Euphrates, for except for a small part they all, Babylon and of the other satrapies those where the land within their confines is highly fertile, have Jewish inhabitants.

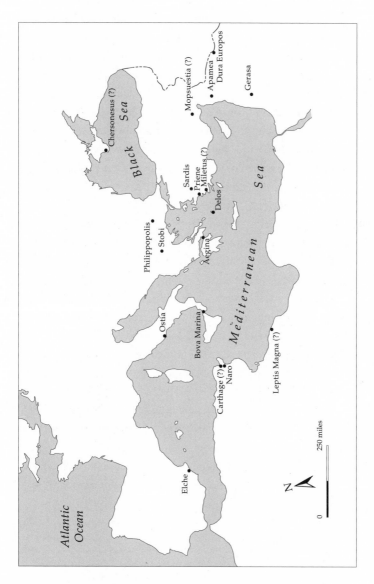

Fig. 7. Map of the archeological remains of Diaspora synagogues in the Roman-Byzantine period.

Diaspora Jews, who in the first century c.e. numbered in the millions (together with those in Judaea, reaching perhaps 10 percent of the Roman Empire's population),[24] not only made substantial monetary contributions to Jerusalem and its Temple, but also offered gifts of enormous value. Noteworthy in this regard are the massive Corinthian bronze doors donated by Nicanor of Alexandria and, according to a recently published inscription, a stone pavement in the Temple area donated by a Jew from Rhodes.[25] In addition to the golden objects donated by Queen Helena of Adiabene (a lamp for the Temple and a golden tablet with the text of the suspected adulteress; Numbers 5:11–31) and those of her son Monobaz (handles for the vessels used on Yom Kippur), the family built a number of palaces in the City of David as well as a monumental tomb north of the city. Moreover, in the serious famine of the mid-forties, Helena and her family mobilized massive aid for the city. She herself brought grain from Alexandria and dried figs from Cyprus, while her other son, King Izates, dispatched a large sum of money for use by the Jerusalem authorities.[26]

Of even greater significance to our discussion was the presence of permanent communities of Diaspora Jews in Jerusalem. The existence of these communities is attested by three independent sources. Rabbinic literature takes note of a synagogue of Alexandrians in Jerusalem (*t. Megillah* 2:17), and the well-known Theodotus inscription speaks of a synagogue in Jerusalem almost certainly founded by Jews from Rome (intended to serve, inter alia, as a hostel for visitors from abroad).[27] The most important source

24. Baron, *Social and Religious History* 1, pp. 167–79, 370–72; cf. also first edition of this work (New York: Columbia University Press, 1937), 1, pp. 128–43.

25. Nicanor: see *m. Middot* 1:4, 2:3, 6, and elsewhere; B. Isaac, "A Donation for Herod's Temple in Jerusalem," *IEJ* 33 (1983): 86–92.

26. *m. Yoma* 3:10; Josephus, *Antiquities* 20.49–55. For a tradition relating to Helena's personal piety, see *m. Nazir* 3:6.

27. L. Roth-Gerson, *The Greek Inscriptions from the Synagogues in Eretz-Israel* (Jerusalem: Yad Ben-Zvi, 1987), pp. 76–86 (Hebrew).

is Acts 6:9, which lists Diaspora synagogues in the city established by Jews from Alexandria, Cyrene, Asia, Cilicia, and a synagogue of freedmen, perhaps a reference to Jews from Rome. The precise effect of these permanent Diaspora communities in the city is unknown, but together with the constant stream of visitors from abroad throughout the year, their influence on city life and affairs was undoubtedly considerable.

GRECO-ROMAN INSTITUTIONS AND PRACTICES IN HERODIAN JERUSALEM

In an attempt to assess in greater depth the nature and extent of Hellenistic-Roman influence on Jerusalem, we will examine five different aspects of life in the city during the Herodian–early Roman period, i.e., at the end of the Second Temple period.

Entertainment Institutions

In a relatively detailed account, Josephus records the existence of three major entertainment institutions in Herodian Jerusalem—a theater, amphitheater, and hippodrome (*Antiquities* 15.267–79).[28] The theater was the setting for dramatic and musical performances, the amphitheater for bloody spectacles between gladiators, animals, or gladiators and animals, while the hippodrome featured chariot (and perhaps foot) races (see fig. 8). Herod constructed these buildings with the intention of introducing typical Roman institutions into his capital, thus placing Jerusalem in the cultural forefront along with other major urban centers of the East. No sizable Roman city with any modicum of civic pride would do with-

---

28. M. Lämmer, "Griechische Wettkämpfe in Jerusalem und ihre politischen Hintergrunde," *Kölner Beiträge zur Sportwissenschaft* 2: *Jahrbuch der deutschen Sporthochschule Köln* (1973): 182–227.

Fig. 8. Hippodrome, located south of the Temple Mount
(model, Holyland Hotel).

out one or more of these institutions, much as any respectable modern city would be unwilling to do without cultural centers, museums, and major sports facilities. However, Herod was not content with simply erecting these structures; he also allocated considerable sums of money to promote quadrennial spectacles to which he invited the foremost athletes and performers of the time. Josephus offers us a vivid description of the various competitive events that were held in Jerusalem, as well as of their lavishness:

> For this reason Herod went still farther in departing from the native customs, and through foreign practices he gradually corrupted the ancient

way of life which had hitherto been inviolable. As a result of this we suffered considerable harm at a later time as well, because those things were neglected which had formerly induced piety in the masses. For in the first place he established athletic contests every fifth year (every four years by our reckoning) in honour of Caesar, and he built a theatre in Jerusalem, and after that a very large amphitheatre in the plain, both being spectacularly lavish but foreign to Jewish custom, for the use of such buildings and the exhibition of such spectacles have not been traditional (with the Jews). Herod, however, celebrated the quinquennial festival in the most splendid way, sending notices of it to the neighbouring peoples and inviting participants from the whole nation. Athletes and other classes of contestants were invited from every land, being attracted by the hope of winning the prizes offered and by the glory of victory. And the leading men in various fields were assembled, for Herod offered very great prizes not only to the winners in gymnastic games but also to those who engaged in music and those who are called *thymelikoi*. And an effort was made to have all the most famous persons come to the contest. He also offered considerable gifts to drivers of four-horse and two-horse chariots and to those mounted on race-horses. And whatever costly or magnificent efforts had been made by others, all these did Herod imitate in his ambition to see his spectacle become famous. All around the theatre were inscriptions concerning Caesar and trophies of the nations which he had won in war, all of them made for Herod of pure gold and silver. As for serviceable objects, there was no valuable garment or vessel of precious stones which was not also on exhibition along with the contests. There was also a supply of wild beasts, a great many lions and other animals having been brought together for him, such as were of extraordinary strength or of very rare kinds. When the practice began of involving them in combat with one another or setting condemned men to fight against them, foreigners were astonished at the expense and at the same time entertained by the dangerous spectacle, but to the natives it meant an open break with the customs held in honour by them. For it seemed glaring impiety to throw men to wild beasts for the pleasure of other men as spectators, and it seemed a further impiety to change their established ways for foreign practices. But more than all else it was the trophies that irked them, for in the belief that these were images surrounded by weapons, which it was against their national custom to worship, they were exceedingly angry.

That the Jews were highly agitated did not escape Herod's notice, and since he thought it inopportune to use force against them, he spoke to some of them reassuringly in an attempt to remove their religious scruples. He did not, however, succeed, for in their displeasure at the offenses of which they thought him responsible, they cried out in unison that although everything else might be endured, they would not tolerate images of men, i.e., trophies being brought into the city, for this was against their national custom. Herod, therefore, seeing how perturbed they were and that they could not easily be persuaded if they did not get some reassurance, summoned the most eminent among them. Leading them to the theater, he showed them the trophies and asked just what they thought these things were. When they cried out, "Images of men," he gave orders for the removal of the ornaments and showed the people the bare wood. As soon as the trophies were stripped, they became a cause of laughter. What contributed most to the confusion of these men was the fact that up until then they had themselves regarded the ornamentation as a disguise for images.[29]

While Josephus' description above paints a clear picture of Herod's personal agenda for Jerusalem, it is important to try and assess the reaction of Jerusalemites to this phenomenon. Again, Josephus' account must provide the basis for such an assessment. Taking his narrative at face value, beginning with the declaration made at the outset, it seems that most Jerusalemites were opposed to these institutions and the events held therein, as both were considered anathema to Jewish law and custom. However, such a conclusion becomes somewhat less clear when Josephus, or the source upon which he draws, spells out some of the specific objections. These are directed at the bloody events held in the amphitheater, which are described as both immoral and in direct conflict with the basic tenets of Jewish faith (*Antiquities* 15.273–74). Such a declaration with respect to the amphitheater is more than understandable,

29. *Antiquities* 15.267–79.

and the sentiment, moreover, would probably be echoed by most people in the East who were unfamiliar with this type of institution. As a matter of fact, of all Greco-Roman institutions of entertainment, the amphitheater made the least headway in penetrating the East. Little wonder, therefore, that of the three structures erected by Herod, the amphitheater alone was located outside the city walls, or as Josephus phrases it, "in the plain" (*Antiquities* 15.268).[30]

In marked contrast to the performances of the amphitheater, no specific reservations are reported with regard to the hippodrome or theater—only that the events there were foreign to earlier Jewish custom, which is, of course, true. Furthermore, our assessment of the reaction of the Jerusalem populace becomes even more uncertain when we read further on of the protest organized by some Jerusalemites (referred to by Josephus as "the Jews"). What both-

---

30. On the Roman amphitheater, see L. Friedländer, *Roman Life and Manners under the Early Empire* (reprint; New York: Barnes and Noble, 1968), 2, pp. 40–90; G. E. Smith, *A Guide to the Roman Amphitheatre* (Los Angeles: Westland, 1984); and generally J. C. Golvin, *L'Amphithéatre romain: Essai sur la théorisation de sa forme et de ses fonctions* (2 vols., Paris: Publications du Centre Pierre, 1988). Regarding the other entertainment institutions, cf. Friedländer, *Roman Life*, pp. 19–40, 90–117; E. Frézouls, "Recherches sur les théatres de l'orient syrien," *Syria* 36 (1959): 202–27 and 38 (1961): 54–86; J. H. Humphrey, *Roman Circuses: Arenas for Chariot Racing* (London: Batsford, 1986), pp. 438–539. Cf. also R. MacMullen, "Roman Imperial Building in the Provinces," *HSCP* 64 (1959): 207–35; A. Segal, "Theatres in Ancient Palestine during the Roman Byzantine Period (An Historical-Archaeological Survey)," *SCI* 8–9 (1989): 145–65.

On the basis of the latest archeological evidence from Jericho and Caesarea, there is now a tendency among some scholars to assume that the amphitheater and hippodrome mentioned by Josephus (*War* 1.415; *Antiquities* 16.137; 17.193–94) were, in reality, one building. Whatever the merits of this suggestion for Caesarea and Jericho, it was clearly not the situation in Jerusalem. Josephus gives the general locations of both the hippodrome (south of the Temple) and amphitheater ("in the plain"); there is little likelihood that they were one and the same place.

*Fig. 9. Theater in the Upper City of Herodian Jerusalem
(model, Holyland Hotel).*

ered these people more than anything else was the suspicion that
Herod had adorned the theater with statues and images, as was customary elsewhere in the Roman world (see fig. 9). Herod pro-
ceeded to invite a delegation of their leaders to the theater and
dramatically uncovered the objects in question, which turned out
to be trophies and not statues. We are then told that all laughed at
the mistaken suspicion, and that "most were inclined to change
their attitude and not to be angry any longer" (*Antiquities* 15.280),
although Josephus does note that some continued to resent Herod's
innovations and a few even plotted to murder him (*Antiquities*
15.280–91).

It would seem from this narrative as a whole that the institutions in question were themselves less of a problem than at first imagined, and that it was the sensitivity toward figural representations in the holy city which was, in fact, of paramount concern to the dissident Jerusalemites. Whatever opposition continued to simmer appears to have been centered in a very small fringe group. The story of the trophies clearly points in this direction. If this be the case, then the sentiment reflected in Josephus' opening statement quoted above was not reflective of all, or perhaps even most, of the city's inhabitants. The fact that by the first centuries c.e. such institutions (the amphitheater excepted) existed in other Jewish cities, e.g., Tiberias, Sepphoris, Tarichaeae, and Jericho—not to speak of their attendance by Diaspora Jews—indicates that Jewish presence in them was not all that unusual. How, then, can we explain the harsh and critical description of these institutions appearing in Josephus? It may be suggested that in his description of the Jerusalem institutions, Josephus was drawing upon an anti-Herodian, anti-Roman source and that he copied the source's description as well as its negative editorial comments.[31]

Funerary Remains

Funerary remains constitute a large percentage of the archeological finds from any ancient city. Because graves were usually placed out-

---

31. The issues regarding Josephus' use of sources, as well as his own aims and prejudices in writing his various works, are many and complex. See, inter alia, M. Stern, *Studies in Jewish History*, pp. 378–413; S. J. D. Cohen, *Josephus in Galilee and Rome: His Vita and Development as a Historian* (Leiden: Brill, 1979), pp. 3–180; H. W. Attridge, "Josephus and His Works," in *Jewish Writings of the Second Temple Period*, ed. M. E. Stone (Assen: Van Gorcum, 1984), pp. 185–232; S. Mason, *Josephus and the New Testament* (Peabody, MA: Hendrickson, 1992), pp. 53–84; J. J. Price, *Jerusalem under Siege: The Collapse of the Jewish State 66–70 c.e.* (Leiden: Brill, 1992), pp. 180–93.

side the city walls, they were not affected by the ravages of war. Furthermore, being located underground and in caves, they were more likely to survive intact over the centuries. Jerusalem is no different in this regard (see fig. 10). As was the case in the earlier Hasmonean period, the city's burial remains from the first century C.E. offer clear evidence of Hellenistic influence; the funerary monuments in the Qidron Valley, such as the so-called Absalom and Zechariah tombs (see fig. 11) are typical of Hellenistic monuments found throughout the Roman East. Wealthy Jerusalemites copied the finest examples of Hellenistic architecture when building these bold and magnificent funerary monuments, featuring solid square bases, columns, capitals, architraves, and cornices, all conforming to Greek styles. The monuments might have had a *tholos* or a pyramid, both ubiquitous elements in the Hellenistic Roman East. The universal use of *kukhim* (*loculi*) in the Jerusalem necropolis, as already noted, made its way into Palestine in the early Hellenistic period, eventually reaching Jerusalem by the late second or early first century B.C.E.[32]

Moreover, Diaspora Jews expended sizable sums of money for funerary memorials in Jerusalem. Nicanor of Alexandria, who contributed a magnificent gate to the Temple, also built an impressive tomb on the crest of Mount Scopus, while what may have been the most magnificent tomb of all in the city was that of Queen Helena of Adiabene and her royal family. Pausanias mentions her tomb together with that of King Mausolus of Halicarnassus, whose mau-

---

32. *NEAEHL* 2, pp. 747–57; N. Avigad, "The Rock-Carved Facades of the Jerusalem Necropolis," *IEJ* 1 (1950–51): 96–106; and bibliographies of Purvis, *Jerusalem* 1, p. 498; L. Y. Rahmani, *A Catalogue of Jewish Ossuaries in the Collections of the State of Israel* (Jerusalem: Israel Antiquities Authority and Israel Academy of Sciences and Humanities, 1994), pp. 264–80. See also the doctoral dissertation of A. Kloner, "The Necropolis of Jerusalem in the Second Temple Period" (Hebrew University of Jerusalem, 1980) (Hebrew).

Fig. 10. Tombs from the Herodian period in the Qidron Valley, east of the Old City. Left: "Absalom's tomb"; right: Zechariah's tomb; center: tomb of Bnei Ḥezir (photograph from 1869).

soleum became one of the seven wonders of the world: "I know many wonderful graves, and will mention two of them, the one at Halicarnassus and one in the land of the Hebrews."[33]

The early Herodian period witnessed the beginning of the extensive appearance of ossuaries used for the secondary burial of

33. *Description of Greece* 7.16.4–5, in M. Stern, *Greek and Latin Authors* 2, p. 196.

Fig. 11. "Absalom's tomb" in the Qidron Valley.

bones. Well over two thousand such ossuaries have been found to
date, deriving from a variety of burial settings, of the wealthy and
poor alike, and in all areas around Jerusalem. Some ossuaries were
decorated (see figs. 12, 13) or bore multiple inscriptions. Some were
located in *kukhim*, others on shelves encircling the room at the entrance. The use of such ossuaries flourished for about one hundred

Fig. 12. Ossuary decorated with an amphora flanked by two rosettes, first century C.E.

years, largely disappearing after the destruction of 70 C.E., although traces were still in evidence into the third century.[34]

Given the popularity of ossuaries for secondary burial in Jerusalem, questions arise as to the origin and significance of this custom. Two very different approaches have been suggested. One posits that the appearance of ossuaries was essentially an internal development; their use in secondary burials evolved in response to the growing belief in the resurrection of the body, and the belief that a deceased person's fate was ultimately decided after twelve months,

34. Kloner, "Necropolis," pp. 250–53; E. M. Meyers, *Jewish Ossuaries: Reburial and Rebirth* (Rome: Biblical Institute Press, 1971).

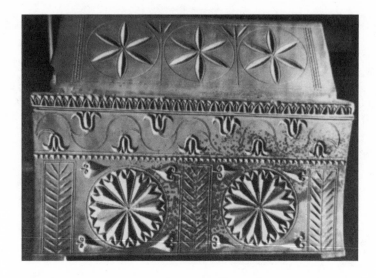

Fig. 13. Ossuary decorated with alternating columns of palm branches and rosettes, first century C.E.

when the flesh disintegrated and the bones were ready for final burial. Ancient sources attribute these beliefs to the Pharisees or later rabbis.[35]

This suggestion, however, flies in the face of other historical data. Such an assertion would have us assume that almost all Jews during this period were Pharisees or that they at least accepted their doctrines, an assumption generally rejected by historians over the last generation. Moreover, this theory does not explain why the custom was introduced when it was (one hundred years after the first appearance of the Pharisees!) and, more crucially, why it began to

35. L. Y. Rahmani, "Ancient Jerusalem's Funerary Customs and Tombs I–IV," *BA* 44 (1981): 171–77, 229–35; 45 (1981): 43–53; 45 (1982): 109–19; idem, *Catalogue*, pp. 53–59; idem, "Ossuaries and Ossilegium (Bone-Gathering) in the Late Second Temple Period," in *Ancient Jerusalem Revealed*, ed. H. Geva (Jerusalem: Israel Exploration Society, 1994), pp. 191–206.

disappear precisely when Pharisaic influence was on the rise, i.e., following the destruction of the Temple. Moreover, if this practice was, in fact, connected to the belief in individual resurrection and immortality, then why do so many ossuaries contain more than one set of bones, including those of priests (Sadducees?)?

A second explanation posits the introduction of ossuaries from non-Jewish origins. It is known that the Romans used such small stone boxes—along with the better-known urns—for their secondary burials. The main difference from Jewish burials, however, is that Roman secondary burial was performed after cremation, when ashes—and not bones—were placed in these receptacles. Viewing this Roman practice as the inspiration for the Jews' use of ossuaries can best explain the dating of this widespread Jerusalem burial custom. It appeared in the Herodian era, reflecting the profound impact Rome was having on the city. Such a theory would also explain the timing of this custom's disappearance. Once the city was destroyed, the social and cultural context that had supported and sustained it also disappeared.

If the above argument is granted, then the introduction of ossuaries may be construed less as a statement of particular Jewish religious beliefs than as a social convention that the relatively affluent Jerusalem society borrowed from Roman practice. The adoption of such a practice required several adjustments: depositing bones and not ashes, waiting twelve months for the flesh to decompose, and accompanying this act with burial customs appropriated from the primary Jewish funerary setting. The extent to which we accept this second explanation determines whether we have further evidence for the influence of Roman customs on a most central Jewish funerary practice from late Second Temple Jerusalem.[36]

---

36. L. I. Levine, "From the Beginning of Roman Rule to the End of the Second Temple Period," in *The History of Eretz Israel 4: The Roman Period from the Conquest to the Ben Kozba War (63 B.C.E.–135 C.E.)*, ed. M. Stern (Jerusalem:

The Jerusalem Temple

The pièce de résistance of Herod's building projects in the city was the rebuilding of the Temple. The king's munificence in this regard knew few bounds. He doubled the size of the Temple Mount area, creating the largest *temenos* (sacred precinct) known in the ancient world. Around three sides of this *temenos* he built porticoes, and a monumental basilica (royal stoa) measuring well over 250 meters along the fourth (see fig. 14). This basilica was the largest-known building of its kind at the time. In the overall plan of the complex, Herod utilized a recognized Hellenistic model. Similar *temenoi*, with their artificial platforms, porticoes, basilicas, and temples, are known from North Africa, Syria, and Asia Minor, and this type of building, referred to as a Caesareum, is described by Philo and other Greco-Roman authors of the period. Herod thus adopted a well-known architectural model for his showpiece Temple.[37]

Other aspects of the Temple complex likewise reflect Hellenistic

---

Keter, 1984), pp. 66–67 (Hebrew); N. Rubin, "Secondary Burials in the Mishnaic and Talmudic Periods: A Proposed Model of the Relationship of Social Structure to Burial Practice," in *Graves and Burial Practices in Israel in the Ancient Period*, ed. I. Singer (Jerusalem: Yad Ben-Zvi, 1994), pp. 248–69 (Hebrew). On Jewish customs regarding secondary burial ossuaries, see D. Zlotnick, ed., *The Tractate "Mourning"* (New Haven: Yale University Press, 1966), pp. 80–88.

37. B. Mazar, "The Archaeological Excavations near the Temple Mount," in *Jerusalem Revealed: Archaeology in the Holy City, 1968–1974*, ed. Y. Yadin (New Haven: Yale University Press, 1976), pp. 25–40; idem, "The Temple Mount," in *Biblical Archaeology Today: Proceedings of the International Congress on Biblical Archaeology, Jerusalem, April 1984* (Jerusalem: Israel Exploration Society and Israel Academy of Sciences and Humanities, 1985), pp. 463–68; M. Ben-Dov, *In the Shadow of the Temple: The Discovery of Ancient Jerusalem* (Jerusalem: Keter, 1985), pp. 73–147; *NEAEHL* 2, pp. 736–44.

On the Hellenistic *temenos* as a model for Herod's Temple Mount, see E. Sjøqvist, "Kaisareion," *OR* 1 (1954): 86–108; J. B. Ward-Perkins, "The Caesareum at Cyrene," *PBSR* 26 (1958): 175–86; G. Foerster, "Art and Architecture in Palestine," in *The Jewish People in the First Century*, ed. S. Safrai and M. Stern (Philadelphia: Fortress, 1976), 2, p. 980.

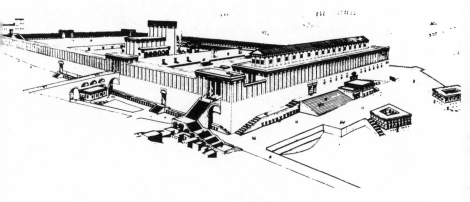

Fig. 14. Reconstruction of the Temple Mount and the buildings surrounding it, as built by Herod.

influence. The architectural components of buildings found in archeological excavations conform to regnant Greek traditions; the columns, capitals, basilical plan, lintels, and gates all follow Greek architectural models. There should be nothing particularly revolutionary in such a realization. As noted, Jews have never possessed an architectural tradition of their own, and their buildings borrowed heavily from the architectural and artistic styles in vogue in contemporary society. Even Solomon's Temple was patterned after a typical Phoenician temple plan (on the synagogue, see chapter IV).

Moreover, certain practices known from Greek and Roman temple precincts also appear in connection with the Jerusalem Temple and its related activities. For example, the Temple Mount itself functioned as a forum or agora where a plethora of judicial, political, social, economic, and cultural activities took place. Specific parallels relating to the religious dimension of the Temple Mount can also be noted. For instance, the Temple Mount was planned in such a way that the main approaches to the sacred

*Fig. 15. Monumental staircase leading to the Ḥuldah Gates
(model, Holyland Hotel).*

precincts were designated for one-way traffic only, as was common in the ancient world. In Jerusalem, the main entrances to the sacred Temple precincts were from the two southern Ḥuldah Gates; the Mishnah relates that the one on the right, the eastern gate, was used for entrance, while the left, or western, gate was for exit.

Archeological finds have indirectly confirmed this arrangement. A monumental thirty-step staircase measuring circa 65 meters in width was discovered in front of the western Ḥuldah Gate (see fig. 15), while another set of stairs, 15 meters wide, was located in front of the eastern gate. The striking difference in size of these two staircases is readily explained by their specific functions. Because the eastern gate was for entry, it did not have to be very wide, as people did not generally enter the Temple area en masse. In contrast, the gate for exit demanded a wide set of stairs to handle the heavy traffic of those leaving at more or less the same time, i.e., at the conclusion of the Temple ceremony. The arrangement is much the same today, when additional exits are made available for the quick exit of a crowd at the conclusion of a theater presentation or sports event.

In a very different vein, the weaving of Temple-related fabrics by virgins was a known practice in non-Jewish sanctuaries as well as in the Jerusalem Temple.[38] Metal spikes attached to the parapet on a building's roof to keep birds away were also common to such settings (*m. Middot* 4:6). Moreover, certain religious customs that appear to have crystallized during the Second Temple period are remarkably similar to those of pagan temples and clearly have their origins in the outside world. A most striking example is the ceremony of bringing the first fruits (*bikkurim*) to Jerusalem. According to the Mishnah, these ceremonies involved a festive procession into the city with the decorated horns of animals, particularly oxen:

> Those living near [Jerusalem] brought fresh figs and grapes, and those living far away brought dried figs and raisins. Before them went an ox, with its horns overlaid with gold and a wreath of olive-leaves on its head. The flute was playing before them (the procession) until they came near the city. (*Bikkurim* 3:3)

Another example of a celebration that evolved in the later Second Temple period is the Simḥat Bet Hasho'evah (water-drawing cele-

---

38. S. Lieberman, *Hellenism in Jewish Palestine* (New York: Jewish Theological Seminary of America, 1962), pp. 144–46, 164–79.

bration) held during the Sukkot holiday. These celebrations lasted for several days and were characterized by all-night festivities that included singing and dancing, juggling and acrobatics, mass processions (often with torches), and carrying items such as willow branches and water libations. All of these activities have striking parallels in contemporary pagan holiday celebrations; clearly some sort of borrowing took place here.[39]

Thus, even the most sacred building in Jewish life, the Jerusalem Temple, was influenced to some degree by the Hellenistic world. While this influence is most pronounced in the physical and material dimension, we have seen that it was present in ceremonial practices and customs as well. Even the most particularistic practice of the Jerusalem Temple—its exclusion of the other, in this case the non-Jew—was not unknown in pagan sanctuaries. In Egypt, for example, aliens such as Phoenicians, Greeks, and Bedouins were forbidden to enter certain local temple precincts.

Languages of Jerusalem

Four different languages could be heard in Second Temple Jerusalem throughout the year, though in sharply varying degrees: Aramaic, Greek, Hebrew, and Latin.[40] They are all attested in epi-

39. J. L. Rubenstein, *The History of Sukkot in the Second Temple and Rabbinic Periods* (Atlanta: Scholars, 1995), pp. 145–48.

40. Fitzmyer, "Languages of Palestine," pp. 501–31. See also J. M. Grintz, "Hebrew as the Spoken and Written Language in the Last Days of the Second Temple," *JBL* 79 (1960): 32–47; R. H. Gundry, "The Language Milieu of First-Century Palestine: Its Bearing on the Authenticity of the Gospel Tradition," *JBL* 83 (1964): 404–8; J. N. Sevenster, *Do You Know Greek? How Much Greek Could the First Jewish Christians Have Known?* (Leiden: Brill, 1968); K. Treu, "Die Bedeutung des Griechischen für die Juden im römischen Reich," *Kairos* 15 (1973): 123–44; B. Z. Wacholder, *Eupolemus: A Study of Judaeo-Greek Literature* (Cincinnati: Hebrew Union College, Jewish Institute of Religion, 1974), pp. 259–306; Ch. Rabin, "Hebrew and Aramaic in the First Century," in *The Jewish People in the First Century*, ed. S. Safrai and M. Stern (Philadelphia: Fortress,

graphical remains, and we know of literary works from the city that are written in at least three of the above languages. Much of Jerusalem's population was probably familiar with, if not fluent in, the first two or three of these languages. Archeological remains from the Judaean Desert and Qumran, and those relating to Bar Kokhba and Babatha, as well as several rabbinic traditions (*j. Megillah* 1.71b; *Sifre–Deuteronomy* 343), clearly indicate the complex linguistic situation in Palestine and Arabia throughout the first and second centuries C.E.[41]

Latin. Of the four languages mentioned above, Latin was the least common and was restricted largely to Roman soldiers and Imperial officials. As a result, it was used only in certain places in the city at certain times, for example, in the Antonia fortress on pilgrimage festivals when large contingents of soldiers were brought in to keep order, or in the procurator's residence when he visited the city. There is always the possibility that some Jews from Rome, Italy, or the western provinces of the Empire visited Jerusalem. However, their numbers were probably quite small, and even then many of them were probably Greek-speakers. Of the approximately six hundred catacomb inscriptions from Rome in the later Empire, only 21 percent were in Latin, while 78 percent were in

---

1976), 2, pp. 1007–39; G. Mussies, "Greek in Palestine and the Diaspora," ibid., pp. 1040–64; Rajak, *Josephus*, pp. 46–58; J. Barr, "Hebrew, Aramaic and Greek in the Hellenistic Age," in *The Cambridge History of Judaism* 2, pp. 79–114; M. Hengel, *The "Hellenization" of Judaea in the First Century after Christ* (London: SCM Press, 1989), pp. 7–18; Schürer, *History* 2, pp. 20–28, 74–80; H. B. Rosén, *Hebrew at the Crossroads of Cultures: From Outgoing Antiquity to the Middle Ages* (Leuven: Peeters, 1995), pp. 5–39; N. M. Waldman, *The Recent Study of Hebrew: A Survey of the Literature with Selected Bibliography* (Cincinnati: Hebrew Union College Press, 1989), pp. 79–135; T. Rajak, "The Location of Cultures in Second Temple Palestine: The Evidence of Josephus," in *The Book of Acts in Its First Century Setting* 4: *The Book of Acts in Its Palestinian Setting*, ed. R. Bauckham (Grand Rapids: Eerdmans, 1995), pp. 1–14.

41. H. M. Cotton, E. H. Cockle, and F. G. B. Millar, "The Papyrology of the Roman Near East: A Survey," *JRS* 85 (1995): 227–31.

Greek, and the remaining 1 percent in Hebrew and Aramaic. Other than the specifically mentioned populations, occasions, and settings, it seems safe to say that the use of Latin at the time was negligible in the city's life.

Hebrew. Relative to Latin, Hebrew was more commonly used in the city, although it is impossible to gauge to what extent. Other than funerary inscriptions, we have little evidence for the use of this language among the population in general. Even the funerary inscriptions are only partially helpful in this respect; it is often difficult to distinguish between Hebrew and Aramaic, as most of the inscriptions consist of names only. And even when we are sure that an inscription is in Hebrew, it does not necessarily indicate that Hebrew was spoken, but rather that the language may merely have been used for identification in a funerary context. Similarly, with regard to the "Hebrews" of the early Jerusalem church referred to in Acts (6:1), it is not clear whether this term refers to the language spoken or to these people's Semitic/Palestinian origins. Furthermore, even if the word does refer to a language, it is generally assumed that Aramaic, and not Hebrew, was intended.[42]

We have only scattered traces of spoken Hebrew in Jerusalem. The statements ascribed to pre-70 sages in rabbinic literature are almost all in Hebrew and may be relevant (assuming that they are not merely a second-century C.E. tannaitic formulation). The first chapters of the *Ethics of the Fathers* is a case in point. The two Aramaic statements found there, quoted in Hillel's name (1:13, 2:6), are striking exceptions that may highlight, even prove, the rule that

42. Cf., for example, W. F. Arndt and F. W. Gingrich, eds., *A Greek-English Lexicon of the New Testament and Other Early Christian Literature* (Chicago: University of Chicago Press, 1957), p. 212; D. A. Fiensy, "The Composition of the Jerusalem Church," in *The Book of Acts in Its First Century Setting 4: The Book of Acts in Its Palestinian Setting*, ed. R. Bauckham (Grand Rapids: Eerdmans, 1995), pp. 230–36. For a broad perspective on the use (and nonuse) of Hebrew in antiquity, see S. Schwartz, "Language, Power and Identity in Ancient Palestine," *Past and Present* 148 (1995): 3–47.

Hebrew was used primarily in limited circles, such as the Pharisees. Of more direct relevance are references in the New Testament and in Josephus' writings to the speaking of "Hebrew" in Jerusalem, as, for example, when Paul addresses a crowd before being taken to the barracks, or when Josephus speaks to the city's inhabitants (Acts 21:40, 22:2; *War* 6.96). If Paul's remarks were indeed in Hebrew, this may be understood, at most, as a demonstration of his Jewishness. However, in light of other evidence that seems to point to the predominance of Aramaic in the city, most scholars have interpreted this word as designating a Semitic language, in this case Aramaic.

Other than several works probably written in Jerusalem during the Hellenistic-Hasmonean period, such as Ben Sira, Jubilees, Judith, Psalms of Solomon, and possibly other books of the Apocrypha and Pseudepigrapha, the most telling evidence for the widespread use of Hebrew in Jewish circles of the first century comes from outside Jerusalem. The written material found in the Judaean Desert, relating to both Qumran and Bar Kokhba, attests to the use of Hebrew not only as a literary language but also, in the case of the latter, as a living tongue used in letters and documents. However, the relevance of this data to the question of languages spoken in Jerusalem is unclear. It is also not at all certain what percentage of the Qumran population hailed from Jerusalem; the Bar Kokhba fighters certainly did not. Moreover, the highly developed religious-nationalistic ideologies of both of the above-noted groups argue for a greater emphasis on Hebrew than in the rest of Judaea's population.

Mishnaic Hebrew has often been invoked as evidence for a spoken language, but even if this be granted, any direct connection with Jerusalem is tenuous. Mishnaic Hebrew's roots may well have been in the Galilee or rural Judaea in this earlier period. In fact, it was rural Judaea, not Jerusalem or the Galilee, that was the geographical context associated with a Hebrew clause in the *ketubah*, the Jewish marriage contract (*m. Ketubot* 4:12). Finally, the wording of at least one document preserved in the Mishnah and purportedly describing a Second Temple setting—the *prozbol*, giving the court the right to collect debts after the sabbatical year—was in Hebrew (*Shevi'it* 10:4).

Greek. We are on more secure ground in trying to assess the use of Greek in Jerusalem. The epigraphical evidence is clear in this regard. More than one-third of the inscriptions found in and around the city are in Greek. Of the 233 inscriptions recently published by L. Y. Rahmani in his catalogue of ossuaries, 73 are in Greek only and another 14 bilingual—in Greek and either Aramaic or Hebrew, i.e., about 37 percent (see fig. 16).[43] Thus, we can safely set this number as the minimum percentage of those inhabitants in the city who preferred Greek. Undoubtedly, there were many others who used Greek regularly, yet wished to have their Hebrew names recorded in a funerary setting—much as is the case in the Diaspora today. Since most of these inscriptions were found on ossuaries and sarcophagi, primarily for the practical purpose of identification, it is likely that the families and relatives of the interred were most familiar with the Greek language.[44]

43. Rahmani, *Catalogue,* pp. 12–13.

44. Although, at first glance, epigraphical statistics appear to constitute hard data, they are nevertheless problematic when used as a basis for generalizations regarding the languages spoken in a given society. The issue, of course, is how representative such evidence is. What percentage of the population had inscriptions made (what MacMullen terms the "epigraphical habit" in "The Epigraphic Habit in the Empire," *American Journal of Philology* 103 [1982]: 233–46), and what percentage of these inscriptions has been discovered? Obviously there is no way of ascertaining these numbers. Nevertheless, epigraphical evidence should not be summarily dismissed. It is not an insignificant quantity (over 250 inscriptions for Second Temple Jerusalem), and the inscriptions come from all parts of the Jerusalem necropolis, from both simple tombs to more elaborate ones. This spread, it would seem, should provide a sample of important strata within Jerusalem society, certainly the middle and upper classes.

Fig. 16. Greek inscription on an ossuary found on Mount Scopus:
"These are the bones of Nicanor the Alexandrian who made
the gates." The last line (in Aramaic) is incomplete:
"Nicanor the Alex[andrian]"; first century C.E.

Diaspora Jews who had settled in Jerusalem were clearly responsible for some of these Greek inscriptions. The custom of bringing the bones of the deceased to the Land of Israel for burial is only attested in the post Bar Kokhba period, i.e., from the second century C.E. onward. The most salient example of a Diaspora Jewish family having taken up residence in Jerusalem is reflected in the monumental Theodotus inscription, which records three generations of synagogue leaders called *archisynagogoi*. This family appears to have come to Jerusalem from Rome and established a synagogue, presumably as a kind of *Landsmannschaft*. Such an institutionalized Diaspora presence in Jerusalem is likewise reflected in Acts 6 which, in addition to identifying one wing of the nascent Jerusalem church as Hellenists (Greek-speaking Jews from the Diaspora), refers, as noted above, to a series of Diaspora synagogues in the city, serving Jews from Alexandria, Cyrene, Asia, Cilicia, and freedmen possibly from Rome.

However, most of the Greek funerary inscriptions noted above probably originated in Jerusalem's middle and upper classes. We have no way of knowing if, and to what extent, the lower classes knew Greek. Other than a smattering of isolated terms, this seems doubtful, as reflected in the Roman tribune's question to Paul: "Do you know Greek?" (Acts 21:37). Having just rescued Paul from a threatening crowd, this official may well have regarded him as a local rabble-rouser.

That many native-born Jerusalemites had some command of Greek may well be indicated by Josephus in a revealing though somewhat enigmatic passage, in which he takes pride in his Jewish learning. He also seems to imply that to know Greek was so common among his fellow Jews that it was of no particular significance:

> For my compatriots admit that in our Jewish learning I far excel them. I have also laboured strenuously to partake of the realm of Greek prose and poetry, after having gained a knowledge of Greek grammar, although

the habitual use of my native tongue has prevented my attaining preci-
sion in the pronunciation. For our people do not favour those persons
who have mastered the speech of many nations, or who adorn their style
with smoothness of diction, because they consider that not only is such
skill common to ordinary freemen but that even slaves who so choose
may acquire it. But they give credit for wisdom to those alone who have
an exact knowledge of the law and who are capable of interpreting the
meaning of Holy Scriptures. (*Antiquities* 20.263–64)

Other than Josephus himself, however, we know of no one else
in first-century Judaea who wrote in Greek other than Justus of
Tiberias, who composed several histories in that language.

There is some rather telling evidence for the knowledge of Greek
among Jerusalem's Jews in the Hasmonean period, and perhaps
earlier. Eupolemos, apparently to be identified with one of Judah
Maccabee's emissaries to Rome in 161 B.C.E., wrote a history of biblical Judaea in Greek. According to the *Letter of Aristeas*, probably
written in the latter half of the second century B.C.E., Jerusalem
boasted enough Greek culture that Ptolemy wrote to the high priest,
asking for a delegation of those versed in the Hebrew text and
knowledgeable in Greek to come to Alexandria and translate the
Bible. Although the *Letter of Aristeas* itself is in large part fanciful
and legendary, the author clearly presumed that Greek was known
in Jerusalem. Moreover, the grandson of Ben Sira, who migrated to
Egypt in 132 B.C.E., translated his work into Greek, presumably having gained at least a rudimentary knowledge of that language while
in Hasmonean Jerusalem. At about the same time, a Greek epitome
known as 2 Maccabees was being created—very likely in Jerusalem—
from Jason of Cyrene's five-volume history of Judah Maccabee.
Several Greek letters were added to this epitome, purportedly written by the authorities in Jerusalem to Alexandria in 143 B.C.E., again
in 124 (and perhaps a third one as early as 161). From about the turn
of the first century B.C.E., the book of Esther (with additions) was
translated into Greek by one Lysimachus son of Ptolemy of Jeru-

salem and sent to Alexandria. Finally, later rabbinic literature knows of a halakhic controversy between Sadducees and Pharisees from some time in the later Second Temple period wherein the works of Homer were used as an example of not defiling the hands (*m. Yadaim* 4:6).

To fully account for the Greek spoken in Jerusalem, one must also consider the thousands of visitors who spent time in the city during pilgrimage festivals and on other occasions. Of those coming from the Roman Diaspora, the overwhelming majority's mother tongue was assuredly Greek. Approximately 70 percent of the entire corpus of Jewish inscriptions from the Greco-Roman and Byzantine periods, in both the Diaspora and Palestine, is in Greek. Even within the Temple precincts, certain chests set aside for donations were marked with Greek letters (*m. Sheqalim* 3:2). Moreover, the number of non-Jews who frequented the city and Temple—and who assuredly spoke either Greek or Latin—was not negligible, as is attested by the Greek and Latin inscriptions placed on the parapet (*soreg*) surrounding the Temple's sacred precinct designed to prevent gentiles from entering (*War* 5.193–94). While it is difficult to assess what percentage of the population spoke Greek, or even understood it, the use of Greek in Jerusalem appears to have been far more widespread than either Latin or Hebrew. That some rabbis sought to ban the teaching of Greek in the early second century C.E. while others facilitated a Greek translation of the Bible by Aquilas further indicates the widespread use of the language (*m. Sotah* 9:14; *j. Megillah* 1.11.71c).

Aramaic. There can be little question that the most ubiquitous language of first-century Jerusalem was Aramaic. Evidence for its extensive use comes from a number of sources. Many funerary inscriptions are in Aramaic (see fig. 17), including one indicating the reburial of King Uziah's bones in the Second Temple period. As noted above, Greek references to Hebrew by Josephus (*War* 6.96)

Fig. 17. Aramaic inscription on an ossuary found in southern Jerusalem: "Yehosef son of Qafa"; first century C.E.

and in the New Testament (Acts 21:40, 22:2) may well refer to Aramaic. The use of Aramaic by the populace at large, reflected either in the name of a place (Gabath Saul, *War* 5.51) or in phrases ascribed to Jesus (*talita kumi*, Mark 5:41; or *lama shabaktani*, Matthew 27:46), is striking testimony for how widespread Aramaic was at the time.

Three types of evidence should be considered decisive in according Aramaic primacy among the languages used in the city. The first is the use of Aramaic translations of the Scriptures in this period—in synagogue settings, at the very least. This custom is well known from rabbinic literature of the second century C.E., but it probably existed beforehand as well. Greek translations of biblical books, as well as an expanded Aramaic midrash known as *Genesis Apocryphon*, have been discovered at Qumran. Rabbinic tradition also speaks of an Aramaic translation of Job that was found on the Temple Mount in the time of Rabban Gamaliel the Elder (ca. 30–50 C.E.), and of another that came to the attention of Rabban Gamaliel II in Tiberias (ca. 100 C.E.; *t. Shabbat* 13:2). The fact that such translations existed and played a central role in the synagogue liturgy of the time indicates the degree to which the populace at large did not understand Hebrew and thus required an Aramaic translation. Perhaps this was one of the reasons why the Torah-reading cycle in the synagogues of Judaea was spread over three to three and one-half years.

A second indication of Aramaic's predominance in the city at this time can be found in the literary works written in this language. The last part of Daniel was composed in Aramaic circa 165 B.C.E. and thus serves as a case in point from the mid-second century. During the Hasmonean period, a number of apocryphal and pseudepigraphal books were presumably originally composed or soon translated into Aramaic; 1 Enoch, Tobit, and the Testaments of the Twelve Patriarchs seem to fit this category. Moreover, Alexander Jannaeus' dated coins bear Aramaic inscriptions: "King Alexander, year 25."[45] From the first century C.E., we have a list of holidays during which mourning was prohibited, with a brief indi-

---

45. J. Naveh, "Dated Coins of Alexander Jannaeus," *IEJ* 18 (1968): 20–25.

cation of their origin; this list became known as *Megillat Ta'anit* and is written in Aramaic.

The third, but far from least important, piece of evidence, is a series of public documents in Aramaic relating specifically to Second Temple Jerusalem. Aramaic versions of the marriage contract (*ketubah*)—at least one explicitly associated with Jerusalem—are quoted in the Mishnah (*Ketubot* 4:7–12), and letters sent by Rabban Gamaliel the Elder from the Temple Mount area to Jews throughout Palestine and the eastern Diaspora regarding tithes and the intercalation of the year were likewise written in Aramaic (*t. Sanhedrin* 2:6).

Among the many ancillary indications of Aramaic's prominence in first-century Jerusalem is the well-documented reality of the third century C.E. and onward, when Aramaic reigned supreme in the Galilee—in synagogue inscriptions, the Jerusalem Talmud, early midrashim, and the continually evolving targumic literature. It may be assumed that the prominence of Aramaic in the later Empire was, in large part, a continuation from earlier centuries.[46]

In summary, by far the two most prominent languages of first-century Jerusalem were Aramaic and Greek. Thus, except for Hebrew, which appears to have been limited to highly defined circles, the languages of Jerusalem were those common to the peoples throughout the East. Just as Greek could have easily been used

46. We have not introduced into our discussion of Jerusalem the evidence from Qumran, for despite their proximity, the connection between these sites remains unknown. Nevertheless, this evidence should be noted. Fragments of Greek translations of the Bible have been found there, as well as Greek words in a number of Qumran scrolls. See J. Fitzmyer, *The Dead Sea Scrolls: Major Publications and Tools for Study* (rev. ed., Atlanta: Scholars, 1989), pp. 11–75, esp. pp. 22 and 41–42; Hengel, "*Hellenization*," p. 21; L. Schiffman, *Reclaiming the Dead Sea Scrolls: The History of Judaism, the Background of Christianity, the Lost Library of Qumran* (Philadelphia: Jewish Publication Society, 1994), pp. 170–76, 212–13.

throughout the Empire and even beyond its borders, so, too, written Aramaic could have served as a bond between a Buddhist emperor, a Parthian dynast, and the Jewish high priest in Jerusalem. In short, throughout the Roman East, Jerusalem included, these two languages were the most important channels of communication from the time of Alexander to the Arab conquest.

Political Institutions

The Jerusalem political scene appears to have been significantly influenced by Greco-Roman models, namely, the first-century *polis* form of government on the one hand and the Hellenistic *synedrion* (Hebrew: *sanhedrin*) on the other. While the question of their existence in Jerusalem is of enormous consequence, the evidence for each requires clarification.

A wide range of sources—rabbinic literature, Josephus, the New Testament, and the Roman historian Cassius Dio—all allude, in one way or another, to the existence of typical Greek political institutions in Jerusalem, such as archons (rulers) and a *boule* (city council). Josephus also speaks of a *demos*, a distinct citizens' group within the city. The single most telling source in this regard is an official letter from the emperor Claudius, quoted by Josephus, in which he addresses "the *archontes, boule,* and *demos* of Jerusalem" (*Antiquities* 20.11). Another institution of the *polis* is the "ten leading men" (*dekaprotoi, Antiquities* 20.194; *War* 5.532), and several sources note the existence of a council building (*bouleuterion*) within the city (*War* 6.354; *j. Yoma* 1.38c), members of a *boule* (*War* 2.405; *j. Ta'anit* 4.69a; Mark 15:43; Cassius Dio 66.6, 2), and a *boule* secretary (*War* 5.532).

Such a *polis*-like municipal structure was not new to Hellenistic-Roman Palestine. Many pagan cities were organized as *poleis* (Gaza, for example, as early as the second century B.C.E., *Antiquities* 13.364), as was at least one Jewish city, Tiberias (*Life* 12.64; *War*

2.641), and possibly Sepphoris as well. It is not clear when such a *polis* system was introduced into Jerusalem; opinions range from the time of Herod to that of Agrippa I.[47]

The earlier scholarly consensus regarding the existence of a Jerusalem *polis* was questioned a generation ago, when Tcherikover raised a series of penetrating issues regarding the city's status.[48] He claimed that each of the above-noted sources is problematic in one way or another, and if any one of these institutions existed in Jerusalem it was a far cry from the Greek model. Tcherikover believed that the authority of the Jerusalem *sanhedrin*, which incorporated many of the functions associated with the *polis*, was broad and that its jurisdiction went beyond the Jerusalem city limits. Moreover, there is no indication of elections or change of officials, nor of any regular meetings of the *demos*, as was customary in a Greek *polis*. None of the educational institutions usually associated with a *polis*, such as the *gymnasium* or *ephebeion*, is referred to in first-century sources, nor does there seem to have been a distinction between the function of the *boule* on the one hand and the priesthood on the other. Josephus, our primary source in this regard, appears inconsistent and somewhat careless in his use of terminology, thus raising serious doubts regarding his overall reliability; he may have used these Greek terms solely for the benefit of his Greco-Roman readers. Tcherikover thus concludes that what existed in Jerusalem were traditional Jewish institutions (*sanhedrin*, priesthood, and so on) with, at the very most, a Hellenistic veneer, i.e., the labels of Greek institutions.

Despite this critique, the case for the existence of a Jerusalem *polis* cannot be readily dismissed. Not only do a wide variety of sources use specific terms that relate to known political institu-

---

47. See, for example, H. Zucker, *Studien zur jüdischen Selbstverwaltung im Altertum* (Berlin: Schocken, 1936), pp. 76–79.

48. V. Tcherikover, "Was Jerusalem a 'Polis'?" *IEJ* 14 (1964): 61–78.

tions, but Claudius' letter should not be regarded simply as an error on the part of the emperor, or as a Josephan misinterpretation or misrepresentation. Some of Tcherikover's assumptions concerning the traditional first-century Jewish institutions, which supposedly lie behind the Greek terminology, are far from self-evident. As we shall suggest below, the *sanhedrin* at this time was most probably a very different institution from what has often been assumed, having nothing whatsoever in common with a city council (*boule*) or otherwise.

The most problematic link in Tcherikover's argument lies in his methodology. Implicit in his presentation is a comparison of the evidence for city government in first-century Jerusalem with what is known about the classic Greek *polis*. The fact remains, however, that by the first century C.E. few if any *poleis* imitated the Greek model. Centuries of Ptolemaic and Seleucid rule, followed by Roman hegemony, had radically altered the status and functioning of Greek cities. Many of the prerogatives of the *polis* were usurped by the Imperial government, and the Roman tendency to rely on trustworthy local oligarchies became a cardinal element in Imperial policy.[49] On the local level, for example, Herod Antipas appointed Agrippa I *agoranomos* (supervisor of the marketplace) in Tiberias, despite the fact that the city was a *polis*. The presence of a Roman governor in Caesarea undoubtedly affected the workings of the city's municipal government, just as the presence of the Temple and its officials affected the Jerusalem *boule*. As regards regular meetings of the *demos* and its authority, these had almost entirely disappeared by the first century C.E. By this time, most *poleis* of the Roman East had evolved into something far different from their Greek prototypes, exhibiting an amalgamation of both Greek and Eastern elements, with limited local autonomy, and functioning in

---

49. A. H. M. Jones, *The Greek City* (Oxford: Clarendon, 1940), pp. 170–91.

the context of Roman imperialism. Thus, the Jerusalem *polis* was something very different from the classic Greek one, but probably would not have been unusual in the landscape of the Roman East. It thus appeared in Roman eyes—as per Claudius' letter—as similar to other contemporary Greek *poleis*.

That Jerusalem had such an institution is a significant statement regarding the penetration of Greek models into the city by the first century. Its introduction would signal another significant measure of Hellenization among Jerusalem's citizens. One has only to recall the events of 175 B.C.E., when the high priest Jason converted Jerusalem into a *polis*. As far as we can tell, there was no known resistance or negative reaction to this move at the time. At least nothing to this effect is recorded in 2 Maccabees, a source which, given its tendentiousness, probably would not have ignored any expression of opposition to Hellenization. Chances are that this was also the case 150 to 200 years later, in Roman Jerusalem.

A second political institution of first-century Jerusalem was the *sanhedrin*. The vast literature dealing with this institution is due in part to its presumed importance and in part to the sharply contradictory descriptions it is accorded in various sources.[50] According to rabbinic literature, the *sanhedrin* was an independent, Pharisaic-led institution guided by Pharisaic halakhah and dealing with a wide range of political and religious issues. In contrast, Greek sources (Josephus and the New Testament) describe the *sanhedrin* as a politically oriented institution controlled by a Herodian ruler

---

50. *TDNT* 7, pp. 860–71; for a full review of the literature up to a generation ago, see H. Mantel, *Studies in the History of the Sanhedrin* (Cambridge: Harvard University Press, 1965), pp. 54–101; and esp. A. Büchler, *Das Synedrion in Jerusalem und das Grosse Beth-Din in der Quaderkammer des jerusalemischen Tempels* (Vienna: Israelitisch-Theologische Lehranstalt, 1902); E. Bickerman, "On the Sanhedrin," *Zion* 3 (1938): 356–59 (Hebrew); S. Hoenig, *The Great Sanhedrin* (Philadelphia: Dropsie College, 1953); J. Efron, *Studies on the Hasmonean Period* (Leiden: Brill, 1987), pp. 287–318.

or high priest and governed by a halakhah apparently quite different from that recorded in rabbinic literature. Moreover, the composition of this body was quite diverse and included Sadducees, Pharisees, and members of the Jerusalem aristocracy.

There have been many attempts to resolve this dilemma. Some scholars have been inclined to accept the testimony of one type of source and dismiss the other as untrustworthy, while others have assumed the historicity of each, at least in part. The latter approach, in turn, has given rise to a plethora of theories claiming that there were two *sanhedrins* (a political one as described by Josephus and the New Testament, and a religious one as per rabbinic literature), three *sanhedrins* (the above two as well as the Jerusalem *boule*), or one all-encompassing *sanhedrin* under the high priest with a committee on religious affairs led by the Pharisees. According to these theories, each of our sources seems to describe a different facet of one complex reality.

Faced with such contradictions between the sources and the concomitant array of theories, what conclusions about the actual operation of a *sanhedrin* can we draw? When and in what contexts did this institution function, who headed it, and what was its composition? In other words, the actual activities of the *sanhedrin* are far more important in determining its place and status in society than theoretical statements describing its prerogatives.

Josephus mentions a *sanhedrin* a number of times. Gabinius created five *sanhedrins* when he divided Judaea in 57 B.C.E. (*Antiquities* 14.90–91); Hyrcanus II convoked it in 46 B.C.E. to try Herod for Hezekiah's murder (*Antiquities* 14.175); and Herod summoned a *sanhedrin* to gain an official seal of approval for his plans to execute Hyrcanus II, his own sons Aristobulus and Alexander, Antipater, and the wife of his brother Pherora (*Antiquities* 15.173, 16.357, 17.46, 93). Ananus, a Sadducean high priest, summoned a *sanhedrin* to try Jesus' brother James (*Antiquities* 20.200), while Agrippa II gathered a *sanhedrin* to deal with the Levites' complaints (*Antiquities*

20.216). In all the above instances, the *sanhedrin* appears to have been a council of eminent figures summoned by the ruling power to try specific cases.

Of no less importance to our discussion are the many occasions when the *sanhedrin* is not mentioned by Josephus; it never represents the people vis-à-vis Rome, either in the rebellion of 4 B.C.E. or later on, in the course of the many events that preceded the outbreak of hostilities in 66 C.E. Nowhere do we read of the *sanhedrin* functioning as an autonomous legislative-judicial body, nor is it ever mentioned in any of the crises concerning the various procurators. Moreover, it appears that the *sanhedrin* was not functioning under Agrippa I, nor in Agrippa II's dispute with the Temple authorities over the wall they built (*Antiquities* 20.216-18) — an issue in which it would have been natural for such a body to have been convened had it existed, at least according to the rabbinic description of its prerogatives.

In the New Testament, the *sanhedrin* appears as an arm of the high priesthood as, for example, in the proceedings surrounding Jesus' trial (Mark 14–15 and parallels); on another occasion, a *sanhedrin* was convoked to try James and Peter (Acts 5), then Stephen (Acts 7), and finally Paul (Acts 22–23). The body mentioned in these cases dealt with matters of religious and political import, was convened by the ruling power, and was composed of priests (mostly Sadducees), the aristocracy, and some Pharisees. The *sanhedrin* does not appear as an independent body wielding its own authority. Thus, the weight of evidence from the more contemporary sources, i.e., Josephus and the New Testament, would seem to be decisive in determining a more limited role for the *sanhedrin* in Herodian and first-century Jerusalem.[51]

---

51. D. Goldblatt (*The Monarchic Principle: Studies in Jewish Self-Government in Antiquity* [Tübingen: Mohr, 1994], pp. 103–30) has reached similar conclusions with regard to the status and authority of the *sanhedrin*. See also the

In this light, it is important to note that an institution such as that described by Josephus and the New Testament was well known in the Hellenistic and Roman worlds. An advisory council, often referred to as a *synedrion* (and similar to the Latin *concilium*), was frequently convened by a ruler in order to take counsel on a major issue at hand. Thus, it would appear that with the development of a strong central monarchy in Judaea in the late Hasmonean and Herodian periods, the *gerousia*, a quasi-independent political body, disappeared, only to be replaced by a *sanhedrin* that functioned in an advisory capacity under the direction and the discretion of the ruling power.[52]

Tertullian once asked, "*Quid Athenis et Hierosolymis?*" ("What has Athens in common with Jerusalem?"). On the basis of our examination of the city, its practices, composition, and institutions at the end of the Second Temple period, we would have to answer, a great deal! Jerusalem was affected by Hellenistic and Roman culture as was Athens. Hellenism was clearly in evidence throughout the city by the first century C.E. The question now is whether we can be more specific and home in on certain areas of city life or certain elements of the population that were particularly affected. The answer, I believe, is guardedly affirmative. Let us begin from the most solid evidence at our disposal and then progress to the less certain data.

---

comments of M. Stern, *Greek and Latin Authors* 2, p. 376; and M. Goodman, *The Ruling Class of Judaea: The Origins of the Jewish Revolt against Rome A.D. 66–70* (Cambridge: Cambridge University Press, 1987), pp. 114–16. Rabbinic literature, specifically Mishnah and Tosefta Sanhedrin, thus appears to reflect an idealized picture of an institution that, in fact, never existed in Second Temple Jerusalem. It is blatantly unhistorical in listing such issues as an idolatrous tribe, tribal courts, and an apostate city, all of which had long since disappeared from the Jewish scene.

52. See H. J. Mason, *Greek Terms for Roman Institutions: A Lexicon and Analysis* (Toronto: Hakkert, 1974), pp. 123–24.

There can be little doubt that the upper classes of the city's population were appreciably Hellenized. Their residential quarter in the Upper City, the impressive funerary monuments, and the widespread use of Greek (including Greek names) all point in this direction. In addition, the presence of a theater in the city offered them exposure to cultural performances enjoyed by their contemporaries in other parts of the Empire.

On an official, public level, a number of institutions functioning in the city reflected common Roman provincial practice. The presence of a *polis*-type government, with its *boule* and *bouleuterion* as well as *sanhedrin*, operating in Jerusalem as elsewhere in the Empire, provided the city a Hellenistic stamp that existed side by side with the Temple and priesthood. The physical and functional prominence of the Temple Mount basilica, not to speak of the Herodian *temenos*, constituted yet another link with civic institutions of other cities.

To the above we may add the many other public buildings in the city that were patterned after Hellenistic models and likewise lent a cosmopolitan aura to Jerusalem. In this regard, we can mention the Antonia palace-fortress, Herod's palace, the three towers adjacent to it, probably the Hasmonean palace, the Xystus (possibly a *gymnasium* as well as a place of assembly), and the archive building. The city's entertainment institutions—the hippodrome, amphitheater, and theater—were also an integral part of the city's landscape.

The last-noted institutions lead us to inquire about the impact of Hellenism on yet a third component of city life—the middle and lower classes, which constituted the bulk of Jerusalem's population. Here, admittedly, the evidence is meager. We may assume that several of the entertainment institutions (the hippodrome and amphitheater) catered to more popular tastes, and that the use of Hellenistic and Roman funerary customs was also widespread among the city's entire population and not just the wealthy. This assumption is based on the fact that funerary remains have been discovered around the entire city, although they are especially concentrated to its north and south. These tombs, ranging from more elaborate, ostentatious monuments to very simply hewn cave arrangements, appear to represent a wide spectrum of socio-economic groups. A similar range is also evident with respect to the contents of these tombs and the ornateness of their ossuaries and sarcophagi. Finally, as the overwhelming majority of Second Temple inscriptions come from this funerary setting, the epigraphical evidence may well be representative of a large portion of society and not only of the wealthy class. There is little more that we can say about these social strata in this regard. Given their widely recognized disinclination for cosmopolitan fashion, either for ideological, nostalgic, or economic reasons, we must be careful not to posit what the evidence clearly does not sustain.

We have noted above (chapter I) the distinction between conscious and subconscious borrowing. Obviously, there is a difference between deliberately adopting a foreign mannerism or custom—or at least being conscious of this action after the fact—and merely internalizing a practice prevalent in one's surroundings which may have stemmed at some point from non-Jewish origins. However important such a distinction may be with regard to measuring conscious acculturation, whether on the individual or societal level, the crucial point in describing social and cultural orientation is determining what the daily practice was and how it resembled what transpired in other parts of the Empire. In measuring the urban dimensions of this interplay—from material culture to institutions, languages, and diverse social and religious practices—the impact of Hellenism on Jerusalem must be judged as significant. Indeed, Jerusalem had a great deal in common with its pagan neighbors of the first century.

The study of the influence of Hellenism on Jerusalem has thus proved to be rich. Before we conclude, however, an important caveat is in order. We have examined only one side of the picture, the impact of the surrounding culture on Jerusalem and its population, and thus we have focused on the extent to which these influences were integrated into the Jewish setting. However, there were also many instances when such influences were seriously altered when adapted to Jewish practice, or were rejected entirely because they offended Jewish sensibilities. Moreover, we know of instances in which strong Hellenistic proclivities existed side by side with distinctly Jewish behavior. The hippodrome, for example, seems to have been located close to the Temple, and most homes of the wealthy featured Hellenistic-Roman decorations alongside Jewish ritual baths (see fig. 18). Even Herod himself was careful to avoid any figural representations in his palaces and public buildings (within Jewish Judaea) and also demanded circumcision before allowing female members of his family to marry non-Jews. All these nuances were at play in the city at one and the same time and in a variety of areas. It is important to underscore the need for a balanced picture in order to appreciate the totality of this phenomenon.[53]

Jerusalem was a thoroughly Jewish city in the early Roman period, in population, calendar, holidays, forms of religious worship, historical memories, and more. Walking its streets in the first century, a visitor in all probability could not help but be struck by the absence of idols, statues, and figural art, an absence that distinguished Jerusalem from every other non-Jewish urban center in the Empire. Moreover, the number and variety of ritual baths were unique to the city and attest to the marked emphasis on ritual purity observed by many Jews, by the priests on a regular basis, and by others before entering the holy precincts of the Temple. The extensive use of stone tables and eating utensils within the city likewise

53. For example, the attempt by Feldman in this regard (*Jew and Gentile*, pp. 19–31).

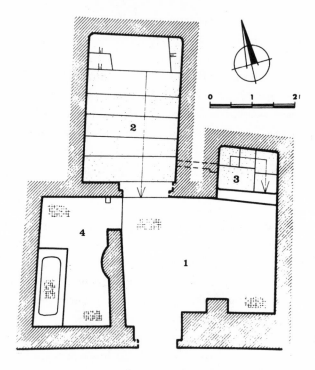

*Fig. 18. Plan of a ritual bath, or miqveh: (1) vestibule; (2) ritual bath;
(3) "store pool"; (4) bathroom.*

attests to punctilious Jewish observance of ritual purity, certainly
by the priests but possibly by others as well. The fact that rabbinic
tradition knows of a dramatic increase in the red heifer sacrifice
(for removing corpse impurity) at this time may well indicate a
greater concern with such issues (*m. Parah* 3:5).

In short, Jerusalem occupied a most unusual position within
Jewish Palestine. On the one hand, it was the most Jewish of its
cities, given the presence of the Temple, the priesthood, and the
leadership of almost every sect and religious group, not to speak of

the many religious observances exclusively associated with this city. On the other hand, Jerusalem was also the most Hellenized of Jewish cities, in terms of its population, languages, institutions, and general cultural ambience. Jerusalem's Janus-type posture made it truly remarkable, both for Jewish society and within the larger Roman world.

CHAPTER III

Rabbinic Judaism in
Its Roman-Byzantine Orbit

JEWISH RELIGIOUS LIFE UNDERWENT A DRAMATIC META-
morphosis in the thousand years between the conquest of Alexander and the ascendancy of the Arabs (332 B.C.E.–640 C.E.). Judaism
in late antiquity, with all its varieties and nuances, was a far cry
from that known and practiced in the First Temple, Persian, or even
early Hellenistic period. Beliefs and practices hitherto marginal or
unknown had now assumed center stage; new forms of religious
leadership and new types of institutions had crystallized; the number and kinds of books considered sacred had expanded greatly;
new holidays were added to the Jewish calendar, and older ones
were recast and given new meanings in light of the evolving tradition and cataclysmic historical events.[1] Below we shall examine
some of these developments in the context of the surrounding
Greco-Roman world, focusing primarily on the emerging world of
the rabbis.

THE UNIVERSAL DIMENSION IN BIBLICAL
AND POSTBIBLICAL JUDAISM

It might seem rather strange at first to raise the issue of foreign influences on the religious dimension of Judaism, for religious con-

---

1. See, for example, S. J. D. Cohen, *From the Maccabees to the Mishnah*
(Philadelphia: Westminster, 1987); L. L. Grabbe, *Judaism from Cyrus to Hadrian*
(2 vols.; Minneapolis: Fortress, 1992); H. Shanks, ed., *Christianity and Rabbinic
Judaism: A Parallel History of Their Origins and Early Development* (Washington, D.C.: Biblical Archaeology Society, 1992).

cerns go to the very heart of the Jewish enterprise and ostensibly distinguish the Jews from the gentile world. If the Jews were different from their neighbors, as assuredly they were, then at the very least it must have been their religious beliefs and practices which set them apart. Such a view is deeply rooted in Jewish texts from the earliest biblical traditions onward; one has only to recall the statement of Bilʿam describing Israel as "a people that dwells alone" (Numbers 23:9). Both the Torah and prophets inveigh time and again against idolatry and the "ways of the nations," a sign that such practices were considered to be in direct contradiction to what was deemed the will of the God of Israel. Some traditions, such as Deuteronomy 7:1–11, go even further and advocate the elimination of certain pagan peoples, while the destruction of idols and places of idolatrous worship is often asserted and not infrequently carried out (2 Kings 18:4–7, 23:4–20).[2]

However, Israelite religion also offered another response to the outside world. While some biblical writers clearly advocated the rejection of anything foreign, others regarded outside influences in a very different light. Although statements sympathetically viewing interaction with pagan society and culture are relatively few, such influences and stimulation were at play from the very beginning of Israel's historical memory. The traditions of Genesis 1–11, for example, are indicative of a broad universalistic panorama, both in their grand scope as well as in their knowledge of other Near Eastern traditions. The epics of Enuma Elish and Gilgamesh, the early Babylonian creation and flood stories, were consciously reworked in the Genesis narratives. Moreover, many of the customs and practices associated with the biblical Patriarchs were known throughout the ancient Near East, as attested by documents

---

2. The fact that these admonitions were often reiterated indicates that many, if not most, of the Jews were often attracted to pagan ways in one form or another. If such practices were not appealing, there would have been little need to constantly admonish the people for wayward behavior.

discovered at Mari and Nuzi. The laws of Hammurabi and other ancient codes of law go a long way in accentuating the nature of Israelite law in Exodus and elsewhere (both in what they had in common and how they differed), while Hittite treaties most probably stand behind at least some of the Deuteronomic legislation. Moreover, biblical wisdom literature and not a few psalms display features strikingly similar to parallel genres found in surrounding cultures.[3]

Alongside the particularistic emphasis and the evidence of de facto influence, there are also traces of a distinctly universalistic strain in biblical thought. Such an outlook involves an awareness of the larger context within which the Jewish people operated, a clear sense of commonality and mutuality between Israel and other nations, and the concomitant downplaying of any sense of superiority or primacy.[4] The statement in Genesis 9:6, "He who spills human blood, his blood will be spilled by another," reflects an awareness of the humanity of all peoples. Deuteronomy recognizes the differences in worship between Israel and other nations as a legitimate phenomenon, one ordained by no less than the God of Israel; He assigned them the constellations of the heavens as objects of worship, just as Israel is to worship Him (4:19–20).

3. N. Sarna, *Understanding Genesis* (New York: Jewish Theological Seminary, 1966), pp. 4–23, 39–59, 86–92, 102–3, 127–29; idem, *Exploring Exodus: The Heritage of Biblical Israel* (New York: Schocken, 1986), pp. 130–89; M. Weinfeld, *Deuteronomy and the Deuteronomic School* (reprint; Winona Lake, IN: Eisenbrauns, 1992), pp. 59–157; and the many stimulating articles appearing in F. Greenspahn, ed., *Essential Papers on Israel and the Ancient Near East* (New York: New York University Press, 1991).

4. M. Greenberg, "The Biblical Grounding of Human Value," in *The Samuel Friedland Lectures, 1960–1966* (New York: Jewish Theological Seminary, 1966), pp. 39–52; idem, "Mankind, Israel and the Nations in the Hebraic Heritage," in *No Man Is Alien*, ed. J. R. Nelson (Leiden: Brill, 1971), pp. 15–40 (reprinted in M. Greenberg, *Studies in the Bible and Jewish Thought* [Philadelphia: Jewish Publication Society, 1995], pp. 369–93); E. E. Urbach, "Humanistic Aspects of Jewish Law," *Immanuel* 18 (1984): 28–42.

Later on, Isaiah gives dramatic expression to this viewpoint in several stunning prophecies. He vividly articulates his vision of the universalistic mission of Israel as a light to the gentiles: "And the many peoples shall go and shall say: 'Come, let us go up to the Mount of the Lord, to the House of the God of Jacob; that He may instruct us in His ways, and that we may walk in His paths.' For instruction (lit. Torah) shall come forth from Zion, the word of the Lord from Jerusalem" (2:3). Isaiah foresaw a period of reconciliation and alliance even with regard to Israel's ancient enemies:

> In that day, there shall be an altar to the Lord inside the land of Egypt and a pillar to the Lord at its border. They shall serve as a symbol and reminder of the Lord of Hosts in the land of Egypt, so that when [the Egyptians] cry out to the Lord against oppressors, He will send them a savior and champion to deliver them. For the Lord will make Himself known to the Egyptians, and the Egyptians shall acknowledge the Lord in that day, and they shall serve [Him] with sacrifice and oblation and shall make vows to the Lord and fulfill them. The Lord will first afflict and then heal the Egyptians; when they turn back to the Lord, He will respond to their entreaties and heal them.
>
> In that day, there shall be a highway from Egypt to Assyria. The Assyrians shall join with the Egyptians and Egyptians with the Assyrians, and then the Egyptians together with the Assyrians shall serve [the Lord].
>
> In that day, Israel shall be a third partner with Egypt and Assyria as a blessing on earth; for the Lord of Hosts will bless them, saying: "Blessed be My people Egypt, My handiwork Assyria, and My very own Israel." (Isaiah 19:19–25)

The open acceptance of non-Jews into Jewish society is reflected by the many "intermarriages" spoken of in this period, such as those of Joseph, Moses, David, and Solomon, and is perhaps most tellingly related in the case of Ruth, whose subsequent status was none other than ancestress of King David.

In the postexilic period, however, tension between particularism

and universalism was evident on a number of levels.[5] Ezekiel and
the prophecies ascribed to Second and Third Isaiah (40–66) adopt
almost diametrically opposed positions on the status of the non-
Jewish world; Ezekiel views this realm in terms of rejection and impurity (36), while Third Isaiah, for example, articulates a more
inclusive universalistic vision (56:6–9). In fifth-century B.C.E. Jerusalem, Ezra, Nehemiah, and other returnees from Babylonia found
themselves in direct conflict with the leading priestly and aristocratic elements of the city over such issues as the legitimacy of
foreign wives and the desirability of ongoing contact with the
non-Jewish world (Ezra 9–10; Nehemiah 13). Diverse views regarding the outside world and the Jews' place in it are likewise evident
in several short books written at about this time; Ruth and Jonah
project a more universal message, while Daniel and Esther emphasize a more particularistic bent. Yet, it should be noted that in each
of these works the dominant attitude espoused is far from exclu-
sive, and contrasting tendencies to each book's main thrust are also
in evidence.

Such diametrically opposed proclivities toward particularism or
universalism, and their resultant tensions, have always been part
and parcel of Jewish history. It stands to reason that a small people,
constantly exposed to outside influences yet with unique traditions
that set it apart, had of necessity to grapple with questions regarding its place within the wider cultural and sociopolitical reality of
the day. On the one hand, there were those who sought to preserve
traditions intact and unadulterated, rejecting all innovation, especially that which originated in a foreign environment. On the other,
there were those who espoused a more open and inclusive view of

5. See Bright, *History of Israel*, pp. 315–19, 335–41; P. R. Ackroyd, *Israel under Babylon and Persia* (Oxford: Oxford University Press, 1970), pp. 62–141;
D. Baltzer, *Ezechiel und Deuterojesaja: Beruehrungen in der Heilserwartung der
beidengrossen Exilspropheten* (Berlin: W. de Gruyter, 1971).

the Jewish enterprise, regarding contacts with and influences from surrounding peoples and cultures as a given, if not a potentially positive source of inspiration and stimulation.

The period we are addressing—the Greco-Roman and Byzantine worlds—was clearly characterized by cultural creativity as well as a flow of ideas in many directions and from different sources. That these technologically advanced and culturally attractive worlds had their fascination for many Jews, as for others, is clear. Nevertheless, these worlds also engendered opposition from those who viewed foreign ways as antithetical to everything Jewish. This dichotomy is already reflected in two statements appearing in the late second century b.c.e., 1 and 2 Maccabees. In the former, the Hellenizers are quoted as giving a theological and historical justification for their program of maximum acculturation: "Come, let us make a covenant with the gentiles around us, because ever since we have separated from them we have suffered many evils" (1 Maccabees 1:11). On the other hand, the author of 2 Maccabees, as already noted, is the first to use the terms *Judaismos* (2:21) and *Hellenismos* (4:13), the latter referring to the adoption of Greek ways, which was anathema. Because of this wholesale sellout to foreign ways, "grievous troubles came upon them (the Jews): the Greeks, whose way of life they admired and whom they wished to ape in every way, became their enemies and the executors of their punishment; it is no light matter to be impious toward the laws of God" (2 Maccabees 4:16–17).

The dilemma posed by the potentially deleterious influence of the non-Jewish world became even more acute toward the end of late antiquity with the rise of Christianity. Here was not just another non-Jewish culture that smacked of idolatrous tendencies (e.g., the Trinity and later the widespread use of icons). Relations were severely complicated owing to diametrically opposed theological claims of Jew and Christian. Judaism's antiquity, and the fact that Jesus himself was Jewish, clearly gave the Jews a unique standing in Christian eyes. Nevertheless, the ongoing tensions and conflicting claims often led to a highly charged atmosphere and strained relations between the two groups. Despite this ever-present potential for conflict (which, indeed, erupted not infrequently on a local level), we are also aware of a wide range of amicable contacts and mutual influences between the two religions in the Byzantine period and even earlier.

A striking expression of the universalistic dimension in Jewish thought appears in the Mishnah, in the context of a discussion on capital punishment:

> Therefore man was created individually, to teach you that he who destroys one soul, Scripture considers it as if he had destroyed a complete world; and he who sustains one soul, Scripture considers it as if he had sustained a complete world . . . and [individual creation also comes] to attest to the greatness of the Holy One Blessed be He. For a man strikes a number of coins with one die and they all resemble each other; [but] the King of Kings, the Holy One Blessed be He, strikes (i.e., creates) each human being with the die (i.e., likeness) of Adam, and not one resembles the other. Therefore, each and every human being is obligated to say: "For me, the world was created." (*Sanhedrin* 4:5)[6]

The universalistic emphasis of this source underscores the value of every human being as a complete world unto himself, as well as the fact that each and every individual is unique despite the many features shared with others. The fact that this tradition refers to people qua human beings and not to the Jewish people in particular is sig-

---

6. While this appears to be the most dramatic articulation of this universalism, the cited statement hardly stands alone. R. ʿAqiva is credited with the following statement: "Man is dear [to God] because he was created in [His] image; even greater was the love in that it was made known to him that he was created in [God's] image" (*m. Avot* 3:14). According to Ben ʿAzzai (*Sifra, Qedoshim* 4.12, ed. Weiss, p. 89a), the greatest principle of the Torah is contained in the verse, "This is the record of Adam's line. When God created man, He made him in the likeness of God" (Genesis 5:1).

nificant. This emphasis—the original intent of the text—was altered in the Middle Ages by the addition "[of] Israel" (it appears so in the printed editions of the Mishnah), thus recasting the entire tradition so that it speaks exclusively about the Jewish people.[7]

This universalistic strain did not hold sway all, or even most, of the time. Extant sources do not emphasize this dimension.[8] What is clear, however, is that this type of outlook was not alien to biblical or postbiblical thought and, in fact, found repeated expression.

Finally, two caveats—one methodological and one contextual—are in order. First, the literary sources at our disposal are religious in essence, composed by a religious elite that ipso facto was conservative for the most part, and thus emphasized a more particularistic posture. It is important, therefore, to note the diversity of

7. For example, the Leiden manuscript. See esp. E. E. Urbach, *The World of the Sages: Collected Studies* (Jerusalem: Magnes, 1988), pp. 561–77 (Hebrew), and, more generally, his *The Sages: Their Concepts and Beliefs* (Jerusalem: Magnes, 1979), 1, p. 217.

8. Note the sweeping statement in *Numbers Rabbah* 10:1: "All the deeds of Israel are different from those of the nations"; and the presentation of S. Stern, *Jewish Identity in Early Rabbinic Writings* (Leiden: Brill, 1994), pp. 1–50, 139–98. Nevertheless, despite the generally assumed discriminatory attitude of rabbinic literature toward the non-Jew in civil law, S. Fraade ("Navigating the Anomalous: Non-Jews at the Intersection of Early Rabbinic Law and Narrative," in *The Other in Jewish Thought and History*, ed. L. Silberstein and R. Cohn [New York: New York University Press, 1994], pp. 145–65) has succeeded in demonstrating the existence of tensions and conflicting opinions with regard to this question within rabbinic literature itself.

On the other hand, I. Knohl ("The Acceptance of Sacrifices from Gentiles," *Tarbiz* 48 [1979]: 341–45 [Hebrew]) has claimed that tannaitic literature—following Second Temple practice—regarded the acceptance of gentile sacrifices at the Jerusalem Temple as legitimate, an attitude that was rejected in later midrashic compilations (*Pesiqta Rabbati, Pirqei d'Rabbi Eliezer, Midrash Tanḥuma–Yelamdenu*).

On the universalistic nature of the Noahide laws in rabbinic thought and legislation, see D. Novak, *The Image of the Non-Jew in Judaism: An Historical and Constructive Study of the Noahide Laws* (Lewiston: Mellen Press, 1983), pp. 28–35, 257–73. See also G. G. Porton, *Goyim, Gentiles and Israelites in Mishnah and Tosefta* (Atlanta: Scholars, 1988).

opinion, even within the ranks of the elite, together with the evidence for outside influences which penetrated these circles. Of no less significance is the need to distinguish between what the elite prescribed and what the people at large were actually doing.

Second, the nature of the larger social and political ambience in which the Jews found themselves often had a direct and profound influence on the balance between these particularistic-universalistic tendencies. In periods of greater isolation and insulation as, for example, in the Persian or Restoration era (538–332 B.C.E.), the forces that advocated distancing the people from foreign influences and contacts clearly had the upper hand. Yet, in an era of greater exposure to and contact with the outside world—political, economical, social, and cultural, as in the Greco-Roman and Byzantine periods—the willingness and even necessity to confront new ideas, influences, and models increased dramatically. This, of course, does not imply a slavish accommodation to or imitation of any and all non-Jewish phenomena. Some outside ideas and practices were accorded a receptive ear; some underwent a measure of adaptation; others had only a very superficial effect; while still others were rejected outright. Most often, if not always, these various processes were going on at one and the same time, and even within the same circles.

Contrasting Views among the Rabbis

The desired degree of openness to the non-Jewish world not only was a source of tension among contemporaneous groups or sects of Jews, but might also have been a divisive factor among those within the same social and religious framework. We are best informed about such issues within Pharisaic and later rabbinic circles, and we shall cite several examples of this internal debate.

A series of traditions associated with Hillel, Shammai, and their followers is instructive in this regard. In one well-known story, we are witness to the contrasting behavior exhibited by Hillel and Shammai toward gentiles who asked a series of questions, some clearly intended to irritate owing to their apparent triviality—for example, why are Africans' feet wide or Babylonians' heads round? (*b. Shabbat* 31a). While Shammai became visibly angry with the interlocutor, Hillel demonstrated exemplary patience and understanding. The positions described are clearly polar and tendentious; given the fact that the stories appear in the Babylonian Talmud centuries after these two sages lived, when Hillel was already considered the leading figure of early rabbinic tradition, their historicity is most dubious. Nevertheless, there can be little question that the issues raised were of ongoing concern to Jews throughout this period, and for this reason such traditions were formulated and preserved.

A similar issue surfaced between the schools of Hillel and Shammai on the eve of the revolt in 66 c.e. Elaborating on a tradition appearing in the Mishnah and Tosefta, the Jerusalem Talmud reports a bitter dispute between these academies over a series of decrees relating to the relationship between Jew and non-Jew. The school of Hillel adopted a moderate position and that of Shammai a much stricter one, advocating a maximal degree of isolation of the Jew from the non-Jewish world.[9] We are on fairly safe ground in assuming a basic historicity for these particular traditions, which are anchored in specific issues and can be linked to a particular historical context. Moreover, they relate to a period—the latter half of the first century c.e.—when rabbinic traditions in general contain much more reliable historical information than for earlier eras. Fi-

9. M. *Shabbat* 1:4; t. *Shabbat* 1:16–22; j. *Shabbat* 1.4.3c–d; b. *Shabbat* 13b–17b. On these decrees, see M. Hengel, *The Zealots: Investigations into the Jewish Freedom Movement in the Period from Herod I until 70 A.D.* (Edinburgh: T. & T. Clark, 1989), pp. 200–6; I. Ben-Shalom, *The School of Shammai and the Zealots' Struggle against Rome* (Jerusalem: Yad Ben-Zvi, 1993), pp. 252–72 (Hebrew).

nally, since this tradition is not at all complimentary in tone (at one point the students of the House of Shammai are reputed to have killed some of their rivals), it would be hard to imagine why later rabbis would have invented it.

The second century C.E. has given us several contrasting traditions from another realm, this time in a cultural-religious vein, revolving around the issue of figural art. In the previous chapter we noted how Jewish attitudes in this regard changed dramatically at the outset of the Hasmonean period. From a rather permissive posture in the First and early Second Temple periods, Jewish attitudes became more polarized and practice more restrictive in the mid-second century B.C.E. and continued as such through the mid-second century C.E. At this later date, the pendulum once again began to shift toward a more open and permissive stance.[10] This transition, however, was not always smooth, and alternative viewpoints are brought into sharp focus in two tannaitic traditions that offer widely differing assessments of this issue. In commenting on the Second Commandment, the tannaitic midrash on Exodus (the *Mekhilta*) states unequivocally that no figural representation is permissible in any way, shape, or form:

> "You shall not make for yourself a sculptured image . . ." (Exodus 20:4). One shall not make one that is graven. But perhaps he may make one that is solid? Scripture says: "Nor any likeness" (ibid.). He shall not make a solid one, but perhaps he may plant something [for idolatrous purposes]? Scripture says: "You shall not plant an *asherah*" (Deuteronomy 16:21). You shall not plant a sapling but may you make something of wood? Scripture says: "Any kind of wood" (ibid.). You shall not make [an idol] of wood, but perhaps one of stone? Scripture says: "Nor shall you place any figured stone" (Leviticus 26:1). You may not make one of stone, but perhaps you may make one of silver or gold? . . . Scripture says:

10. See Urbach, "Rabbinical Laws of Idolatry," pp. 149–65, 229–45; Avigad, *Beth She'arim* 3, pp. 275–87.

"Nor should you make molten golds for yourself" (ibid., 19:4).... Scripture goes to such length in pursuit of the evil inclination towards idolatry in order not to leave room for any pretext of permitting it. (*Masekhet Baḥodesh* 6, ed. Horovitz and Rabin, pp. 224–25)

A very different attitude vis-à-vis the issue of figural art is reflected in a story about Rabban Gamaliel II of Yavneh that took place circa 100 to 120 C.E.:[11]

Proklos the son of Philosophos asked Rabban Gamaliel who was bathing in Acco in the Bath of Aphrodite. He said to him: "It is written in your Torah, 'And nothing of the devoted (forbidden) thing should cling to your hand' (Deuteronomy 13:17). Why are you bathing in the Bath of Aphrodite?" He answered him: "One ought not respond in the bath." When he came out, he (Rabban Gamaliel) said to him: "I did not come into her borders, she came into mine! People do not say, 'Let us make a bath for Aphrodite,' but rather, 'Let us make Aphrodite an ornament for the bath.' Moreover, even if they would give you a large sum of money, you would not approach your idol naked and suffering pollutions, and urinate before it; yet, this goddess stands at the mouth of the gutter and all the people urinate before her. [Lastly,] it is written 'Their gods' (ibid., 12:3), that which they refer to as a god is forbidden and that which is not referred to as a god is permitted." (*m. 'Avodah Zarah* 3:4)

This Mishnah ascribes to Rabban Gamaliel a rather liberal and flexible attitude toward figural art, one that would allow its use in almost all settings, except where idolatry itself is involved. The first two answers that Rabban Gamaliel offers his pagan locutor relate to specific contexts: 1) the purpose of a particular building should determine one's attitude in such matters—if it was meant to be a temple, then any form of contact is forbidden; if not, then one has

---

11. For a different dating of this story, to the time of Rabban Gamaliel III in the early third century, see A. Wasserstein, "Rabban Gamaliel and Proclus the Philosopher (Mishna Aboda Zara 3, 4)," *Zion* 45 (1980): 257–67 (Hebrew).

no need to avoid such images; 2) the way people behave is determinant—if they are respectful toward the statue, then it is forbidden; if not, then the use of such facilities should be permitted. However, Rabban Gamaliel's final comment is the most far-reaching. His statement does not deal with the particular circumstances of the Acco bath or of Aphrodite, but is cast as a general principle applicable anywhere: if the statue is intended for idolatrous purposes, it is forbidden; otherwise it is permitted.

The difference between these almost contemporary traditions regarding figural art is indeed striking. The *Mekhilta* bans outright the making of idols and images, and presumably any contact with them, on the suspicion of potential idolatry.[12] The Rabban Gamaliel account implies a willingness to deal with each situation on its own merit, while inclining toward a very lenient position. Since the absence of figural representation had heretofore constituted one of the cardinal distinctions between Jewish and non-Jewish societies, these different viewpoints reflect the various ways in which the sages (and perhaps Jewish society in general) were grappling with a new reality. The *Mekhilta* advocates a basically conservative approach: what had been the practice among Jews for centuries should continue. Behind this assertion lies the assumption that the greater the distinction between Jew and non-Jew, the better. Rabban Gamaliel—perhaps because of the new historical reality of the post-70 period (i.e., following the destruction of the Second Temple) and the increased contact with non-Jewish society, or ow-

---

12. Scholars generally agree that the ban in the *Mekhilta* was on any kind of figural representation, in continuation of late Second Temple practice; so, for example, E. Goodenough, *Jewish Symbols in the Greco-Roman Period* (New York: Pantheon, 1953–68), 4, pp. 3–24; B. Cohen, "Art in Jewish Law," p. 168; Urbach, "Rabbinical Laws of Idolatry," p. 235. Cf., however, Blidstein ("Tannaim and Plastic Art," pp. 19–20), who claims that the ban applied to cultic objects only.

ing to his own prominent position or personal proclivity—advocated a reassessment of the prohibition to allow greater leeway.

That such questions continued to rivet the attention of later rabbis is clearly reflected in the contrasting views of R. Yoḥanan and Resh Laqish, two leading Palestinian amoraim of the third century.[13] When in Bostra, the capital of Provincia Arabia, Resh Laqish was asked whether it is permissible for Jews to draw water from the local nymphaeum even though it was used from time to time for idolatrous worship and despite the fact that it contained many statues, especially that of Aphrodite. Resh Laqish forbade such usage, thus forcing observant Jews to walk some distance in order to draw water. However, when he told his teacher and colleague, R. Yoḥanan, what had happened, Yoḥanan responded by ordering Resh Laqish to return immediately to Bostra and rescind his decision. R. Yoḥanan then ruled that any statue or image in the public domain (such as a nymphaeum, which generally stood at the main intersection of a city) was not to be considered idolatrous. In other words, in order to enable Jews to function within any given Roman city of the third century, allowance had to be made for the many statues that inevitably graced its streets and plazas, the overwhelming majority of which were for aesthetic, and not necessarily religious, purposes.

The above examples clearly indicate that rabbinic circles encompassed a broad range of attitudes toward the outside world and its culture. Such issues would inevitably find advocates for contrasting and often conflicting positions, a situation in many ways similar to that of the church fathers. While Clement more readily embraced the larger Hellenistic-Roman world and mediated its seemingly

13. *J. Shevi'it* 8.11.38b–c; *b.* *'Avodah Zarah* 58b–59a, and G. Blidstein, "R. Yohanan, Idolatry and Public Privilege," *JSJ* 5 (1974): 154–61; Lieberman, *Hellenism*, pp. 132–33.

conflicting claims, Tertullian tended to emphasize the dichotomy and its inherent irreconcilability.[14]

HELLENIZATION AMONG THE RABBIS: SOME METHODOLOGICAL CONSIDERATIONS

When we turn to specific examples of Hellenistic influence on religious practice, we are confronted with a perplexing situation. With rare exceptions, at one time or another over the past century and a half scholars have detected traces of foreign influence in rabbinic literature, whether Hellenistic, Roman, or Byzantine-Christian. In the Second Temple period, each of the three main sects—the Pharisees, Sadducees, and Essenes, including the Qumran sect—has been described (following Josephus, *Life* 12; *Antiquities* 15.371) as being influenced in some way by the surrounding culture. As noted in chapter I, Qumran itself is a stunning case in point, as many of its basic ideological components and organizational patterns appear to have been drawn from outside models.[15] Hellenistic in-

14. R. Greer, "Alien Citizens: A Marvellous Paradox," in *Civitas: Religious Interpretations of the City*, ed. P. S. Hawkins (Atlanta: Scholars, 1986), pp. 39–56. Cf., however, S. Stern, who claims that the rabbinic attitude toward figural art throughout antiquity was generally permissive, at least until the sixth or seventh century ("Synagogue Art and Rabbinic Halakhah," *Leʿela* 38 [1994]: 33–37, and in greater detail, "Figurative Art and Halakha in the Mishnaic-Talmudic Period," *Zion* 61 [1996]: 397–419 [Hebrew]).

15. Winston, "Iranian Components," 183–216; B. Dombrowski, "היחד in I QS and τὸ κοινόν: An Instance of Early Greek and Jewish Synthesis," *HTR* 59 (1966): 293–307; S. Shaked, "Qumran and Iran," *Israel Oriental Studies* 2 (1972): 433–46; idem, "Iranian Influence on Judaism: First Century B.C.E. to Second Century C.E.," in *Cambridge History of Judaism* 1, ed. W. D. Davies and L. Finkelstein (Cambridge: Cambridge University Press, 1984), pp. 308–25; Hengel, *Judaism and Hellenism* 1, pp. 228–47; M. Weinfeld, *The Organizational Pattern and the Penal Code of the Qumran Sect* (Fribourg: Éditions Universitaires, 1986), passim; D. Mendels, "Hellenistic Utopia and the Essenes," *HTR* 72 (1979): 207–22.

fluences have been detected in apocalyptic literature as well as other books in the Apocrypha and Pseudepigrapha (e.g., Ben Sira, Wisdom of Solomon). Philonic writings, of course, are steeped in Greek philosophical concepts, and a number of Jewish holidays and festivals, such as Hannukah and the celebrations of military victories listed in *Megillat Taʿanit,* may be indebted, at least partially, to Hellenistic models.[16]

From the post-70 era, examples in this regard have been cited from rabbinic halakhah, aggadah, and midrash. Rabbinic institutions such as the sage and the *bet midrash,* as well as literary genres (legal codes and midrashic collections), have been viewed in the context of more or less parallel developments in the non-Jewish world. Parallels from late antiquity have also been indicated with respect to nonrabbinic Judaism. The ways in which Jewish communities organized their public fast-day observances, the appearance of mysticism in certain Jewish circles and the widespread use of magic, the introduction of piyyut (liturgical poetry) into the synagogue liturgy in Byzantine Palestine, and the flourishing of Jewish art in late antiquity all appear to be related, in varying degrees, to similar phenomena from the surrounding society. The list of studies produced and areas treated is enormous and, taken at face value, would point to an overwhelming impact of the outside world on every conceivable aspect of ancient Judaism.[17]

16. Apocalyptic literature: Collins, "Jewish Apocalyptic," pp. 27–36 (contra R. Hanson, "Jewish Apocalyptic against Its Near Eastern Environment," *RB* 78 [1971]: 31–58). Ben Sira: Sanders, *Ben Sira and Demotic Wisdom,* pp. 27–106; N. Walter, "Jewish-Greek Literature of the Greek Period," in *Cambridge History of Judaism* 2, ed. W. D. Davies and L. Finkelstein, pp. 385–408; idem, "The Apocrypha and Pseudepigrapha of the Hellenistic Period," ibid., pp. 409–503; Wolfson, *Philo,* passim; Bickerman, *From Ezra to the Last of the Maccabees,* pp. 120–21, 131.

17. See the bibliography listed by H. Fischel, "Story and History," pp. 63–65. On the issue of historical periodization in rabbinic thought, see now I. Gafni,

However, in the excitement of discovering possible parallels for one phenomenon or another, it has often been assumed that we are dealing with cases of direct influence and borrowing.[18] Other possibilities have often received short shrift: these parallel phenomena may have had a common source; they may have evolved in several places quite independently, thus eliminating the need to posit direct influence; or these apparent parallels really may have nothing significant in common. The questions, therefore, arise: How can we determine if and when there was influence on the religious sphere? If that influence existed, of what nature and degree was it? What criteria should be invoked before we can safely draw any conclusions?

Several considerations immediately come to mind in dealing with these issues. First, to what extent, if at all, did similar phenomena exist earlier in Jewish history? Could a specific phenomenon have evolved over time so as to account for these later developments? Second, what is the nature of the evidence from the contemporary world? Are similar instances known and, if so, are these sufficiently compelling to warrant positing such a connection? Is there an intrinsic tie between the two? Is there a geographical propinquity or chronological correlation that would help account for such influence? If the first answer (regarding earlier traces in Jewish tradition) is largely negative, and the second (regarding contemporary parallels) positive, then one can begin to make a case for influence—be it outright adoption or some form of adaptation.

To concretize the methodological issues involved, it might be helpful to consider three specific examples from the Pharisaic-rabbinic tradition which appear to reflect a form of Hellenistic in-

---

"Concepts of Periodization and Causality in Talmudic Literature," *Jewish History* 10 (1996): 23–24.

18. See Sandmel, "Parallelomania," pp. 1–13.

fluence. These instances, in turn, will allow us to refine the criteria necessary for establishing a tie between Jewish and non-Jewish phenomena.

Hermeneutical Rules

The hermeneutical rules for interpreting classical Greek literature that were in vogue in Hellenistic rhetorical circles were well known, especially in a major cultural center such as Alexandria. These rules, which include inferences *a minori ad maius*, inferences by analogy, and so on, were widely used among Greek rhetors and appear in the third-century C.E. Tosefta; their introduction into Pharisaic circles is attributed to Hillel, who lived at the end of the first century B.C.E. What are we to make of this coincidence between Greek and Jewish intellectual circles?

Almost a half century ago, D. Daube and S. Lieberman addressed this issue, each adopting a very different position.[19] Lieberman, an avowed minimalist, admits that the terminology itself was borrowed. The rules appearing in both Jewish and Hellenistic traditions are identical; Hillel rendered into Hebrew terms that had already been in use for generations among the Greeks. However, the polemic between Daube and Lieberman is not whether the rabbis borrowed the terms themselves, but whether they also appropriated the hermeneutical methodology associated with these terms. Daube adopts a maximalist position, claiming that these rules were first introduced into rabbinic circles under the influence of Greek models. Moreover, he proposes a possible tie between Hillel and Alexandria, citing a tradition in which Hillel deals with a halakhic issue involving Alexandrians (*t. Ketubot* 4:9). This, how-

19. Daube, "Rabbinic Methods," pp. 239–64; idem, "Alexandrian Methods," pp. 27–44; Lieberman, *Hellenism in Jewish Palestine*, pp. 47–82.

ever, would not necessarily account for Hillel's adoption of the sophisticated hermeneutics employed by contemporary Alexandrian rhetors. Daube instead utilizes a later Babylonian tradition which claims that Hillel's predecessors and teachers, Shemaʿya and Avtalion, were converts from Alexandria (*b. Gittin* 57b; *b. Yoma* 71b) and that they provided the conduit by which such Hellenistic practice reached Jerusalem and, more specifically, Pharisaic circles.

This point appears to be a weak link in Daube's argument. By accounting for the way in which such ideas were transferred to Jewish society, Daube would certainly help to close the circle and strengthen his argument. However, he has not done this; the above-mentioned Babylonian traditions are too distant chronologically from the events they purport to describe and too nonhistoric in nature to be of any value here. Besides, if these two sages were, in fact, responsible for such a transmission, why, then, are they not so credited by later rabbinic tradition? Why is only Hillel mentioned?

Lieberman, on the other hand, denies that the rabbis were beholden to the Greeks for the method itself. In his opinion, it is impossible to imagine any serious midrashic activity that did not employ such methods; he further holds that such activity had been going on throughout the Second Temple period:

> The early Jewish interpreters of Scripture did not have to embark for Alexandria in order to learn there the rudimentary methods of linguistic research. To make them travel to Egypt for this purpose would mean to do a cruel injustice to the intelligence and acumen of the Palestinian sages. Although they were not philologists in the modern sense of the word, they nevertheless often adopted sound philological methods.[20]

20. Lieberman, *Hellenism in Jewish Palestine*, p. 53. Cf. also D. Weiss Halivni, *Midrash, Mishnah, and Gemara: The Jewish Predilection for Justified Law* (Cambridge: Harvard University Press, 1986), pp. 9–37.

Despite Lieberman's disclaimer, the prior existence of such methods is precisely the issue at hand. Was this type of hermeneutical activity indeed practiced within Pharisaic (or any other Jewish) circles before the first century B.C.E.? There is no indication of this in any earlier source, either biblical or postbiblical. Nor do we encounter any indirect evidence. We know of no exegesis that might be best explained by assuming the existence of these hermeneutical rules. Later biblical books have some material that appears to be based on a midrashic interpretation of earlier sources, as do a number of books from the Apocrypha, Pseudepigrapha, and Qumran scrolls. However, in none of these instances have traces of hermeneutical rules been detected.[21] Thus, Lieberman's assertion that midrashic methods similar to those of the Greeks were to be found among Palestinian sages remains an assumption only. Probably whatever midrashic activity did take place among the early Pharisees was intuitive and strictly ad hoc, with no theoretical underpinning as the later hermeneutical rules provided.[22]

Thus, it is very possible that this area of midrashic activity among Pharisees began to develop significantly and dramatically only in Hillel's time with the aid of well-defined Greek hermeneutical rules that not only widened the parameters of such inquiry but also, by their very crystallization, motivated others to work in a similar fashion. If this be granted, then Hillel himself may well have been associated with such an innovation, and in all probability he appropriated both the methodology and terminology, heretofore

21. Cf. S. Fraade, "Interpretive Authority in the Studying Community at Qumran," *JJS* 54 (1993): 66–67.

22. See J. L. Kugel and R. Greer, *Early Biblical Interpretation* (Philadelphia: Westminster, 1986), pp. 27–102; M. Fishbane, "Use, Authority and Interpretation of Mikra at Qumran," in *Mikra*, ed. M. J. Mulder (Assen: Van Gorcum, 1988), pp. 339–77; D. Dimant, "Use and Interpretation of Mikra in the Apocrypha and Pseudepigrapha," ibid., pp. 379–419; Y. Fraenkel, *Darchei Haaggadah V'hamidrash* (Givataim: Massada, 1991), pp. 464–80.

unknown among Jews. In fact, at one point in his argument, Lieberman himself seems to hedge with regard to the possibility of a more substantial Hellenistic influence:

> Hillel the Elder and the Rabbis of the following generations used to interpret not only the Torah but also secular legal documents. Most likely general standards for the interpretation of legal texts were in vogue which dated back to high antiquity. But it was the Greeks who systematized, defined and gave definite form to the shapeless mass of interpretations. . . .
>
> Literary problems were solved in a similar way in the schools of Alexandria and those of Palestine. The methods of the rhetors and their discussions had at least a stimulating effect on serious treatment of legal texts.[23]

The Ketubah

Methodological issues regarding the possible connection between a Hellenistic practice and its appearance in a Jewish context are central to another phenomenon—the introduction of the *ketubah* (marriage contract) into the Jewish wedding ceremony. Rabbinic sources attribute this innovation to Simeon ben Shataḥ, who lived in the early first century B.C.E., during the reigns of Alexander Jannaeus and Salome Alexandra. In one tannaitic tradition (*b. Ketubot* 82b), we learn of several stages in the arrangements of how a groom was to meet his obligations to his wife in case of divorce. Only after

---

23. Lieberman, *Hellenism in Jewish Palestine*, pp. 62, 67–68. W. S. Towner, who adopts a position quite similar to that of Lieberman, also makes allowance for some sort of common awareness: "It seems highly probable that the learned rabbinical interpreters of Hebrew Scripture were at least aware that explicit interpretive methods similar to their own were in use among those intellectuals of the Greek-speaking world who studied Homer and the classics in the hope of extrapolating from them lessons for their own time" ("Hermeneutical Systems," p. 109). Cf., however, the reservations of Feldman (*Jew and Gentile*, pp. 31–38) on this as well as other issues related to Greco-Roman culture and the sages.

a series of unsuccessful attempts did ben Shataḥ implement a contract which apparently proved much more successful in preventing quick divorces. Beforehand, an agreement involved the parents, and the sum to be paid by them in case of divorce was set aside at the time of the marriage. Simeon ben Shataḥ introduced a radical change in these two elements: the marriage contract would not involve the parents, but rather would be arranged between bride and groom only; and the sum given to the divorced wife would not be set aside at the outset, but would be taken from the husband's property at the time of the divorce. This stipulation would make it harder for him to part with some of his possessions and thus lead to greater attempts at reconciliation.

In his study of matrimonial arrangements in the ancient Near East, M. Geller has suggested that the Jewish practice outlined in *b. Ketubot* 82b was patterned after well-known models from the ancient world.[24] The first stages of Jewish matrimonial arrangements follow ancient Mesopotamian practice. However, the innovation that rabbinic sources associate with ben Shataḥ is, in fact, first attested only in fourth- and third-century B.C.E. Egyptian Demotic matrimonial contracts, i.e., that the agreement is between the bride and groom, and the sum owed in the event of divorce is specified but not set aside until the actual time of divorce. Thus, it is clear that our Pharisaic sage is credited with proposing something that had already been in practice for several centuries in Egypt, and possibly elsewhere as well.

Whether Simeon ben Shataḥ actually initiated this change himself is difficult to say. To put it differently, how reliable the Babylonian Talmud is in citing a tannaitic source—and how reliable that tannaitic source is in preserving an accurate historical picture—is impossible to determine with any degree of certainty. The use of the

24. Geller, "New Sources," pp. 227–45.

ketubah was well in place by the first century c.e., as attested by tannaitic literature (*m. Ketubot* 4:12). Moreover, a modicum of credence might be accorded this rabbinic source, which itself is clearly aware of historical development; an innovation of this magnitude probably required the backing of a person of stature in order to give it legitimacy. In addition, the wider historical context of ben Shataḥ's era makes the likelihood of contact between Alexandria and Hasmonean Judaea quite strong.[25] In contrast to the previously cited example regarding Hillel, there is solid evidence of Pharisaic presence in Egypt. Alexander Jannaeus' persecution of his opponents, which included the Pharisees, led many to flee abroad. While ben Shataḥ appears to have hidden within the country, many of his colleagues, including Judah ben Tabbai, fled to Alexandria (*j. Ḥagigah* 2.2.77d). It is tempting to assume, though impossible to substantiate, that ben Shataḥ became acquainted with this custom via Judah ben Tabbai or others who had returned from Egypt, and then incorporated it into Jewish practice.[26]

Methodologically speaking, this example of the *ketubah* provides us with two important factors that were missing from the previous instance dealing with Hillel and Hellenistic hermeneutical rules. First, rabbinic literature itself claims that there was a major innovation in this regard at the time of ben Shataḥ. Therefore, one cannot argue that the use of a *ketubah* was a Jewish practice from time immemorial. Second, accounting for the transference of this practice from Hellenistic Egypt to the Jewish realm may be easier in this

25. See, for example, the letters prefacing 2 Maccabees and the colophon at the end of the additions to the Greek Esther, both works appearing in editions of the Apocrypha.

26. I am thus accepting the talmudic attribution, although with some reservation, being fully aware of the problematics involved, namely, the tendency of later generations to attribute changes to leading figures of the past for purposes of validation and legitimation. In this particular case, certitude is impossible.

case, since some Pharisees spent a good deal of time (years, if not a decade or more) in Egypt, thus facilitating the transfer of an Alexandrian custom back to Hasmonean Palestine.

Finally, we should mention in this context a statement penned several centuries prior to ben Shataḥ, which seems to refer to earlier instances of these kinds of influence. Hecataeus of Abdera, a Hellenistic ethnographer in the court of Ptolemy I, offered his impressions regarding various aspects of Jewish society. He discusses, inter alia, the degree to which the Jews kept to themselves and maintained their unique customs, though he notes two areas in which their ancestral practices were affected by those of the surrounding peoples: burial and marriage.[27] This is indeed fascinating testimony, which may serve as a precedent and backdrop to what ben Shataḥ was to do some two hundred years later.

The Seder

A final example of outside influence on Jewish religious behavior focuses on the major customs of the Passover seder which are recorded in the *Haggadah* and in Mishnah Pesaḥim and Tosefta Pesaḥim. In examining these texts, it seems most likely that the ceremonies described therein crystallized in the postdestruction era, i.e., the Yavnean period (70–130 C.E.). All the sages mentioned in these sources (with the exception of Hillel, who is noted in connection with the custom of eating a *maror* [bitter herbs] sandwich) hail from this period. The rabbis who spent the entire night in Bnai Beraq relating the story of the Exodus lived at this time, as did those who expounded on the miracles at the Sea of Reeds (often referred to as the Red Sea); finally, it is Rabban Gamaliel of Yavneh who ex-

27. M. Stern, *Greek and Latin Authors* 1, p. 29.

plained the principal symbols of the Passover meal and, in effect, answered the questions asked at its outset.[28] Thus, the basic framework of the *Haggadah* derives from this period, and the seder as recorded in the above sources, and as we largely know it today, was developed in Yavneh.

This internal evidence dovetails neatly with the larger historical context. The main thrust of the Passover celebration prior to the Temple's destruction in 70 was bringing the paschal sacrifice to the Jerusalem Temple and the ensuing family meal. Specific foods were consumed—the paschal sacrifice itself, *matzot*, and perhaps also bitter herbs. The nature of the liturgy accompanying this meal in Temple days, if one indeed existed, is unknown.

Following the destruction of the Temple, there was a need to fill the vacuum of the Passover celebration with a practice that could be performed anywhere, and it was this desideratum that the sages of Yavneh addressed when they discussed the seder customs. This was not the only area in which the sages sought to fill a vacuum in the aftermath of the Temple's destruction. A new communal liturgy was also created as a substitute for the now defunct sacrificial system. Many significant innovations were also made in the Rosh Hashanah and Yom Kippur liturgy, two holidays (especially the latter) that previously had been largely bound up with the Temple ritual.

28. Scholarly opinion has been divided over the identity of the Rabban Gamaliel mentioned in the Mishnah and *Haggadah*. Are we speaking of Gamaliel the Elder who flourished in the first half of the first century C.E., or Gamaliel II of Yavneh at the turn of the second century? Among those opting for the former identification are J. N. Epstein, *Prolegomena ad Litteras Tannaiticas* (Jerusalem: Magnes, 1957), pp. 334, 514 (Hebrew); E. D. Goldschmdit, *The Passover Haggadah: Its Sources and History* (Jerusalem: Bialik, 1960), p. 51, n. 1 (Hebrew). Preferring the later date are G. Alon, *The Jews in Their Land in the Talmudic Age* (Jerusalem: Magnes, 1980), 1, pp. 261–65; S. Safrai, *In Times of Temple and Mishnah: Studies in Jewish History*, 2d ed., 2 (Jerusalem: Magnes, 1996), pp. 612–14 (Hebrew); Bokser, *Origins of the Seder*, pp. 37–49. While this is not the place to argue the matter in detail, the latter opinion is to be preferred.

The rabbis drew their inspiration in shaping the seder ritual from elements of popular Jewish practice at the time and, particularly in this case, the well-known institution in Greco-Roman society—the symposium. The symposium framework consisted of a banquet and philosophical discussion held on various occasions during the year, on a holiday, in honor of the emperor's birthday, or on some other festive occasion. A number of sources, e.g., Plato, Plutarch, and Athenaeus, describe such celebrations, so that we are relatively well informed on this institution.

Based on this literature, S. Stein has suggested that the main elements of the seder ritual as incorporated in the *Haggadah* were borrowed from these symposia: questions about food at the outset of the evening; the types of food eaten before the meal (greens, apples and nuts mixed with wine); a cup of wine to initiate the evening, followed by others; a description of those in attendance at a particular symposium; a midrash referring to a classical text, around which much of the discussion focused; and concluding hymns of praise to the god or king to whom the evening was dedicated.[29] The custom of reclining while eating is another practice at the seder that is clearly of Greco-Roman origin.

Thus, to anyone familiar with the Passover *Haggadah* it becomes eminently clear that the main outlines of this ceremony have been cast in a mold strikingly similar to the Greco-Roman symposium model. Of course, some elements of the Passover celebration as described in tannaitic literature may well have had roots in Jewish tradition for many generations, if not centuries, prior to Yavneh.[30]

29. Stein, "Influence of Symposia Literature," pp. 13–44.

30. See Bokser (*Origins of the Seder*, pp. 50–66, and esp. pp. 61–62), who emphasized this diachronic dimension:

> To summarize my argument, the meal appears prominent among several Jewish groups as the context to celebrate key religious moments, both for Passover and for other occasions. The groups in question are not identical in their conception of the meal though they draw upon analogous notions. All of the groups assume the importance of the temple, and draw upon

However, there is a high degree of probability that, when formulating this ritual around the turn of the second century, the rabbis were influenced—directly or indirectly—by contemporary Roman practices.[31]

Moreover, evidence that the rabbis themselves were very much aware of the parallels between their seder practices and those of contemporary Roman society is reflected in their statement, "One does not conclude the Passover celebration (the seder) with the *afikoman*" (*m. Pesaḥim* 10 : 8). Later Jewish tradition interpreted the term *afikoman* as referring to the middle of the three *matzot* placed on the Passover table, and the phrase was taken to mean that this piece of *matzah* must be the very last item eaten at the seder meal, that is, one is to conclude the seder by eating the *afikoman*. Lieberman, however, has shown that this term is, in fact, of Greek derivation and means "after dinner activities," referring to the par-

---

temple concepts and earlier examples of extra-temple practices, which they perceive in terms of the temple. The Hellenistic culture these groups shared in common contributed to their increased receptivity to alternatives to a central temple and may have influenced their choice of the features to be developed from the ancient heritage. It is therefore not surprising that rabbinic circles may have drawn upon banquet practices to enrich what they were doing. It is unlikely, however, that they were prompted to expand the biblical tie by their observation of Hellenistic symposia or on account of their knowledge of the symposia literature.

See also J. Tabory, "The Passover Eve Ceremony: An Historical Outline," *Immanuel* 12 (1981): 32–43; idem, *The Passover Ritual throughout the Generations* (Tel Aviv: Hakibbutz Hameuchad, 1996), pp. 367–77 (Hebrew).

31. Mention should also be made of a recent article by I. J. Yuval, whose thesis is that the seder ceremony formulated at Yavneh was largely in response to contemporary Passover celebrations of redemption within the early church, as practiced by the Quartodecimans or Jewish-Christians; see his "The Haggadah of Passover and Easter," *Tarbiz* 65 (1995): 5–28 (Hebrew). However, the problematics in dating some rabbinic traditions—and establishing the *Sitz im Leben* of early Christian practices—are well nigh insurmountable, as is the attempt to account for the actual channels of communication and influence between the rabbis of Yavneh and Jewish-Christian practice around the turn of the second century c.e.

ticipants concluding the symposium by getting drunk, going from house to house for further indulgence, taking to the streets to seek women companions, and generally conducting themselves in a boisterous and bawdy fashion.[32]

By instructing the seder participants not to follow the Greek custom, the rabbis were, in effect, saying two things. First, they wished to keep the seder evening as sacred and home-oriented as possible, which was a far cry from the symposium setting. The seder indeed differed from its Greco-Roman model in several significant ways: it was family-oriented (not for males only, as was the case with the symposium), and it had a historically focused theme, the story of the Exodus (as against the philosophical discussion of most symposia). The second implication of the rabbinic statement is the one most relevant to our discussion: the rabbis themselves were aware that the seder celebration was quite similar to the Roman symposia, and thus they drew a clear line between the two by indicating which aspects of the symposium setting were unacceptable and to be studiously avoided.[33]

32. S. Lieberman, *Tosefta Ki-Fshutah* (New York: Jewish Theological Seminary, 1962), 4, p. 655; idem, *Hayerushalmi Kiphshuto* (Jerusalem: Darom, 1935), pp. 521–22; C. Albeck, *Commentary to the Mishnah–Mo'ed* (Jerusalem: Bialik, 1949), 2, pp. 179–80 (Hebrew); Bokser, *Origins of the Seder*, pp. 65–66; Segal, *Rebecca's Children*, pp. 139–40.

33. It may also be noted that the parallels between the symposium and seder go even beyond the points raised by Stein. In the symposium, the custom was traditionally to have the meal first and then the discussion; this order was reversed toward the end of the second century C.E. The same change appears to have been implemented for the seder. According to the Mishnah, our earliest source in this regard, the meal came first; children would then be prone to ask questions on the basis of the unusual foods and customs. By the amoraic period, in the third century, the order had been reversed, which caused not a little confusion among amoraim (*b. Pesaḥim* 115b). For another explanation that relates this change to the Jewish-Christian polemic, see D. Daube, *The New Testament and Rabbinic Judaism* (London: University of London, Athlone Press, 1956), pp. 192–95.

The three examples we have discussed—the hermeneutical rules of Hillel, the *ketubah* initiated by Simeon ben Shataḥ, and the Passover seder as crystallized at Yavneh—all relate to issues involved in positing a connection between Jewish religious practice and that of the contemporary world. Each case is unique and has components not found in the others, but the parallels are evident. The question is, how much is outright cultural borrowing rather than the use of labels or isolated elements, or merely parallel developments? What is clear is that Jewish practice was constantly evolving at this time owing to internal religious developments, traumatic political and social events, the influence of outside models, or a combination of these factors. However, there can be little doubt that influences from the outside were crucial in these developments: as the main source of inspiration (the *ketubah*), as a helpful stimulus and organizing factor for an activity already current among Jewish sects (hermeneutical rules), or as a new framework for a traditional Jewish practice that was being dramatically transformed by cataclysmic changes within Jewish society (the seder). It is clear that these developments cannot be fully understood or appreciated without reference to the larger cultural context in which the rabbis found themselves.

Rabbinic Attitudes toward Greco-Roman Culture

The seder celebration at Yavneh touches on an important dimension of the rabbis' response to the non-Jewish culture in second- to fourth-century C.E. Roman Palestine. Granted that there were various kinds and degrees of influences (conscious and unconscious), the question arises as to the attitude of the rabbis in the post-70 era to foreign culture, both of the pagan and Christian varieties.

At first glance, the views expressed in rabbinic literature seem clear and unequivocal. Jews were warned to steer clear of the distinctive mores and fashions of Roman culture, except for the more superficial, external aspects. In the tannaitic midrash on Leviticus—*Sifra*—the following admonition is offered:

> "Do not follow the practices of the land of Egypt or those of the land of Canaan" (adapted from Leviticus 18:3). Does this mean that they should not build buildings and plant trees like them? Scripture says: "Do not follow their practices" (ibid.)—I intended [to forbid] only those practices which have been legislated for them, their fathers and their fathers' fathers (i.e., are deeply embedded in pagan society). And what were they wont to do? A man would marry another man, and a woman [would marry] a woman, a man would marry a woman and her daughter and a woman would be married to two [men]—thus it is written: "Do not follow their practices." (*Aharei Mot, Parsha* 9:8, ed. Weiss, p. 85b)

Later on in the *Sifra*, there is a warning to avoid gentile social norms, which are understood by some to refer to their theaters and circuses. R. Judah ben Bathyra, however, interprets this phrase to mean stabbing someone or wearing one's hair in the style characteristic of pagan society (*Pereq* 13:9, ed. Weiss, p. 86a). Wearing a toga or certain kinds of ornamentation common in Roman society was also discouraged by the rabbis:

> You should not say: since they go out in a toga, so, too, will I wear a toga; since they go out in purple, so, too, will I wear purple; since they go out in round hats, so, too, will I—"And I too will do this." (*Sifre–Deuteronomy* 81, ed. Finkelstein, p. 147)

Elsewhere *Sifre–Deuteronomy* lists another half-dozen types of garments which, according to the rabbis, should not be worn by Jews, but obviously were (*Sifre–Deuteronomy* 234, ed. Finkelstein, pp. 266–67). The rabbis' tendency to distance themselves and others from Greek culture seems clear-cut when one adds to these traditions the apparent prohibition against teaching Greek (*m. Sotah* 9:14), which allegedly resulted from the "War of Kitos" (115–17 C.E.), but which other sources date either to the Hyrcanus II–Aristobulus II rift in 63 B.C.E. (*b. Sotah* 9b and parallels) or, according to R. Simeon bar Yoḥai, to the revolt of 66 C.E. (*j. Shabbat* 1.4.3c).

The prohibition against attending pagan institutions of entertainment is accorded lengthier treatment in the Tosefta, where the practice is forbidden for a number of reasons: pagan worship often accompanied these theater performances (according to R. Meir); such places were also considered a waste of time, coming at the expense of studying Torah; and undesirable elements were in attendance, about whom it was said, "One should not sit in the seat of scorners" (Psalms 1:1). The circus was forbidden to the Jews because of the bloody spectacles held there, although at least one sage permitted attendance if it meant being able to save someone's life, as was often determined by those in attendance (*t. 'Avodah Zarah* 2:5–7).[34]

Without denying the historical validity of the above sources, the attitude of rabbinic Judaism toward non-Jewish culture cannot be easily categorized, as it was indeed far from monolithic. We have already had occasion to note the contrasting attitudes of sages to Roman material civilization as well as to the issue of figural art.[35] A similar range of views can be found in other cases as well, for example, with regard to the Septuagint translation; some rabbis praised it, while others condemned it (*b. Megillah* 9a; *Masekhet Soferim* 1.7, ed. Higger, pp. 101–5). Moreover, side by side with the prohibition against teaching Greek, we know of three translations of the Torah into that language dating to the second century C.E., at least one of which seems to have been carried out by those closely associated with rabbinic circles. Aquilas is reputed to have been ei-

---

34. See S. Stern, *Jewish Identity*, pp. 170–94.
35. On some rabbinic assessments of Roman material culture, see *b. Shabbat* 33b. On rabbinic attitudes toward figural art, see above.

ther a disciple or a close associate of the Yavnean sages R. Joshua and R. Eliezer, who praised him with the verse, "You are fairer than all men (your speech is endowed with grace; rightly has God given you an eternal blessing)" (Psalms 45:3; *j. Megillah* 1.11.71c). A second translator, Symmachus, lived toward the end of the second century and has been identified by some with Somachus, reportedly a student of R. Meir (*b. ʿEruvin* 13b).[36]

Given this widespread use of Greek, it is not surprising that the rabbis sanctioned the use of this and other languages (e.g., Aramaic) for a series of liturgical readings (*m. Sotah* 7:1). Interestingly, all important prayers are included in this listing, from the morning service (the *Shemaʿ*, its accompanying blessings, and the *ʿAmidah*), to the blessings after meals, to oaths concerning testimony and deposits. In contrast, all the prayers to be recited in Hebrew relate only to the Temple or biblical prescriptions, some of which were no longer relevant in mishnaic times (*m. Sotah* 7:2). Moreover, the second-century Rabban Simeon ben Gamaliel II allowed Torah scrolls to be written only in Greek and Hebrew (*m. Megillah* 1:8). While some sages seem to have permitted the use of other languages as well, Rabban Simeon's ruling appears to have become the norm (*j. Megillah* 1.11.71c).

This rabbinically sanctioned use of Greek throws into question the above-noted prohibition against teaching that language. Lieberman argued that the prohibition was intended for children only and did not refer to adults.[37] Even this decree was set aside in the case of R. Judah the Prince, who is specifically noted as having taught his children Greek (*j. Shabbat* 6.1.7d), and two generations

---

36. E. Tov, *Textual Criticism of the Hebrew Bible* (Minneapolis: Fortress, 1992), pp. 146–47. Cf. also L. L. Grabbe, "Aquila's Translation and Rabbinic Exegesis," *JJS* 33 (1982): 527–36.

37. Lieberman, *Hellenism in Jewish Palestine*, pp. 100–14.

later R. Abbahu advocated the teaching of Greek to one's daughter (see below).

Moreover, there were individuals and groups within rabbinic society whose use of Greek and knowledge of "Greek wisdom" were well known. First and foremost in this category were the Patriarchs and their households. The most striking source in this regard is the testimony of Rabban Simeon ben Gamaliel II, who claimed that the house of his father, Rabban Gamaliel II of Yavneh, boasted five hundred students studying Torah and five hundred studying Greek (*b. Sotah* 49b). These numbers cannot be taken literally; a school of that size would have been an enormous institution for those times. What may possibly be derived from this source is some sort of parity that existed in the studies conducted at Rabban Gamaliel's academy; students studied Greek language and wisdom no less than the Torah. The Talmud further explains this emphasis by claiming that the Patriarch needed to train people in order to maintain contact with the Roman government. Undoubtedly, there is much to say for this explanation. However, it also may be true that this type of acculturation was not all that unusual for Jewish aristocratic circles and that we have here cultural norms not necessarily subscribed to by many—or even most—other sages.

Fascinating testimony regarding the Patriarch's Hellenistic proclivities comes from the fourth century, in correspondence between several Patriarchs and the famous Antiochan rhetor, Libanius.[38] Nine of the latter's epistles to several Patriarchs have been preserved; unfortunately, no responses have survived. The very fact that such correspondence took place between the Patriarch and one of the leading intellectuals of the age is in itself significant. There is little question that all such correspondence, i.e., that written by the Patriarch as well, was in Greek; this was the language of Libanius'

---

38. M. Stern, *Greek and Latin Authors* 2, pp. 580–99, and esp. p. 596.

letters, and the Patriarch undoubtedly responded in kind. Of interest for our discussion is Libanius' reference in one of his letters to the Patriarch's son, who had been sent to him to receive an advanced Greek education after first studying with one Argeius. The Patriarch in this case was Gamaliel V, but it is quite possible that others, too, considered Greek education so important so as to send a child away for a period of time. This tells us much about the cultural and intellectual priorities and expectations of the holders of this office, and undoubtedly of those associated with his circle. Of the acumen of the Patriarch in more general areas of study we have one brief, enigmatic, but thoroughly intriguing piece of information. In a tradition preserved in Marcellus' *De Medicamentis*, written at the beginning of the fifth century, the author speaks of a medicine "recently" invented by Gamaliel, presumably referring to Gamaliel VI.[39]

Of all the rabbis of the talmudic period, R. Abbahu appears to have been the most acculturated.[40] He was known to his contemporaries as such. In the above-noted tradition concerning the desirability of Greek education for daughters, he was accused by Simeon bar Abba of inventing a tradition in order to justify his own preferences: "Because he wants to teach his daughters Greek, he ascribes [this tradition] to R. Yoḥanan!" (*j. Peah* 1.1.15c). In fact, this criticism may, indeed, have been correct; if so, it would further highlight R. Abbahu's Hellenistic proclivities. He apparently wished to assure his daughters a Greek education. Lieberman has described him as "a man of high Hellenistic culture."[41] His facility with the Greek language was considerable, as attested by his fre-

---

39. Ibid., 2, pp. 582–83.

40. L. I. Levine, "Rabbi Abbahu of Caesarea," in *Christianity, Judaism and Other Greco-Roman Cults: Studies for Morton Smith at Sixty,* ed. J. Neusner (Leiden: Brill, 1975), 4, pp. 56–76.

41. Lieberman, *Greek in Jewish Palestine*, p. 21.

quent phonetic plays on Greek (as well as Aramaic) words (*Genesis Rabbah* 14:2).

As was common in Greco-Roman society, R. Abbahu took great pride in his physical appearance. He apparently possessed unusual strength and frequented the baths of his native Caesarea and other cities. His handsome features impressed his contemporaries: "And Mar said: 'The beauty of R. Kahana is like the beauty of R. Abbahu, the beauty of R. Abbahu is like the beauty of father Jacob, the beauty of father Jacob is like the beauty of Adam'" (*b. Bava Metzia* 84a; *b. Bava Batra* 58a).

The Hellenization of R. Abbahu, however, ran far deeper than his extensive acquaintance with Greek culture and mores. On several occasions he remarked how mathematical science aided him in solving various halakhic questions (*j. Terumot* 5.3.43c; *j. Sukkah* 5.8.55d). Hellenistic proclivities affected, in turn, the shaping of at least some of his halakhic decisions and personal behavior. It was R. Abbahu, for example, who quoted older authorities in order to justify the translation of the Bible into Greek and, when necessary, reading the scroll of Esther in a language other than Hebrew (*b. Megillah* 9b; *j. Megillah* 2.1.73a).

R. Abbahu's more cosmopolitan tendencies are strikingly portrayed in one source describing the behavior of several sages during communal fast prayers in synagogues having decorated mosaic floors:

> Rav instructed the house of R. Aḥa and R. Ami instructed his own household not to bow down, as is customary when they go [to the synagogue] on a fast day [so as not to appear to be bowing to the images decorating the synagogue]. R. Yonah bowed sideways, as did R. Aḥa. R. Samuel said: "I saw R. Abbahu bow as usual." R. Yose said: "I asked R. Abbahu: Is it not written, 'And a figured stone [you shall not place in our land to bow down upon it]'?" (Leviticus 26:1). [The difficulty concerning R. Abbahu's behavior] should be solved [by assuming that it is appropriate]

where one has a fixed place [in the synagogue] for bowing. (*j. 'Avodah Zarah* 4.1.43d)[42]

Setting aside the last statement, which the editor of the Jerusalem Talmud provided, it appears that R. Abbahu was not troubled by the fact that he was prostrating himself (as was customary on public fast days) on a decorated synagogue floor; but other rabbis clearly were. The above passage is therefore illustrative of his tolerance and ease vis-à-vis figural art, a quality undoubtedly engendered by his Hellenistic acculturation.

STUDIES AND ISSUES OF HELLENISM AND RABBINIC JUDAISM

Beyond individual rabbis with a greater or lesser receptivity toward Hellenistic culture, several primary areas of rabbinic intellectual literary activity likewise display varying degrees of acquaintance with Hellenistic literary genres, ideas, and motifs.[43] In this regard, Lieberman's studies *Greek in Jewish Palestine* and *Hellenism in Jewish Palestine* were pioneering and revolutionary contributions. The phenomenon is particularly apparent in rabbinic aggadah. The number of parallels scholars claim to have discovered between rabbinic motifs and those of the surrounding world is legion. Not all these parallels are of equal cogency. E. Halevi, for example, amassed an enormous repertoire of supposed parallels, many of which may

42. See G. Blidstein, "Prostration and Mosaics in Talmudic Law," *Bulletin of the Institute of Jewish Studies* 2 (1974): 19–39, and esp. pp. 33–37.

43. For a general statement in this regard, see Lieberman, *Greek in Jewish Palestine*, pp. 15–28. On talmudic law in relation to ancient Near Eastern legal systems, see S. Friedman, "The Case of the Woman with Two Husbands in Talmudic and Ancient Near Eastern Law and Literature," *Israel Law Review* 15 (1980): 530–58.

be considered tenuous.[44] In contrast, H. Fischel focused on fewer, more select examples that demonstrate a remarkable familiarity with Greek *chria* (short stories) by the rabbis, who reworked and used them for their own purposes. He notes a striking story wherein Hillel solves a halakhic issue regarding the offering of the paschal sacrifice on the Sabbath, and demonstrates how this account was recast in terms of the founder-of-a-school motif, well known in Greco-Roman tradition; every stage of the Hillel account parallels this type of *chria*.[45]

Similar parallels have been discovered between rabbinic exegesis and that of the church fathers. The subject of related exegetical materials among the writings of the church fathers and rabbinic aggadah was first addressed almost a century ago by L. Ginzberg in his *Die Haggada bei den Kirchenvätern*. Since then, and particularly

---

44. See, for example, the following works by Halevi, all of which have appeared in Hebrew only: *The World of Aggadah: The Aggadah in Light of Greek Sources* (Tel Aviv: Dvir, 1972); *Studies in Aggadah in Light of Greek Sources* (Tel Aviv: Armoni, 1973); *Historical-Biographical Aggadah in Light of Greek and Latin Sources* (Tel Aviv: Dvir, 1975); *Aggadot of Amoraim: Biographical Aggadah of Palestinian and Babylonian Amoraim in Light of Greek and Latin Sources* (Tel Aviv: Dvir, 1976); *Values in the Aggadah and Halakha in Light of Greek and Latin Sources* (4 vols.; Tel Aviv: Dvir, 1979); *The Gates of Aggadah in Light of Greek and Latin Sources* (Tel Aviv: Dvir, 1982).

45. Fischel, "Story and History," pp. 59–88, and his *Rabbinic Literature and Greco-Roman Philosophy*, where, inter alia, he notes:

It is fortunate that at this stage of scholarship no further defense has to be made for the assumption that Greco-Roman situations were well-known to the creators of the Midrash, i.e., the literature that modifies the world and the world of Scriptures by interpretation, explicitly or implicitly. Rather, the problem is how far this knowledge went, how much of Greco-Roman academic procedure and philosophical quest was used in that on-going process in which the culmination of the tannaitic culture, c. 200 A.D. (the codification of the Mishnah) and that of Palestinian amoraic culture, c. 400 (Jerusalem Talmud) were important stages. (p. xi)

For an insightful comparison of a Hillel *chria*, this time from the perspective of the church fathers, see B. Visotzky, *Fathers of the World: Essays in Rabbinic and Patristic Literatures* (Tübingen: Mohr, 1995), pp. 160–68.

in the last few decades, many studies have appeared on this general topic, as well as a number focusing on the writings of specific authors, such as Origen, John Chrysostom, and Jerome. E. E. Urbach has persuasively argued in a series of articles that rabbinic midrash was influenced by the views adopted by the church. Figures such as Melchizedek or the inhabitants of Nineveh, who had merited a positive evaluation in tannaitic literature, were much more critically presented in later amoraic midrashim, presumably after the church had adopted these biblical figures as exemplars of religious behavior or as precursors of Jesus himself.[46] Finally, a number of articles over the last decade have highlighted common motifs and traditions in the writings of the rabbis and church fathers that all point to channels of communication between these religious elites.[47]

The area of halakhah has likewise merited important studies on the relationship between Jewish and Roman law. We have had occasion to note above several important instances of this influence (the *ketubah*, the Passover *Haggadah*), but these only begin to

---

46. Origen: N. de Lange, *Origen and the Jews: Studies in Jewish-Christian Relations in Third-Century Palestine* (Cambridge: Cambridge University Press, 1976); John Chrysostom: R. L. Wilken, *John Chrysostom and the Jews* (Berkeley: University of California Press, 1983); Jerome: J. Braverman, *Jerome's Commentary on Daniel: A Study of Comparative Jewish and Christian Interpretations of the Hebrew Bible* (Washington, D.C.: Catholic Biblical Association, 1978).

E. E. Urbach's *The World of the Sages* collects his most important articles in this regard. See also idem, "The Homiletical Interpretations of the Sages and the Expositions of Origen on Canticles, and the Jewish-Christian Disputation," *SH* 22 (1971): 247–75; R. Kimelman, "Rabbi Yohanan and Origen on the Song of Songs: A Third Century Disputation," *HTR* 73 (1980): 567–95.

47. See, for example, P. R. Davies, "Passover and the Dating of the Aqedah," *JJS* 30 (1979): 59–67; M. Hirshman, "The Greek Fathers and the Aggada on Ecclesiastes: Formats of Exegesis in Late Antiquity," *HUCA* 59 (1988): 137–65; idem, *Mikra and Midrash: A Comparison of Rabbinics and Patristics* (Tel Aviv: Hakkibutz Hameuchad, 1992) (Hebrew); Visotzky, *Fathers of the World*; Yuval, "Haggadah"; and the bibliographies found in each of the above.

scratch the surface. In civil and criminal law, family matters, and religious ceremonies, parallels with Roman law codes or folk practices are undeniable, and some sort of influence is possible, and even quite likely. A remarkable parallel has also been pointed out between the crystallization of the matrilineal principle in rabbinic circles and a similar process taking place in contemporary Roman law.[48]

The Jewish fast-day ceremonies described in the Mishnah include many practices known from Tertullian's description of pagan North African customs: closing baths and shops, a procession that included the notables of the community, and communal prayer while standing barefoot and covered with ashes and sackcloth. However, the degree to which such ceremonies were under rabbinic auspices is uncertain.[49]

One final dimension of rabbinic society and activity deserves mention. The timing of certain developments within rabbinic society, especially with regard to internal organization and compilation of various corpora, both aggadic and halakhic, has interesting parallels with what was transpiring at the time in Roman and later Byzantine society. Is it coincidental, for instance, that the earliest Pharisaic schools of Hillel and Shammai crystallized at the time of Augustus, when legal training was becoming formalized in Rome

48. See the studies on the subject by B. Cohen, many conveniently collected in his *Jewish and Roman Law*; and Alexander, "Quid Athenis et Hierosolymis?" pp. 109–17; S. J. D. Cohen, "Origins of the Matrilineal Principle," pp. 19–53; idem, "The Matrilineal Principle in Historical Perspective," *Judaism* 34 (1985): 5–13. See also T. Friedman, "Parallels: Ancient Greek and Rabbinic Culture," in *Threescore and Ten: Essays in Honor of Rabbi Seymour J. Cohen on the Occasion of His Seventieth Birthday*, ed. A. Karp, L. Jacobs, and C. Z. Dimitrovsky (Hoboken: KTAV, 1991), pp. 47–54.

49. Fast days: D. Levine, "Public Fasts in Talmudic Tradition: Palestinian and Babylonian Contexts," *Proceedings of the Eleventh World Congress of Jewish Studies*, division C, volume 1 (Jerusalem: World Union of Jewish Studies, 1994), pp. 63–64 (Hebrew).

in the early Roman law schools founded by Labeo and Capito? Or that R. ʿAqiva and his colleagues began collecting and organizing rabbinic traditions under Hadrian, when Julianus, Celsus Pomponius, and others were actively involved in making similar compilations in Rome? Or that Rabbi Judah the Prince compiled and edited his Mishnah, and tannaitic midrashim were collected under the Severans, at a time when Gaius, Papinianus, Paulus, and Ulpianus were likewise compiling codices and responsa of Roman law and commenting on earlier legal material? The argument that these recurring parallel activities in Roman and Jewish societies might be related is more compelling when we realize that both Roman jurists and the rabbis centered their activities in schools of higher learning, and that at least one of the most famous Roman schools was located in Berytus, not far from the center of rabbinic activity in the Galilee.[50]

The same parallel literary activity continued in later amoraic midrashic compilations as well. The major thrust in this regard took place in Byzantine Palestine with the editing of *Genesis Rabbah*, *Leviticus Rabbah*, *Pesiqta d'Rav Kahana*, and other works. The fact that the church fathers were engaged in similar activity at the time may well have influenced this type of rabbinic activity, if not in essence, then at least in its timing.[51]

It is irrefutable that many parallels existed between rabbinic culture and the wider world. The question remains, however, whether in each case it was an instance of rabbinic borrowing, either direct or

---

50. F. Schulz, *History of Roman Legal Science* (Oxford: Clarendon Press, 1946), pp. 102–10, 119–23, 272–77; H. F. Jolowicz, *Historical Introduction to the Study of Roman Law* (Cambridge: Cambridge University Press, 1961), pp. 4–6, 369–72, 384–403, 471–78; Alexander, "Quid Athenis et Hierosolymis?" pp. 109–15; O. Tellegen-Couperus, *A Short History of Roman Law* (London: Routledge, 1993), pp. 94–105.
51. See Hirshman, "Greek Fathers and the Aggada."

indirect. Or is it rather a question of parallel developments in two cultures within the same historical framework? How much does the Roman context itself account for these developments among its constituent peoples? Did the overall political, social, and cultural ambience of the Roman and Byzantine Empires have a significant effect on this process? Answers to these questions are not easy to determine and, in fact, there may be no one single answer; they might well differ from case to case. Nevertheless, the ultimate direction is clear. With the steadily increasing number of studies being produced, not only with respect to rabbinic culture per se but also with regard to the ties between Jews and their cultural milieu (e.g., magic, mysticism, synagogue art and architecture, community officials), there is increasing cogency to the argument that many, if not most, of these parallels reflect ongoing contact with the outside world. They can therefore legitimately be viewed as instances of influence—either direct or indirect—on the Jews.

While we have been able to trace a variety of responses among the rabbis through much of the talmudic period, a more systematic diachronic view is harder to come by. We are hampered, for example, in assessing the differences between the pre- and post-70 periods by the paucity of evidence from the earlier era. The post-70 talmudic period, i.e., the later Roman and Byzantine-Christian eras, is also problematic. Practically all ascribed rabbinic sources date to the former, but the overwhelming majority of rabbinic texts were edited in the latter. Several sources seem to indicate a shift from a relatively universalistic posture in the third century (e.g., the last section of the ʿAlenu prayer) to a much more restricted, nationalistic outlook under Christian rule, as reflected in the piyyutim of Yose ben Yose (fourth or fifth century).[52] A similar de-

---

52. A. Mirsky, *Yosse ben Yosse: Poems* (Jerusalem: Bialik, 1977), pp. 16–17, 92, 94; R. L. Wilken, *The Land Called Holy: Palestine in Christian History and Thought* (New Haven: Yale University Press, 1992), pp. 141–42.

velopment occurred with respect to the legitimacy of gentile sacrifices in the Jerusalem Temple; whereas tannaitic opinion was overwhelmingly favorable, later midrashim take a very different tack and oppose such practice.[53] Despite this accelerated introversion, at least in Byzantine Palestine, influences of the Christian church and of Byzantine society are identifiable in a wide range of areas and will become apparent in the following chapter.[54]

It has long been assumed, especially in nonacademic circles, that the one area of Jewish life unaffected by Greco-Roman culture was that of religion. Such an assertion is both true and false. If one understands religion in its narrow sense of worshiping pagan gods, erecting shrines, and participating in pagan cults, then the statement is undoubtedly correct. If, however, we understand religion as a broad area of cultural life that includes diverse forms of worship, beliefs, practices in both the home and community, artistic expression, literary activity, and more, then the above claim is patently false. In many areas that could be considered religious, most Jews, and the rabbis as well, incorporated patterns of behavior, ideas, values, and other religious models whose origins lay outside the Jewish framework. The metaphor of the shell versus the kernel is often invoked in this regard. The shell refers to social, political, and economic manifestations as being more open to influence; the kernel to Judaism, its beliefs and practices, as remaining largely unadulterated and unaffected. Taken as an absolute distinction, such a bifurcation is inaccurate and misleading. It can only be of value if we are speaking about degrees of influence.

Whether by choice or by necessity, whether through the initiative of the religious elite or the people, and whether done consciously or unconsciously, Jewish religious life evolved its own

---

53. See Knohl, "Acceptance of Sacrifices," pp. 341–45.

54. In this regard, see the brief remarks of A. Funkenstein, "Jewish History among Thorns," *Zion* 60 (1995): 342–43 (Hebrew).

unique forms, blending particularism with elements drawn from the surrounding culture, thus providing a wide range of models throughout the course of antiquity. A very significant element in this dynamic was the ongoing contact and interaction between the Jewish and non-Jewish worlds.

CHAPTER IV

The Ancient Synagogue

ALTHOUGH ITS PRECISE ORIGINS ARE SHROUDED IN MYS-
tery, the ancient synagogue emerged as a distinct institution both
in Palestine and the Diaspora sometime in the Hellenistic period. It
functioned first and foremost as the central communal institution
in each community—the Jewish public building par excellence,
a house of assembly, as both its Hebrew (*bet knesset*) and Greek
(*synagoge*) names signify. By the first century C.E., both literary and
archeological sources indicate that the synagogue had become a
universal Jewish institution, playing a central role in Jewish communal life throughout the Empire, save perhaps in pre-70 Jerusalem, where the Temple and Temple Mount area continued to be
focal.[1]

Archeologically speaking, we know of relatively few synagogue
buildings from the pre-70 period: Gamla, Masada, and Herodium
in Roman Palestine, and Delos in the Diaspora. However, from late
antiquity onward the number rises geometrically (see fig. 19). Over
one hundred synagogues have been found in Palestine alone, and at
least thirteen in the Diaspora, from Dura Europos in the East to
Elche (Spain) in the West.

As the meeting place of the community, the synagogue served a
plethora of functions, from social and political to educational and

---

1. *TDNT* 7, pp. 806–41; L. I. Levine, "The Nature and Origin of the Palestinian Synagogue Reconsidered," *JBL* 115 (1996): 425–48.

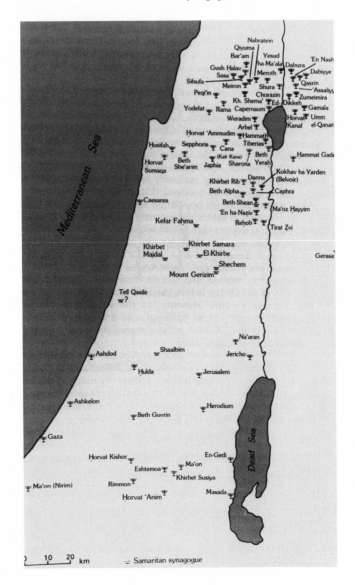

Fig. 19. Map of synagogues in Roman-Byzantine Palestine.

religious. Originally, religious activity was limited to Sabbaths and holidays, when synagogue worship focused almost exclusively on the reading of sacred Scriptures followed by their study and inter- pretation. This form of worship was indeed sui generis; nowhere else in the ancient world do we hear of a congregation reading and studying a holy text on a regular basis. Thus, synagogue worship was unique not only within the Jewish religious context as it had evolved over the previous thousand years (i.e., with no sacrificial component), but also vis-à-vis the pagan world generally.[2]

One of the earliest sources relating to a synagogue, the Theo- dotus inscription from Jerusalem, attests to this unique religious function, and others:

> Theodotus son of Vettenus, priest and *archisynagogos*, son of an *archi- synagogos*, grandson of an *archisynagogos*, built the synagogue for pur- poses of reciting the Law and studying the commandments, and the hostel, chambers, and water installations to provide for the needs of vis- itors from abroad, and whose father, with the elders and Simonides, founded the synagogue.[3]

This synagogue inscription is also significant for what it tells us about the larger cultural context of this particular synagogue. First of all, it is written in Greek, as were about 35 percent of all Jerusa- lem inscriptions from the Second Temple period (see chapter II). About the same percentage of Palestinian synagogue inscrip- tions from late antiquity were likewise in Greek. Outside of Greco- Roman Palestine, however, Greek was all-dominant, with the vast majority of Diaspora synagogue inscriptions being written in that

2. L. I. Levine, "The Second Temple Synagogue: The Formative Years," in *The Synagogue in Late Antiquity*, ed. L. I. Levine (Philadelphia: American Schools of Oriental Research, 1987), pp. 7–31; idem, *The Ancient Synagogue: The First Thousand Years* (New Haven: Yale University Press, forthcoming).

3. For a full discussion of this inscription, see Roth-Gerson, *Greek Inscrip- tions*, pp. 760–86.

language.[4] Moreover, the *synagoge* was a recognized Hellenistic entity; such a framework functioned in the Greco-Roman world, fulfilling social, professional, and religious needs, and was adopted by the Jews for their own purposes. The term *proseuche* (house of prayer), prevalent in non-Jewish Hellenistic and early Roman Diaspora contexts as well, was likewise adopted by the Jews from the pagans, and, over time, came to be associated primarily with the Jewish community.

The titles of synagogue officials in the Theodotus inscription were likewise taken from contemporary non-Jewish society. The archisynagogue (head of a synagogue) and presbyter (elder) are well known from pagan frameworks: clubs, *Landsmannschaften*, and professional (artisans, merchants) guilds. Other terms for synagogue officials that appear regularly in inscriptions, i.e., *archon*, *pater* and *mater*, *phrontistes*, and *grammateus*, are similarly well attested in the larger Greco-Roman context.

ARCHITECTURAL EVIDENCE

Let us explore both the material and religious-liturgical components of the ancient synagogue. As we have noted above, the Jews never possessed an independent architectural tradition, either private or public, and thus they were forced to borrow heavily from the regnant architectural styles of contemporary society. A visit to the Museum of the Diaspora in Tel Aviv provides a striking illustration of this rule in its replicas of synagogue buildings through-

---

4. These figures are based on the following: Rahmani, *Catalogue*, p. 11; Avigad, *Beth Sheʿarim* 3, p. 230; P. W. van der Horst, *Ancient Jewish Epitaphs* (Kampen: Pharos, 1991), pp. 22–23; Roth-Gerson, *Greek Inscriptions*, passim; J. Naveh, *On Stone and Mosaic* (Jerusalem: Israel Exploration Society, 1978), passim (Hebrew).

out the ages, each constructed and decorated in the tradition and style of its particular time and place.

Thus, in late antiquity, Galilean and Golan synagogues generally boasted a monumental facade, with a single or tripartite entrance, decorated lintels and doorposts, friezes, Syrian gables, windows, and arches (see fig. 20). Such elements are well attested for Roman public buildings and temples (similar facades were also used for monumental tombs and triumphal arches) and in a number of Syrian Byzantine churches.[5] It was therefore almost impossible to distinguish a synagogue from a non-Jewish edifice merely by its exterior, a fact not only evident on the basis of archeological remains, but also reflected in a rabbinic tradition that tells of someone passing a pagan temple and, thinking it was a synagogue, bowing before it in deference (*b. Shabbat* 72b). The sages debated whether such a person was guilty of committing an intentional sin (he, in fact, meant to pay respect to the building) or an unintentional one (the person had assumed that it was a synagogue and not a pagan temple). The halakhic aspects of this discussion are not relevant here, but the historical reality behind this pericope is germane. These rabbis imagined a situation where someone walking in the streets of a town or city would not be able to differentiate between a pagan temple and a synagogue merely by the building's exterior. This story confirms what the archeological finds indeed suggest, namely, the striking similarity in the external features of Jewish and non-Jewish religious buildings.

Debate among archeologists regarding the origin of the plans of early synagogues has generally revolved around which non-Jewish model was their source of inspiration. With regard to the Second

5. G. Foerster, "The Art and Architecture of the Synagogue in Its Late Roman Setting," in *The Synagogue in Late Antiquity*, ed. L. I. Levine (Philadelphia: American Schools of Oriental Research, 1987), pp. 139–46; G. Tchalenko, *Villages antiques de la Syrie du Nord* (Paris: Geuthner, 1953–58), 2, pl. xi.

Fig. 20. Above: *facade of the Bar'am basilica-plan synagogue;*
below: *reconstruction of the synagogue with its unusual
entrance portico.*

Temple synagogue at Masada, for example, Yadin has suggested that it followed the plan of Hellenistic meetinghouses (e.g., the *bouleuterion*); alternatively, Foerster has speculated that it followed the plan of the *pronaos* as evidenced in a number of Dura Europos temples. A range of opinions has likewise been advanced regarding the architectural origins of the Galilean synagogue: a Roman basilica (a large rectangular hall divided by two or four rows of columns); Nabatean temple courtyards; Herodian palaces as evidenced in Jericho; or a development of the earlier Masada synagogue. Even according greater weight to Jewish architectural creativity in the shaping of the Galilean synagogue, one must still grant the dominance of Greco-Roman architectural elements in this creation.[6]

The same indebtedness to contemporary models holds true with regard to the plans of basilica-type Byzantine synagogues as well (see fig. 21). Patterned after contemporary Christian churches, many of these synagogues featured a courtyard (atrium), tripartite entrances to a narthex or entrance corridor which led, in turn, into the main hall with a nave, side aisles, and an apse aligned with the building's orientation. The extent of Jewish borrowing from the Christian basilical model is dramatically illustrated by the adoption of the chancel screen into synagogue architecture from a church context. Such a chancel screen was intended in the latter as a parapet built of stone slabs fitted into the grooves of posts, serving to separate the clergy, altar, and presbyterium from the congregation. Unlike in the church setting, however, such a screen had no discernible function in the synagogue, as there was no comparable

6. See the views of Y. Yadin, G. Foerster, N. Avigad, E. Netzer, and Z. Ma'oz in L. I. Levine, ed., *Ancient Synagogues Revealed* (Jerusalem: Israel Exploration Society, 1981), pp. 19–51; Y. Tsafrir, *Eretz Israel from the Destruction of the Second Temple to the Muslim Conquest 2: Archaeology and Art* (Jerusalem: Yad Ben-Zvi, 1984), pp. 165–89 (Hebrew).

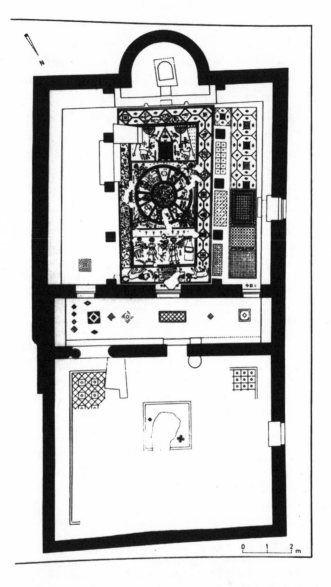

Fig. 21. *Bet Alpha synagogue, closely approximating the plan of a Byzantine church basilica, sixth century.*

Fig. 22. Synagogue parapet (soreg) from Ashkelon with geometric designs and Jewish symbols (menorah, shofar, lulav, and ethrog), seventh century.

division between clergy (i.e., prayer leaders, preachers, or Torah-readers) and congregation there. Thus, the appearance of a chancel screen in a Jewish context is a striking example of the incorporation of a foreign architectural element which, to the best of our knowledge, served no practical purpose. Once borrowed, however, the synagogue chancel screen was often decorated with Jewish symbols, floral and geometric decorations, as well as dedicatory inscriptions in a fashion similar to its Christian counterpart (see fig. 22). Whether the synagogue chancel screen eventually acquired any symbolic meaning of its own is debatable.[7]

7. On parallels with contemporary churches, see idem, "The Byzantine Setting and Its Influence on Ancient Synagogues," in *The Synagogue in Late Antiquity*, ed. L. I. Levine (Philadelphia: American Schools of Oriental Research, 1987), pp. 147–57. See also M. J. Chiat, "Synagogues and Churches in Byzantine Beit She'an," *JJA* 7 (1980): 6–24.

For a suggestion on the significance of the chancel screen in Christian and Jewish contexts, see J. Branham, "Vicarious Sacrality: Temple Space in Ancient

Until now we have been referring to Palestinian synagogues of the late Roman and Byzantine periods, from the third to seventh centuries. The Jewish communities of the Diaspora from late antiquity invariably built their synagogues in consonance with their local contexts and regnant styles. So, for example, the well-established and highly integrated Sardis community constructed its monumental synagogue building on the main street of the city in a structure that had been intended originally as a wing of the local *palaestra* and was later converted into a civic basilica. The synagogue building that had evolved by the fourth century was based on this earlier basilica. Its atrium measured approximately 20 meters in length, and the main hall 60 meters, with an apse at the western end providing seating for synagogue and community leaders. In contrast, the community at Dura Europos located its far more modest synagogue in a private home on the western fringes of the city. This was the case with the nearby church and Mithraeum as well. The pattern of converting private homes into synagogues recurred in a number of other Diaspora communities, such as Delos, Priene, and Stobi. The Dura building provides a striking example of significant contextual influence, since its urban surroundings have been revealed through the extensive excavations carried out in the 1930s. The synagogue, particularly in its second phase, adopted and adapted patterns drawn from nearby pagan shrines. Its hall and courtyard, as well as the series of adjacent rooms, are reminiscent of a number of Duran temples. The synagogue *aedicula* housing the Torah was a close approximation of Duran temple *aediculae*, with the significant distinction being that the former contained a Torah scroll and not the statue of a deity.[8]

Synagogues," in *Ancient Synagogues: Historical Analysis and Archaeological Discovery*, ed. D. Urman and P. Flesher (Leiden: Brill, 1995), 2, pp. 319–45.

8. A. Seager and A. T. Kraabel, "The Synagogue and the Jewish Community," in *Sardis from Prehistoric to Roman Times*, ed. G. M. A. Hanfmann (Cam-

Synagogue Art

In light of the extensive remains from Byzantine Palestine and the Diaspora, information about synagogue art is rich, ranging from instances of slavish imitation of outside models to remarkable originality. In terms of technique (mosaics, frescoes, stone moldings) and types of representations (floral, faunal, geometric, human), the Jewish communities of this era had little in their own tradition from which to draw. Thus, outside influence in these areas was considerable. When it came to specific motifs, however, Jewish creativity was often expressed through a process of selection. Blatantly pagan representations were eschewed, while neutral patterns were more easily assimilated. As a result, geometric and floral patterns, including inhabited scrolls (vines stemming from amphorae and creating a series of circles in which animals and baskets of food are often represented), were ubiquitous, and figural representations of animals, birds, and fish were also quite common.[9]

Two examples of this selection of motifs are particularly instruc-

---

bridge: Harvard University Press, 1983), pp. 168–90; C. Kraeling, *The Excavations at Dura-Europos: The Synagogue* (New Haven: Yale University Press, 1956), pp. 7–33; L. M. White, *Building God's House in the Roman World* (Baltimore: Johns Hopkins University Press, 1990), pp. 60–101; A. Perkins, *The Art of Dura-Europos* (Oxford: Clarendon, 1973), pp. 23–32.

9. Goodneough, *Jewish Symbols*, passim; B. Narkiss, "Pagan, Christian, and Jewish Elements in the Art of Ancient Synagogues," in *The Synagogue in Late Antiquity*, ed. L. I. Levine (Philadelphia: American Schools of Oriental Research, 1987), pp. 183–88; Hachlili, *Jewish Art and Archaeology*, pp. 199–382; A. Ovadiah, "Art of the Ancient Synagogues in Israel," in *Ancient Synagogues: Historical Analysis and Archaeological Discovery* 2, ed. D. Urman and P. Flesher (Leiden: Brill, 1995), pp. 301–18; G. Foerster, "Allegorical and Symbolic Motifs with Christian Significance from Mosaic Pavements of Sixth-Century Palestinian Synagogues," in *Christian Archaeology in the Holy Land: New Discoveries— Essays in Honour of Virgilio F. Corbo, OFM*, ed. G. T. Bottini et al. (Jerusalem: Franciscan Printing Press, 1990), pp. 545–52. See also M. Smith, "The Image of God: Notes on the Hellenization of Judaism, with Especial Reference to Goodenough's Work on Jewish Symbols," *Bulletin of the John Ryland's Library* 40 (1958): 473–512.

tive. The first is the remarkable similarity between the mosaic floors of the synagogues in Gaza and nearby Maʿon (Kibbutz Nirim) and that of the Shellal church (see fig. 23), all three dating to the later Byzantine period. Because these three sites are geographically contiguous and their patterns so similar (almost identical inhabited scrolls), Avi-Yonah once suggested that all three floors might have originated in the same Gazan workshop. Although this suggestion has met with reservation, there is little disagreement as to the remarkable resemblance between these mosaic floors.[10] A second example of parallel motifs is that of the Temple facades appearing in a sixth-century church on Mount Nebo and on the synagogue floor at Susiya in southern Judaea. Foerster has suggested, quite plausibly, that the synagogue artisan borrowed this pattern from the church.[11]

Nevertheless, not all borrowing can be viewed as a judicious selection of neutral motifs. Several instances have had a stunning effect on the scholarly world when first discovered. Such was the case with the mosaics in the House of Leontis at Bet Shean that feature scenes from Homer's *Odyssey*, a depiction of Alexandria, and a

10. M. Avi-Yonah, "Une école de mosaïque à Gaza au sixième siècle," in *Colloque international pour l'étude de la mosaïque classique*, 2: *La mosaïque romaine* (Paris: Picard, 1975), pp. 377–83; idem, "The Mosaic Floor of the Maʿon Synagogue," *EI* 6 (1961): 77–85 (Hebrew); R. Hachlili, "On the Mosaicists of the 'School of Gaza,'" *EI* 19 (1987): 46–58 (Hebrew); idem, *Jewish Art and Archaeology*, pp. 310–16; N. Stone, "Notes on the Shellal Mosaic ('Ein ha-Besor) and the Mosaic Workshops at Gaza," in *Jews, Samaritans and Christians in Byzantine Palestine*, ed. D. Jacoby and Y. Tsafrir (Jerusalem: Yad Ben-Zvi, 1988), pp. 207– 14 (Hebrew); A. Ovadiah, "The Mosaic Workshop of Gaza in Christian Antiquity," in *Ancient Synagogues: Historical Analysis and Archaeological Discovery* 2, ed. D. Urman and P. Flesher (Leiden: Brill, 1995), pp. 367–72. For similarities between Jewish and Christian artistic expression in Rome of late antiquity, with the possibility that both communities used the same workshops, see L. V. Rutgers, *The Jews in Late Ancient Rome: Evidence of Cultural Interaction in the Roman Diaspora* (Leiden: Brill, 1995), pp. 50–99.

11. Foerster, "Allegorical and Symbolic Motifs," pp. 545–52.

Fig. 23. Mosaic floor of the Shellal church, near Gaza, sixth century (?).

Nilotic scene including a semiclad god of the Nile (see fig. 24). To date, it is still an open question whether the Leontis hall was part of a Jewish private home, a communal building complex or—less likely—an actual synagogue hall.[12]

Of far greater importance is the discovery of five clearly attested zodiac representations on mosaic floors from the synagogues of Ḥammat Tiberias, Bet Alpha, Ḥuseifa, Naʿaran, and Sepphoris—to which we might add Susiya and, less likely, Yafia. Moreover, a zodiac list, without figural representations, appears in an inscription on the mosaic floor of the ʿEin Gedi synagogue. While reverberations from the discovery of zodiac designs have been felt in synagogue studies for well over half a century, the precise meaning and significance of this design in this context remains elusive (see fig. 25). The pagan origin of the zodiac motif is well known, and its exclusion from the decorations of the Jerusalem Temple centuries earlier is clearly attested (Josephus, *War* 5.214). Thus, placing such a figural representation in the very center of a synagogue floor is striking; before the discovery of Naʿaran in 1920 and Bet Alpha in 1928–29, the appearance of this motif in such a setting would have seemed unimaginable. To date, this phenomenon has been replicated often enough so as to mute surprise.[13]

12. Ibid., pp. 547–50; Hachlili, *Jewish Art and Archaeology*, p. 301; L. Roussin, "The Beit Leontis Mosaic: An Eschatological Interpretation," *JJA* 8 (1981): 6–19.

13. Goodenough, *Jewish Symbols*, 8, pp. 167–218; R. Hachlili, "The Zodiac in Ancient Jewish Art: Representation and Significance," *BASOR* 228 (1977): 61–77; idem, *Jewish Art and Archaeology*, 301–9; E. Netzer and Z. Weiss, *Zippori* (Jerusalem: Israel Exploration Society, 1994), pp. 56–58. On the above-named synagogues, see the relevant articles in *NEAEHL*, passim. On the representation of the zodiac in the Second Temple, see Josephus, *War* 5.214, 5.217. For other theories regarding the zodiac, see A. Steinberg, *The Zodiac of Tiberias* (Tiberias: Ot, 1972), pp. 11–119 (Hebrew); M. Dothan, *Hammath Tiberias: Early Synagogues and the Hellenistic and Roman Remains* (Jerusalem: Israel Exploration Society, 1983), pp. 43–49; G. Foerster, "Representations of the Zodiac in Ancient Synagogues and Their Iconographic Sources," *EI* 18 (1985): 380–91 (He-

The representation of Helios in the center of the zodiac circle is of especial significance. The most stunning example comes from the Ḥammat Tiberias synagogue of the fourth century C.E., at a time when the symbolic representation of Helios had acquired widespread significance. For almost a century, Roman emperors had been invoking this symbol to represent themselves, and by the fourth century the church had likewise appropriated it, depicting Jesus as a *kosmokrator* in the guise of Helios. What, then, did this Jewish community in Tiberias intend by using this motif? Was it merely for aesthetic reasons? Perhaps Helios, along with the representation of the zodiac and the four seasons, was symbolic of the calendar and its centrality to Judaism? Or did Helios have a distinct religious connotation alluding, for example, to his representation as a superangel as described in the fourth-century magical text *Sepher ha-Razim*? All these suggestions and more, from conservative approaches to radical ones, have been put forth to date.[14]

One major point of dispute among scholars in this respect is how much emphasis ought to be put on the issue of Hellenistic influence and symbolic interpretation. Should one try to fit the Helios motif into the framework of Jewish tradition as expressed in rabbinic sources, or might this symbol indeed reflect a more extensive degree of Hellenization than hitherto imagined? Were the Jews borrowing ideas and concepts, and not merely external forms?

---

brew); idem, "The Zodiac in Ancient Synagogues and Its Place in Jewish Thought and Literature," *EI* 19 (1987): 225–34 (Hebrew).

14. Goodenough, *Jewish Symbols* 8, pp. 214–15; Dothan, *Hammath Tiberias,* pp. 39–43; idem, "The Figure of Sol Invictus in the Mosaic of Hammath-Tiberias," in *All the Land of Naphtali: The Twenty-Fourth Archaeological Convention, October, 1966,* ed. H. Z. Hirschberg (Jerusalem: Israel Exploration Society, 1967), pp. 130–34 (Hebrew); L. I. Levine, "Ancient Synagogues: A Historical Introduction," in *Ancient Synagogues Revealed,* ed. L. I. Levine (Jerusalem: Israel Exploration Society, 1981), p. 9.

Fig. 24. *Mosaic floor donated by Leontis in Bet Shean,*
fifth–sixth centuries. Above: *scenes from Homer's Odyssey;*
center: *Greek dedicatory inscription;* below: *Nilotic scenes.*

Fig. 25. Central panel of Ḥammat Tiberias mosaic floor depicting zodiac signs with Helios in the center, fourth century. The mosaic was damaged by the wall of a later synagogue.

While most artistic representations in the ancient synagogue, from the geometric and floral designs to the figural representations of the zodiac, are clearly borrowed, some noteworthy instances of uniquely Jewish art deserve mention. In most synagogues, either individual Jewish symbols or entire compositions revolving around

Fig. 26. Mosaic panel from the Ḥammat Tiberias synagogue depicting religious symbols: a Torah ark flanked by menorahs, lulavs, ethrogs, shofars, and incense shovels, fourth century.

Jewish motifs can be found. The Galilean-type synagogue is exceptional in this regard; practically no Jewish art appears therein. Elsewhere, for the most part, a small number of Jewish symbols (the Torah ark, menorah, shofar, lulav, and ethrog) constituted the main vehicles of Jewish identification. A number of synagogues feature these Jewish symbols arranged impressively around a representation of a Torah shrine in a mosaic panel located adjacent to the bimah (see fig. 26). Interestingly enough, this cluster of Jewish symbols was not infrequently placed adjacent to a depiction of the zodiac. In a number of places (e.g., Ḥammat Tiberias, ʿEin Gedi, and

Sardis), remains of menorahs, which probably were used in the synagogue, were found.[15]

Of no less significance, although far less frequently displayed than the above-noted symbols, are biblical scenes. Only a handful is known from ancient Palestine: David at Gaza and possibly also at Meroth, Daniel at Na'aran and Susiya, the 'Aqedah (binding of Isaac) scene at Bet Alpha, and a recently discovered 'Aqedah scene at Sepphoris together with a scene of Abraham and the three angels (Genesis 18). Diaspora synagogues, too, are markedly reticent in this regard, having but a few biblical depictions. Gerasa (Jordan) features representations of the Noah story, as does Mopsuestia in Asia Minor, although the latter may well have been a church and not a synagogue. Ḥammam Lif (Naro) in North Africa may contain a scene from the creation story, but this is unclear. The major exception to this generally sparse picture is the stunning synagogue of Dura Europos in Syria, whose four walls were once richly covered with biblical scenes (see fig. 27). This synagogue is so exceptional as to defy explanation. It is obvious that such a small community on the periphery of the Empire could not have created these motifs or the exigetical traditions on which they are based. Yet, to date nothing even beginning to resemble this rich collection of scenes has been found elsewhere. Following the practice in a number of other Dura houses of worship, the Jews decorated their walls with murals intended to inspire the congregation and, as with the nearby church and Mithraeum, instruct it in its *Heilsgeschichte*.[16]

The meeting of Jewish and non-Jewish elements is nowhere more vividly expressed than in synagogue art. The varieties and

15. Hachlili, *Jewish Art and Archaeology*, pp. 234–85. Remains of *menorot* have also been found at three synagogues in southern Judaea: Ma'on, Eshtemoa, and Susiya.

16. Ibid., pp. 287–300; Kraeling, *Dura-Europos*, pp. 54–239.

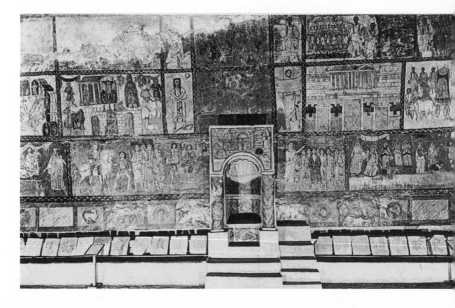

Fig. 27. Three registers of wall paintings on the western wall of the Dura Europos synagogue depicting biblical scenes, third century.

permutations of such motifs are almost as numerous as are the synagogues themselves, reflecting the enormous range of tastes among these communities. Palestinian communities appear to have been more liberal in their use of pagan motifs than their Diaspora counterparts (the zodiac, for instance, never appears in the latter). Yet even within Palestine, conservatism and liberalism with regard to art forms are discernible—between different regions of the country and also side by side in a given urban setting (see below).[17]

17. See my "Diaspora Judaism of Late Antiquity and Its Relationship to Palestine: Evidence from the Ancient Synagogue," in *Studies on the Jewish Diaspora in the Hellenistic and Roman Periods*, ed. B. Isaac and A. Oppenheimer (Tel Aviv: Ramot, 1996), pp. 139–58.

Moreover, rabbinic sources, when examined in light of the archeological data, allow us to view the dramatic changes occurring within Jewish society with regard to art forms influenced by foreign models. Two examples are of particular relevance. The Mishnah (*'Avodah Zarah* 3:1) explicitly forbids the use of certain symbols, including a sphere (representing Earth) and a scepter. Urbach has explained this prohibition as an attempt by the rabbis to distance the Jews from any contact with emperor worship.[18] Yet, just three years after the appearance of Urbach's article, in 1961, the Hammat Tiberias synagogue was discovered, containing mosaics with representations of Helios holding these very symbols! Thus, the Jews who built this particular synagogue about one hundred years after the redaction of the Mishnah either did not know of the rabbinic prohibition or simply ignored it.

A second source, the Jerusalem Talmud, supplemented by a Genizah fragment, describes several rabbinic reactions to the gradual introduction of figural representations into Jewish society: "In the days of R. Yohanan (third century C.E.), they began depicting [figural representations] on walls, and he did not protest; in the days of R. Abun (fourth century C.E.), they began depicting [such figures] on mosaic floors, and he did not protest" (*j. 'Avodah Zarah* 3.3.42d). The introduction of figural representation on mosaics throughout the East followed the above-noted progression; the fourth century witnessed the increasing use of such depictions on mosaic floors of civic and private buildings, a process which had already begun a century or two earlier. The Jews clearly followed suit, and the above sages, while not pleased by such developments, decided that the phenomenon was not of such consequence as to require vigorous opposition. Thus, we have firsthand evidence from

18. Urbach, "Rabbinical Laws of Idolatry," pp. 238–45.

the above sources for the penetration of Hellenistic artistic patterns into Jewish society in general and the synagogue in particular.

SYNAGOGUE LITURGY

There can be little question that Jews of the Diaspora worshiped in the vernacular, although evidence in this regard is largely inferential. We know of some prayers with an apparently Jewish orientation that have been preserved in early church documents, although we cannot be certain that their source was synagogue liturgy.[19] Clear-cut evidence for the use of Greek is preserved in Justinian's famous *Novella* 146 of 553 C.E., wherein it is stated that Jews read the Torah in Greek:

> We decree, therefore, that it shall be permitted to those Hebrews who want it to read the Holy Books in their synagogues and, in general, in any place where there are Hebrews, in the Greek language before those assembled and comprehending, or possibly in our ancestral language (we speak of the Italian language), or simply in all the other languages, changing language and reading according to the different places; and that through this reading the matters read shall become clear to all those assembled and comprehending, and that they shall live and act according to them. We also order that there shall be no license to the commentators they have, who employ the Hebrew language to falsify it at their will, covering their own malignity by the ignorance of the many. Furthermore, those who read in Greek shall use the Septuagint tradition, which is more

19. On possible Diaspora prayers, see J. H. Charlesworth, "Jewish Hymns, Odes, and Prayers (ca. 167 B.C.E.–135 C.E.)," in *Early Judaism and Its Modern Interpreters*, ed. R. A. Kraft and G. W. E. Nickelsburg (Atlanta: Scholars, 1986), pp. 411–36; D. A. Fiensy and D. R. Darnell, "Hellenistic Synagogal Prayers (Second to Third Century A.D.)," in *The Old Testament Pseudepigrapha* 2, ed. J. H. Charlesworth (Garden City, NY: Doubleday, 1985), pp. 671–97; and especially D. A. Fiensy, *Prayers Alleged to Be Jewish: An Examination of the Constitutiones Apostolorum* (Chico: Scholars, 1985).

accurate than all the others, and is preferable to the others particularly in reason of what happened while the translation was made, that although they divided by twos, and though they translated in different places, nevertheless they presented one version.[20]

Rabbinic literature as well has preserved evidence in this regard, although how much refers to the Diaspora rather than to the more Hellenized parts of Roman Palestine is uncertain. The Tosefta (*Megillah* 3:13) specifically addressed itself to a congregation reciting prayers in a language other than Hebrew (probably Greek): "A synagogue of non-Hebrew speakers, if there is someone among them who can read [the Torah] in Hebrew, he should commence and conclude in Hebrew [reading the middle part in Greek]. If only one person is able to read, then only he should read." Moreover, tannaitic material is quite clear in its assertion that the important components of Jewish liturgy can be recited in any language (though perhaps not optimally in rabbinic eyes), referring to Greek, at the very least. The Jerusalem Talmud has preserved a revealing anecdote about two rabbis who entered a synagogue in Caesarea around the turn of the fourth century and found Jews reciting the most basic of prayers—the *Shema'*—in Greek. When one of the sages, astounded by the scene, wished to stop the service, the second replied that it was preferable for the congregation to recite these prayers in Greek than not at all![21] There can be little question that in synagogues such as this one, sermons and the expounding of Scriptures were also conducted in Greek.

In contrast to Greek's successful penetration into synagogue worship in the Diaspora and the Hellenized centers of Palestine, it

20. Translation by A. Linder, in *The Jews in Roman Imperial Legislation* (Detroit: Wayne State University Press, 1987), p. 408.

21. On the recitation of prayers in any language, see *m. Sotah* 7:1 and *t. Sotah* 7:7; the Caesarean story is found in *j. Sotah* 7.1.21b.

does not appear to have played a role in the worship context of either the Galilee or Judaea. This, at least, is the implication to be drawn from rabbinic sources, assuming, of course, that they in large measure reflect the current practice. Everything in these sources seems to indicate that prayer was conducted and some sermons delivered in Hebrew (although the *Sitz im Leben* of the latter may have been the academy and not the synagogue, or these sermons may, in fact, be literary creations). Aramaic was often used in various parts of the liturgy. A number of Aramaic prayers, at least one of which became central to the liturgical context (i.e., the *Kaddish*), were incorporated into the service, and Aramaic piyyutim were being composed in Byzantine Palestine side by side with the more predominant Hebrew compositions. Many midrashim have been preserved in Aramaic, and some of this material may have originally been delivered in one form or another in a synagogue setting. The most significant evidence for the importance of Aramaic in the liturgy, however, are the targumim which were used in most Palestinian synagogues throughout late antiquity. As we have noted above with regard to Second Temple Jerusalem (chapter II), there can be no more eloquent testimony of the linguistic status of Jewish society in both Palestine and Babylonia than the need for such translations of Scripture into Aramaic.[22]

A further area of inquiry relates not to the language of Jewish

22. On Aramaic prayers, piyyutim, and targumic material, see A. Shinan, "Hebrew and Aramaic in Synagogue Literature," in *Tura–Studies in Jewish Thought: Simon Greenberg Jubilee Volume* (Tel Aviv: Hakibbutz Hameuchad, 1989), pp. 224–32 (Hebrew); M. Sokoloff and J. Yahalom, "Aramaic Piyyutim for the Byzantine Period," *JQR* 75 (1985): 309–21.

For a very different—and engaging—view on the function of Aramaic targumim in the synagogue, see S. Fraade, "Rabbinic Views on the Practice of Targum, and Multilingualism in the Jewish Galilee of the Third–Sixth Centuries," in *The Galilee in Late Antiquity*, ed. L. I. Levine (New York: Jewish Theological Seminary, 1992), pp. 253–86.

worship, but to worship itself. How much of Jewish worship in late antiquity flowed directly from Jewish precedents, and how much was a product of outside influences? Influence in this case might mean adopting a worship component in both form and content (an unlikely occurrence), borrowing a form but utilizing traditional material, or being stimulated by outside models to create something new but exhibiting no sign of overt borrowing.

Within the context of Jewish worship, there is a wide range of components, some that appear uniquely Jewish in their form and content, and others which may well have derived from external stimuli. The former is represented by Torah reading and its accompanying study. As noted above, this function was the earliest and the most characteristic form of Jewish worship. While it is true that there are sporadic indications of study and the recital of sacred texts in temples and other religious contexts, such activity usually involved priests only or, at most, a limited coterie of initiates. Nowhere in the ancient world is there evidence that the main communal expression of a religious community focused on this type of study on a regular basis.[23] The church, of course, comes closest to this model, but here it appears to have been clearly influenced by the synagogue.

At the other extreme, i.e., liturgical forms exhibiting some sort of borrowing, is the sacred poem (piyyut), which entered the synagogue's liturgical repertoire sometime in the fourth or fifth century. This was a new dimension in synagogue worship, and those who account for its origins in earlier Jewish liturgical forms are

---

23. A. Momigliano, *On Pagans, Jews, and Christians* (Middletown, CT: Wesleyan University Press, 1987), pp. 89–91. On study and learning within pagan religious contexts, see J. G. Griffiths, "Egypt and the Rise of the Synagogue," *JTS* 38 (1987): 7–14; R. MacMullen, *Paganism in the Roman Empire* (New Haven: Yale University Press, 1981), pp. 10–12.

hard put to delineate and define how and why such forms evolved into the piyyut at this particular time.[24] In the final analysis, the evidence seems to point in but one direction—horizontally—to the influence of contemporary Christian practice.

It was at precisely this time that the church was introducing the sacred poem into its liturgy. The poet Romanus was prominent in this field, and similarities to his liturgical pieces in early Jewish piyyut have been noted.[25] There are several powerful arguments for assuming Jewish adoption and adaptation of such an outside model: this liturgical form appeared in the synagogue context soon after its introduction into the church; the Hebrew terms have exact equivalents in Greek (piyyut deriving from *poema* or *poesis*, and paytan [piyyut composer] from *poetes*); similar stylistic principles appear in both Hebrew and Greek versions; and this new practice was one of many instances of Jewish borrowing of church architectural, artistic, and even epigraphical forms. The fact that most piyyutim are in Hebrew and their themes derive from the Bible and midrash should not be surprising. This creative process of borrowing (as against slavish imitation)—which is characteristic of most cultural transmission—resulted in the creation of a liturgical form. Piyyutim constituted an integral, and at times dominant, part of many prayer services and flourished for well over a millennium.

Between these two polar examples—Torah reading and piyyut—are other elements of Jewish worship. Regular and obligatory com-

---

24. See, for example, Z. M. Rabinowitz, *Halakha and Aggada in the Liturgical Poetry of Yannai* (Tel Aviv: A. Kohut Foundation, 1965), pp. 12–23 (Hebrew); A. Mirsky, *Ha'Piyut: The Development of Post Biblical Poetry in Eretz Israel and the Diaspora* (Jerusalem: Magnes, 1990), pp. 1–76 (Hebrew); E. Fleischer, "Early Hebrew Liturgical Poetry in Its Cultural Setting (Comparative Experiments)," in *Moises Starosta Memorial Lectures—First Series*, ed. J. Geiger (Jerusalem: School of Graduate Studies, Hebrew University, 1993), pp. 63–97 (Hebrew).

25. J. Yahalom, *"Piyyut* as Poetry," in *The Synagogue in Late Antiquity*, ed. L. I. Levine (Philadelphia: American Schools of Oriental Research, 1987), pp. 111–26.

munal prayer, which became a basic component in Jewish worship in later antiquity, is an intriguing—and as yet enigmatic—phenomenon with regard to its Jewish and possibly non-Jewish origins. The phenomenon of prayer, of course, needs little explanation; it has been part and parcel of the human condition since time immemorial. Nevertheless, Jewish communal prayer was negligible in the biblical era, and even by the end of the Second Temple period was quite peripheral to the regular daily ritual of the Jerusalem Temple. Communal prayer first appeared as a basic component in the Hellenistic Diaspora (the term *proseuche*, "house of prayer," was used for the Diaspora synagogue) and entered the Palestinian synagogue worship context (sectarian practice aside) only after 70 C.E. Therefore, questions of why and how such a development took place are quite natural.

In contradistinction to Torah reading and piyyut, which made their appearance either very early or very late in the history of the synagogue in antiquity, regular communal prayer developed in post-70 Roman Palestine in order to fill the vacuum created by the destruction of the Temple. With regard to the first two liturgical components, the issue of outside influence is relatively clear—negative in Torah reading and positive in piyyut. Yet, in the case of prayer the matter remains beclouded. It has usually been assumed that rabbinically prescribed public prayer stemmed from precedents in the Second Temple period. Thus, although scholars have attempted to isolate pre-70 liturgical patterns or clusters of ideas reminiscent of later rabbinic prayer formulations, very few have paid attention to the wider context and its possible role in such a process.

In the Greco-Roman era, organized prayer and the recital of hymns were recognized components of pagan temple worship. Morning prayers were offered in the temple of Dionysius in Theos and those of Aesclepius in Athens and Pergamum. Often such worship settings would include professional singers, choruses, and instrumental music, as well as incense accompanying the recitation of the prayers and hymns.[26] In a short but provocative article, M. Smith suggested that many Jewish prayers praising God with abstract, otherworldly terms and epithets reflect a Hellenistic mode. This type of prayer, he claims, stands in contrast to the earlier Deuteronomic form of prayer, which focused on historical memory. Moreover, several studies on the two basic Jewish prayers—the *Shemaʿ* and the *ʿAmidah*—suggest that they might have been influenced by Hellenistic models. Regarding the *Shemaʿ*, Knohl has noted that the prayer and its accompanying blessings were structured and recited in a fashion similar to Hellenistic royal decrees, with their *acclamatio*, antiphony, and emphasis on observing the king's commands. With respect to the *ʿAmidah*, Bickerman has opined that the source of this prayer was originally a civic prayer for Jerusalem deriving from Ben Sira, and this, in turn, was parallel to and influenced by civic prayers offered daily in Hellenistic cities.[27]

Besides the prayer mode, actual instruction through discourses, sermons, and more general expositions were not unknown in pagan contexts. Such expositions might be of a more popular or theological nature and were found both in pagan temple settings and

26. A. D. Nock, T. S. Skeat, and C. Roberts, "The Gild of Zeus Hypsistos," *HTR* 29 (1936); M. P. Nilsson, "Pagan Divine Service in Late Paganism," *HTR* 38 (1945): 63–69; MacMullen, *Paganism*, pp. 16–17, 149, n. 78.

27. M. Smith, "On the *Yoṣer* and Related Texts," in *The Synagogue in Late Antiquity*, ed. L. I. Levine (Philadelphia: American Schools of Oriental Research, 1987), pp. 87–95; I. Knohl, "'A Parasha Concerned with Accepting the Kingdom of Heaven,'" *Tarbiz* 53 (1983): 11–31 (Hebrew); E. Bickerman, "The Civic Prayer of Jerusalem," *HTR* 55 (1962): 163–85. For an interesting—though somewhat speculative—theory of the influence of Jewish-Christian blessings on a Jewish context, see Y. Liebes, "Mazmiah Qeren Yeshuʿah," *Jerusalem Studies in Jewish Thought* 3 (1983–84): 313–48 (Hebrew). For another suggestion in a similar vein, this time with regard to the Passover seder, see Yuval, "Haggadah," pp. 5–28.

in various religious associations; Jewish worship of the pre-70 era had included this component as well.[28] Whether the sermon in the ancient synagogue owed anything to its pagan counterpart is impossible to assess at present. All substantive literary material regarding Jewish practice is relatively late, while pagan evidence is, at best, meager.

SYNAGOGUE SANCTITY

A salient trait of the synagogue in late antiquity was the sanctity the institution acquired over time. This holy dimension was not inherent in the synagogue from the outset; as noted, it was at first a communal institution in essence. The impetus for the sacred status of the Diaspora synagogue seems to have come in response to its religious, social, and political context. The need for Diaspora Jews to ascribe a degree of sanctity to their local institution would have been important for their own self-identity and self-image, serving as a counterbalance to the ubiquitous pagan temples and other places of worship.

The synagogue's sanctity in the Palestinian setting was a more complex issue. One could easily ascribe its growing sacredness to developments following the Jerusalem Temple's destruction in 70 C.E. As the synagogue began displaying more and more Jewish symbols, particularly those associated with the Temple, a comparable holy status might have followed rather naturally. However, such symbols may well have been the result, and not the cause, of syna-

28. Regarding the pagans, see above, n. 26. On the synagogue setting, see, for example, Luke 4:20–21; Acts 13:15; Philo, *On Moses* 2.215; idem, *Hypothetica* 7.13. See also L. Wills, "The Form of the Sermon in Hellenistic Judaism and Early Christianity," *HTR* 77 (1984): 277–99; C. C. Black II, "The Rhetorical Form of the Hellenistic Jewish and Early Christian Sermon: A Response to Lawrence Wills," *HTR* 81 (1988): 1–18.

gogue sanctity. Moreover, several other internal developments undoubtedly contributed to this sacrality, for example, the permanent presence of Torah scrolls within most synagogues or the gradual institutionalization of communal prayer as an integral part of synagogue worship.[29]

The above factors are undoubtedly necessary components in accounting for the ever-increasing sanctity of the Palestinian synagogue, but they may not be sufficient in and of themselves. Together with these internal factors many pagan and Christian ideologies and worship settings were also moving in the same direction in late antiquity. "Holiness" as a religious category characterizing place, people, and objects was becoming an ever-greater concern in a wide variety of religious circles.[30] The intensive Christian interest in holy places in Palestine, beginning with Constantine's building of churches in Jerusalem, was a phenomenon of which the Jews were undoubtedly aware.[31] Might these developments have in any way influenced the Jews of Palestine and their attitude toward the synagogue? As we have already noted, Byzantine synagogues clearly owed a great deal to their Christian counterparts, both externally and internally. With the dramatic penetration of Christianity into Byzantine Palestine—particularly Judaea—in the fourth century and later, the Jews may well have responded, inter alia, by endowing their central religious institution with an even greater aura of sanctity, thereby counterbalancing the sacred buildings being erected under Christian auspices. The appearance of Jewish symbols in synagogues to a degree hitherto unknown may have served a similar function. It is hard to imagine that the outside

29. See my "Nature and Origin."
30. See, for example, P. Brown, *Society and the Holy in Late Antiquity* (Berkeley: University of California Press, 1982); Wilken, *Land Called Holy*; P. W. L. Walker, *Holy City, Holy Places?* (Oxford: Clarendon, 1990).
31. Wilken, *Land Called Holy*, pp. 82–100.

factors noted above did not play a role—together with internal developments—in creating this sanctity and in transforming the synagogue into a "miniature" Temple (*b. Megillah* 29a).

HELLENIZATION IN ANCIENT SYNAGOGUES

The richness of synagogue data affords us the opportunity to make interesting distinctions regarding the process of Hellenization. In the first place, one is struck by the sheer variety of artistic and architectural forms found within ancient synagogues. Synagogues in the more remote areas of Byzantine Palestine were less affected by outside influences, while urban Jewish communities were generally much more responsive and cosmopolitan than their rural counterparts. Thus, there is less evidence of Hellenization (e.g., the use of Greek or figural representations) in the Upper Galilee as opposed to the Lower Galilee, or in Judaea and the Golan in contrast to Jewish communities in the large Hellenized cities along the coast of Roman Palestine.[32] In the latter, for example, all inscriptions are in Greek, and thus the story of the Caesarea congregation reciting the *Shema'* in that language (see above) is not at all surprising. Similarly, the synagogues discovered in Sepphoris and Tiberias, the two large Jewish urban centers of the Lower Galilee, were clearly Hellenized in a number of significant ways, not the least of which was the use of the zodiac and the appearance of Greek inscriptions.[33]

Nevertheless, even here we must be careful not to overstate our case. Urban Jews were generally more cosmopolitan than those liv-

32. E. M. Meyers, "Galilean Regionalism as a Factor in Historical Reconstruction," *BASOR* 221 (1976): 93–101; idem, "Galilean Regionalism: A Reappraisal," in *Approaches to the Study of Ancient Judaism* 5, ed. W. S. Green (Chico: Scholars, 1985), pp. 115–31.

33. Z. Weiss and E. Netzer, *Promise and Redemption: A Synagogue Mosaic from Sepphoris* (Jerusalem: Israel Museum, 1996). See also Roth-Gerson, *Greek Inscriptions*, pp. 58–75, 105–10.

ing in rural settings, but even within the large cities there were clearly many different types of congregations: those who tended to be more conservative and less inclined to incorporate Hellenistic styles and modes of expression, and others whose constituencies appeared to have been more receptive.

The one locale where such diversity among urban congregations is well attested is Bet Shean. Itself an important Roman city, straddling one of the major trade routes in the Near East, Bet Shean and the surrounding area boasted at least five congregations in late antiquity whose remains have been found: Bet Alpha to the west, Reḥov to the south, Maʿoz Ḥayyim to the east, one synagogue just north of the city wall, and one within the city itself, near its southwestern gate. All five sites were functioning in the sixth century at least, and the range of acculturation, or lack thereof, is striking. Reḥov is extreme in its conservative posture, with no figural representations and with inscriptions in Hebrew and Aramaic only, including the long, and quite exceptional, halakhic inscription (see fig. 28). At the other end of the spectrum is Bet Alpha, with its depictions of the ʿAqedah (binding of Isaac), Helios, zodiac signs, animals, a Greek and Aramaic inscription, and an overall architectural plan clearly borrowed from contemporary church basilical models. Between these two extremes were the other local synagogues, with varying combinations of Jewish and non-Jewish components. Thus, not only within the boundaries of Jewish Palestine as a whole but even in a given urban area, one can find a wide range of possible responses to Hellenization by Jewish communities.[34]

A similar, though not identical, diversity with regard to outside influences exists in the Diaspora. Only with respect to language was

34. Chiat, "Synagogues and Churches," pp. 6–24; F. Hüttenmeister and G. Reeg, *Die antiken Synagogen in Israel* 1 (Wiesbaden: Reichert, 1977), pp. 58–67; G. Fuks, *Scythopolis: A Greek City in Eretz-Israel* (Jerusalem: Yad Ben-Zvi, 1983), pp. 147–59 (Hebrew).

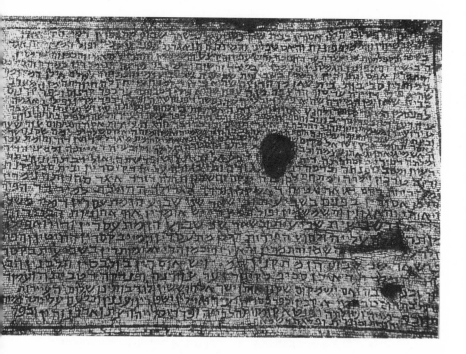

Fig. 28. Twenty-nine line halakhic inscription from the Reḥov synagogue, south of Bet Shean, sixth–seventh centuries.

there unanimity; Greek was predominant, even in the western part of the Empire. Some Latin was used by Jews in the West, and in the East much Aramaic and a little Hebrew. With regard to art and figural representation, differences among Diaspora synagogues are striking. Dura Europos exhibits the most massive use of figural representations, but the synagogues of Sardis, Gerasa, and Naro also have examples, albeit limited, of such art. Particularly striking are the eagle table supports in Sardis flanked by two pairs of lions (see fig. 29), although the enormous mosaic floor of the synagogue hall was entirely aniconic. On the other hand, Diaspora remains from

*Fig. 29. Stone table with an eagle relief from the nave of the Sardis
synagogue, fourth century.*

Stobi, Ostia, Apamaea (Syria), and Aegina had no figural representations whatsoever. The local context was clearly a determining factor in how the Jews decorated their synagogue. A politically secure
and wealthy Jewish community could afford a more imposing type
of building and more elaborate ornamentation executed in a style
consistent with its surroundings. Dura is a classic example of
adopting local styles (a series of registers with wall paintings) to
decorate the synagogue, yet substituting depictions with totally
Jewish (i.e., biblical) content.[35]

35. See the articles on Diaspora synagogues in late antiquity in L. I. Levine,
ed., *Ancient Synagogues Revealed*, pp. 164–90; A. Perkins, *The Art of Dura-
Europos*, pp. 55–65. See also A. T. Kraabel, "The Diaspora Synagogue: Archaeological and Epigraphic Evidence since Sukenik," in *Aufstieg und Niedergang
der römischen Welt* II, 19.1, ed. H. Temporini and W. Haase (Berlin: W. de
Gruyter, 1979), pp. 477–510; as well as my forthcoming *Ancient Synagogue*,
chapter 8; and above, n. 8.

Unique Jewish Components

Until now we have largely focused on the universal dimensions of the ancient synagogue. However, in order to gain a more complete picture of this institution, it is necessary to take note of the synagogue's uniquely Jewish dimensions as well. While most synagogues followed the regnant styles of the time in their architecture, there are some instances of independence and creative adaptation even in this domain. One striking illustration of independence is in the orientation of ancient synagogues, which differed from contemporary religious buildings. Whereas pagan temples and Christian churches almost invariably faced eastward, synagogues located outside of Israel were oriented toward the Holy Land, and those located within Israel faced Jerusalem. This norm, which was undoubtedly based on biblical verses noting that prayers were to be directed toward Jerusalem, was only rarely ignored.[36]

Regarding the creative use of pagan models, we may mention the internal layout of Galilean synagogues. With benches and columns usually on three (in the smaller buildings, only two) sides, the interior focus of attention was directed to the fourth wall facing Jerusalem, thus giving these synagogues a unique internal plan. Roman basilicas had either two or four rows of columns; the use of three rows of columns, with the fourth side of the hall serving as the focus of the worship service, is characteristic of Galilean synagogues, although it can also be seen in several Nabatean temple counterparts and in some Byzantine churches in Syria.[37]

These two categories, independence and creativity, are easily de-

---

36. F. Landsberger, "The Sacred Direction in Synagogue and Church," *HUCA* 28 (1957): 181–203. Striking exceptions to this rule are to be found in Bet Shean (northern synagogue) and Sepphoris.

37. G. Foerster, "The Ancient Synagogues of the Galilee," in *The Galilee in Late Antiquity*, ed. L. I. Levine (New York: Jewish Theological Seminary, 1992), pp. 289–319; idem, "Art and Architecture," pp. 139–46.

tectable with regard to Jewish art. In the former category, Jewish symbols are ubiquitous, individually and collectively, among Jewish communities throughout Byzantine Palestine and the Diaspora. The menorah was especially popular and appears in a wide range of sizes and shapes, including three-dimensional representations.[38] An example of creative use would include a design such as the zodiac which, while adopted from pagan precedents, was given a centrality and importance in many Byzantine synagogues unmatched in contemporary Christian settings.[39]

Another area of Jewish uniqueness finds expression in the functioning of Jewish liturgy within the synagogue setting. Despite the many architectural and artistic similarities between the synagogue and the Byzantine church, there were some very significant differences between the liturgical settings of each. The synagogue offers a very different architectural-liturgical conception from that prevalent in Byzantine Christianity. The focus in the Byzantine church, for example, was almost exclusively on the altar and apse area, the presbyterium, which by the fifth century was augmented by two flanking rooms: the *diaconicon*, which served as a dressing room for officiants as well as a place for votive offerings, and the *prothesis*, where the Eucharist was prepared. The clergy generally remained in the apse area, and it was from there that the Eucharist was offered. Although customs and architecture varied among churches in different regions, generally speaking, the nave—with its *ambo* and *solea*—played a secondary role in church liturgy.[40]

38. Goodenough, *Jewish Symbols* 4, pp. 71–98; A. Negev, "The Chronology of the Seven-Branched Candelabrum," *EI* 8 (1963): 193–210 (Hebrew); Hachlili, *Jewish Art and Archaeology*, pp. 236–56; D. Barag, "The *Menorah* in the Roman and Byzantine Periods: A Messianic Symbol," *Bulletin of the Anglo-Israel Archaeological Society* (1985–86): 44–47.

39. On the zodiac, see above, n. 13.

40. T. F. Mathews, *The Early Churches of Constantinople: Architecture and Liturgy* (University Park: Pennsylvania State University Press, 1971), pp. 105–37.

The contemporary synagogue appears to have been quite different. Synagogue liturgy was not concentrated in any one area, but spread throughout the nave at a number of foci, each featuring a different mode of worship that had evolved over time: the Torah ark was placed against the wall facing Jerusalem, the prayer leader stood on the floor of the nave in front of the ark, and the Torah-reading ceremony appears to have often taken place either on the bimah in the front or in the middle of the hall. The priestly blessing was offered from the front of the hall, but the targum and perhaps sermon were delivered near the place where the Torah was read. The synagogue atrium, or courtyard, was also used for certain ritual-related activities, such as washing hands (and feet?) in a fountain or basin (as in the Temple), greeting mourners, and observing fast-day rituals.[41] Thus, there was a significant degree of architectural and liturgical balance within the synagogue context. The focus might shift from the middle of the building to its front center, and to the Jerusalem wall, depending on which component of Jewish worship was then taking place.

The Byzantine church's seemingly strict division among various populations within the congregation, i.e., clergy, laymen, women, catechumens, and penitents, was unknown in the ancient synagogue.[42] Other than seats of honor for its leaders or specially designated individuals, a relatively status-free ambience seems to have prevailed in the latter.

The same statement is true with regard to the seating of women in the ancient synagogue. In contrast to the contemporary church,

---

41. See my "From Community Center to 'Lesser Sanctuary': The Furnishings and Interior of the Ancient Synagogue," *Cathedra* 60 (1991): 36–84 (Hebrew); Z. Safrai, "*Dukhan, Aron* and *Teva*: How Was the Ancient Synagogue Furnished?" in *Ancient Synagogues in Israel*, ed. R. Hachlili, BAR International Series 499 (Oxford: B.A.R., 1989), pp. 69–84; and my forthcoming *Ancient Synagogue*, chapter 9.

42. Mathews, *Early Churches*, pp. 117–76.

we have every reason to believe that the sexes were not separated here. That women came to the synagogue regularly is well attested,[43] and both archeological and literary sources indicate that men and women sat together. Archeological discoveries have not revealed any traces of a separate area that might even remotely be labeled a women's section; nor has any inscription taking note of a special accommodation for women come to light. In the vast majority of synagogue buildings, only a single room or hall in which the congregation gathered was found, and there was no trace of a balcony. Even when there is evidence for a balcony, such as a staircase or columns of a different size than those on the first story, we have no reason to assume that this balcony served as a women's gallery. Rabbinic sources contain numerous references to nonliturgical activities in the synagogue, some of which are at times associated with a balcony.[44] Finally, rabbinic literature, in the four hundred or so pericopae that relate to the synagogue, never mentions a women's section.[45]

43. Examples of this practice are evident in the following traditions: *t. Megillah* 3:11; *j. Berakhot* 5.9d; *j. Sotah* 1.2.16c, 1.4.16d; *b. Sotah* 22a; *b. 'Avodah Zarah* 38a–b. See also the evidence of John Chrysostom, *Adversus Judaeos* 3.1, 3.2, 7.4. See S. Safrai, "Was There a Women's Section in the Ancient Synagogue?" *Tarbiz* 32 (1964): 329–38 (Hebrew); B. Brooten, *Women Leaders in the Ancient Synagogue* (Chico: Scholars, 1982), pp. 103–38.

44. See, for example, *b. 'Eruvin* 55b, with regard to the *ḥazzan*'s quarters. Other activities might include meals, classes, and court proceedings.

45. One striking example of a woman sitting with men comes from the synagogue in Phocaea in Asia Minor. In response to Tation's generous gift, the synagogue accorded her several honors, one of which was *prohedria*—sitting in the front row of the congregation (P. Trebilco, *Jewish Communities in Asia Minor* [Cambridge: Cambridge University Press, 1971], pp. 110–11). There is no justification for assuming that this refers to the front row of a women's section, or that it refers to some sort of nonliturgical gathering of the community. It is clear from this inscription that, in this community at least, women sitting among men was an accepted practice.

The Byzantine synagogue remained much more congregational in orientation and less "awesome" in appearance than many contemporary churches. The trend of the Byzantine church toward the hierarchical sanctification of basilica space was only partially shared (if at all) by the contemporary synagogue. Moreover, Jewish worship was far more participatory than its Christian counterpart. Whereas a large measure of passivity characterized the latter,[46] the Jewish congregation was either actively engaged (as in prayer) or was the direct object of other activities, e.g., the Torah and haftarah readings, targumim, sermons, and instruction. Very little within the synagogue worship setting required a completely passive mode.

Herein lies another disparity between the church and synagogue of late antiquity. The former aspired not only to be holy (as did the synagogue—see above), but even to acquire a divine status. The church was often considered a *domus dei* and not merely a *domus ecclesiae*. The description of the church building by the eighth-century bishop Germanus is classic:

> The church is heaven on earth, where the God of heaven dwells and moves. It images forth the crucifixion and burial and resurrection of Christ. It is glorified above the tabernacle of the testimony of Moses with its expiatory and holy of holies, prefigured in the patriarchs, founded on the apostles, adorned in hierarchs, perfected in the martyrs.[47]

Hand in hand with this concept of the church as a heavenly, otherworldly edifice is the status of the bishop, who was considered the

---

46. Mathews, *Early Churches*, p. 112.

47. As quoted by R. Taft, "Liturgy of the Great Church: An Initial Synthesis of Structure and Interpretation on the Eve of Iconoclasm," *Dumbarton Oaks Papers* 34–35 (1980–81): 72. On the distinction between *domus dei* and *domus ecclesiae*, cf. V. Turner, *From Temple to Meeting House* (The Hague: Mouton, 1979), pp. 11–12, 304–45.

focus of the community, the representative of God, the mediator, high priest, and earthly father of his flock. No comparable distinctions are known to have existed within the synagogue. No hierarchy governed its proceedings, no set of divinely inspired individuals officiated, whether it be during the Torah and haftarah readings, the targumim, sermons, prayers, piyyutim, or even the priestly blessings; an ordinary Jew had the opportunity to actively participate in almost every aspect of the synagogue ritual. From its often modest size to its sometimes broadhouse dimensions and usually multifocal liturgy, the Byzantine synagogue, in contradistinction to its Christian counterpart, articulated a message of inclusion and involvement. In this sense, the Christian church more closely approximates the hierarchical stratification of the holy that once existed in the Jerusalem Temple. The Jews seemed to have generally shied away from such identification; the Temple was the house of god, the synagogue a communal framework with a modicum of sanctity.

The study of the ancient synagogue thus offers a rich and variegated panorama of the encounter between Judaism and Byzantine Christianity, which was itself a later expression of Hellenistic culture, as defined in chapter I.[48] The large number of archeological remains, together with the rich trove of literary references, afford a nuanced appraisal of the dynamic interaction between these two cultures. It

48. The broader issues of Christianity's impact on Judaism in the Byzantine period have been addressed by J. Neusner on a number of occasions. See, for example, *Judaism and Its Social Metaphors: Israel in the History of Jewish Thought* (Cambridge: Cambridge University Press, 1989), pp. 21–204 (including the early 70–300 period as well); *Judaism in the Matrix of Christianity* (Atlanta: Scholars, 1991), pp. 67–137; *The City of God in Judaism and Other Comparative and Methodological Studies* (Atlanta: Scholars, 1991), pp. 241–78. On Neusner's approach to these issues, see also the comments and reservations of S. Stern, *Jewish Identity*, pp. xxxi–xxxiv.

is hard to imagine another subject offering such a detailed view of this phenomenon, both in the Diaspora and throughout Palestine, in urban as well as in rural areas, and in both the external and internal features of the institution. In some aspects of the ancient synagogue, the Hellenizing component was pervasive; in others it was markedly ancillary. The Jewish component of the synagogue found expression in many ways—architecturally, artistically, and liturgically—but never in quite the same way in each synagogue. If diversity was a hallmark among the synagogues of late antiquity, then to a great extent this was due to the different ways in which each community related to the models and influences stemming from the outside world.

Chapter V

Epilogue

For a millennium, Jews found themselves in the vortex of those ancient cultures that shaped the Greco-Roman and Byzantine worlds. The *oikumene* of that era was indeed multifaceted, though Greek tradition, mediated by the Hellenistic and Roman worlds, remained dominant. The one area in which its influence on the Jewish people can be quantified is in the realm of epigraphy. Some 70 percent of all Jewish inscriptions from this period, including both the Diaspora and Palestine, are in Greek. Even in Rome itself, the Latin-speaking capital of the Empire, almost 80 percent of the six hundred inscriptions found in the local Jewish catacombs are in Greek while only some 20 percent are in Latin (the remaining 1 percent or so is in Aramaic and Hebrew). In Palestine, as we have had occasion to note, the use of Greek was likewise far from inconsequential. About 35 percent of the inscriptions from Second Temple Jerusalem are in Greek, with about the same percentage appearing in the synagogue inscriptions of the Byzantine period. However, when we add to these the funerary inscriptions from Bet She'arim and Jaffa, the two large Jewish necropolises from the late Roman and early Byzantine periods, the overall percentage of Greek inscriptions in Roman-Byzantine Palestine jumps to over 55 percent.

The thrust of our discussion has been to transcend the overly simple question of Hellenism among the Jews—"yes or no?" The type of question that might have been appropriate a generation or two ago should now be regarded as settled: contact between Jews and the outside world was ongoing, often intensive. Jews, like other peoples throughout the East, could in no way remain oblivious to the cultural and social as well as the political and economic forces at work throughout the Empire. Roman material civilization, for example, was a veritable steamroller in the first centuries of the Common Era, shaping urban culture in a myriad of forms. The Jews reacted in various ways, sometimes carefully choosing suitable features to incorporate into their own culture, at other times adopting regnant patterns without much selectivity. In our discussion of rabbinic responses, we have explored the possible routes along which influences from the wider Hellenistic world could have been conveyed to this elite, whose purpose was to maintain and enhance a particularistic way of life. Rabbinic attitudes toward the external trappings of Greek culture varied considerably—as did some rabbis' far-reaching halakhic decisions in the face of real-life situations that called for wisdom and understanding. Their responses involved adaptation and accommodation, at times resulting in rather flexible pronouncements. We have also noted rabbis who consciously responded positively to certain Hellenistic influences, and others who were clearly affected by them, whether consciously or not.

In our discussions of both Jerusalem and the ancient synagogue, the quantity of available data has afforded the opportunity to examine a wide range of phenomena. It became immediately evident that one cannot make a blanket statement about the degree of Hellenization with regard to either of the above topics, but rather each dimension and component must be examined individually. We have noted a number of other factors that influenced the degree of Jewish receptivity to foreign influences, such as regionalism, an urban or nonurban setting, and the particular socioeconomic class involved. As regards Jerusalem, the massive impact of outside material culture on the Jews was one matter; social mores, institutional frameworks, and religious practices were another. Thus, the pace and intensity of outside influence were related in no small measure to which aspect of society was being discussed and which stratum of society was involved.

The chronological factor also proved to be significant in measuring the degree of Hellenization. Often, though not always, the more that Jews were exposed to outside cultures, the greater the impact on Jewish life. Again, turning to the epigraphical evidence, if we compare funerary inscriptions from Second Temple Jerusalem with those from Bet She'arim, Jaffa, or Rome (the latter three from later antiquity), the differences are striking. Whereas, in the first instance 35 percent of the inscriptions were in Greek, in the latter the percentages reach 78 percent, 90 percent, and 78 percent (and including Latin—99 percent), respectively.

Another no less striking example of the penetration of influences over time comes from the realm of artistic representation. When Herod attempted to erect the statue of an eagle over one of the Temple gates, a riot ensued, as such a symbol offended the religious sensibilities of many Jews. Yet, within three hundred years the eagle had become one of the most ubiquitous symbols displayed in the ancient synagogue, appearing on lintels, doorposts, mosaic floors, and building facades! Whatever the reasons for this change, and undoubtedly it resulted from internal as well as external factors, the fact remains that Jewish attitudes in this regard had taken an almost 180-degree turn; what had been considered anathema earlier was now regarded as acceptable, even desirable.

Nevertheless, in each and every case studied, we have taken pains to note the ability of the Jews to absorb and internalize such influences without compromising their unique tradition. Fortified by an ideology that accorded them a special status in the eyes of God (which was, of course, true of other peoples and traditions as well), the Jews were often able to both appreciate and cultivate their inherited tradition while incorporating the ideas, institutions, and patterns of behavior of others as well. The dynamics involved in this interaction were diverse: selectivity, adoption, adaptation, and, at times, outright rejection. Generally speaking, the ability to relate positively to outside influences was in direct correlation to a sense of security and self-confidence. When threatened, the pendulum swung toward self-absorption and self-protection; when secure, the reaction tended to be more responsive. These, however, are broad generalities, and the caveats and distinctions noted throughout our presentation must always be taken into consideration.

Thus, in order to fully understand Jewish society at any given point in history, one must consider both diachronic and synchronic factors, i.e., the forms and practices of Jewish life transmitted from earlier generations as well as the influences and regnant cultural and social mores of the surrounding world. What is patently obvious for the modern world is true of Jewish life in antiquity as well. In some generations, and within certain circles, one component may be more dominant than another, but both vertical and horizontal forces are always at play and must be considered together in order to gain the most complete and comprehensive understanding of the past as possible.

The evolution of Jewish civilization may be compared to a river that widens and increases its capacity as it flows toward the sea. Among the most significant of the tributaries contributing to the river's flow are those influences that the Jews have absorbed from the cultures with which they came into contact. Without such influences, Jewish civilization today would have a radically different appearance. Thus, at any specific stage in its history, Jewish civilization may be viewed as an array of traditions and institutions, many of which had been forged through contact with non-Jewish cultures whose influence had become part and parcel of the Jewish enterprise.

There are those who claim that Jewish life has survived intact and remained vibrant throughout the ages—despite persecution, exile, and discrimination—precisely because the Jews succeeded in maintaining their own particularistic ways, refusing to accommodate any foreign patterns of thinking and behavior. There is certainly some truth in this claim; however, it is only a partial truth, which when taken alone is, in effect, a distortion of the whole. One must also take into account the opposite dimension, namely, that the Jews as a people have survived precisely because of their openness to change—in the light of new conditions and circumstances—in such areas as dress, professions, languages, literary genres, political, social, and cultural institutions, methods of learning, and even religious ideas and practices. Without this ability to change and adapt, Jewish civilization might well have atrophied long ago. The dynamic interplay between cultures—its own and others—is an essential feature of the Jewish historical experience.

Abbreviations

AJS Review	*Association of Jewish Studies Review*
BA	*Biblical Archaeologist*
BAR	*Biblical Archaeology Review*
BASOR	*Bulletin of the American Schools of Oriental Research*
CBQ	*Catholic Biblical Quarterly*
CPJ	*Corpus Papyrorum Judaicarum*, ed. V. Tcherikover, A. Fuks, and M. Stern (3 vols.; Cambridge: Harvard University Press, 1957–64)
EI	*Eretz Israel*
HSCP	*Harvard Studies in Classical Philology*
HTR	*Harvard Theological Review*
HUCA	*Hebrew Union College Annual*
IEJ	*Israel Exploration Journal*
INJ	*Israel Numismatic Journal*
JBL	*Journal of Biblical Literature*
JJA	*Journal of Jewish Art*
JJS	*Journal of Jewish Studies*
JQR	*Jewish Quarterly Review*
JRS	*Journal of Roman Studies*
JSJ	*Journal for the Study of Judaism*
JSQ	*Jewish Studies Quarterly*
JTS	*Journal of Theological Studies*
MGWJ	*Monatsschrift für Geschichte und Wissenschaft des Judentums*

NEAEHL	*New Encyclopedia of Archaeological Excavations in the Holy Land,* ed. E. Stern (4 vols.; Jerusalem: Israel Exploration Society and Carta, 1993)
OR	*Opuscula Romana*
PAAJR	*Proceedings of the American Academy of Jewish Research*
PBSR	*Papers of the British School at Rome*
PEQ	*Palestine Exploration Quarterly*
RB	*Revue Biblique*
RQ	*Revue de Qumran*
SCI	*Scripta Classica Israelitica*
SH	*Scripta Hierosolymitana*
TDNT	*Theological Dictionary of the New Testament,* ed. G. Kittel and G. Friedrich; trans. G. W. Bromiley (10 vols.; Grand Rapids: Eerdmans, 1964–76)
ZDPV	*Zeitschrift des deutschen Palästina-Vereins*

Bibliography

Ackroyd, P. R. *Israel under Babylon and Persia*. Oxford: Oxford University Press, 1970.

Albeck, C. *Commentary to the Mishnah-Moʿed*. 6 vols. Jerusalem: Bialik, 1949 (Hebrew).

Alexander, P. "Quid Athenis et Hierosolymis? Rabbinic Midrash and Hermeneutics in the Graeco-Roman World," in *A Tribute to Geza Vermes: Essays on Jewish and Christian Literature*, ed. P. R. Davies and R. T. White. Sheffield: Sheffield Academic Press, 1990.

Alon, G. *Studies in Jewish History*, 2 vols. Tel Aviv: Hakibbutz Hameuchad, 1958 (Hebrew).

——. *The Jews in Their Land in the Talmudic Age*. 2 vols. Jerusalem: Magnes, 1980–84.

Ariel, D. *Excavations at the City of David 1978–1985*. Qedem 30. Jerusalem: Hebrew University, 1990.

Arndt, W. F., and F. W. Gingrich, eds. *A Greek-English Lexicon of the New Testament and Other Early Christian Literature*. Chicago: University of Chicago Press, 1957.

Attridge, H. W. "Josephus and His Works," in *Jewish Writings of the Second Temple Period*, ed. M. E. Stone. Assen: Van Gorcum, 1984.

Avigad, N. "The Rock-Carved Facades of the Jerusalem Necropolis." *IEJ* 1 (1950–51).

——. *Early Tombs in the Kidron Valley*. Jerusalem: Bialik, 1954 (Hebrew).

——. *Beth Sheʿarim 3*. New Brunswick, NJ: Rutgers University Press, 1976.

——. *Discovering Jerusalem*. Jerusalem: Shikmona, 1980.

Avi-Yonah, M. "The Mosaic Floor of the Maʿon Synagogue." *Eretz Israel* 6 (1961) (Hebrew).

——. *Oriental Art in Roman Palestine*. Rome: University of Rome Press, 1961.

————. "Une école de mosaïque à Gaza au sixième siècle," in *Colloque international pour l'étude de la mosaïque classique* 2: *La mosaïque romaine.* Paris: Picard, 1975.

————. *The Jews of Palestine: A Political History from the Bar Kokhba War to the Arab Conquest.* New York: Schocken, 1976.

Baltzer, D. *Ezechiel und Deuterojesaja: Beruehrungen in der Heilserwartung der beidengrossen Exilspropheten.* Berlin: W. de Gruyter, 1971.

Barag, D. "The *Menorah* in the Roman and Byzantine Periods: A Messianic Symbol." *Bulletin of the Anglo-Israel Archaeological Society* (1985–86).

————. "A Silver Coin of Yohanan the High Priest and the Coinage of Judea in the Fourth Century B.C." *INJ* 9 (1986–87).

————. "A Coin of Bagoas with a Representation of God on a Winged-Wheel." *Qadmoniot* 25, 99–100 (1992) (Hebrew).

Baron, S. *A Social and Religious History of the Jews.* 18 vols. New York: Columbia University Press, 1952–83; first ed., 1937.

————. *History and Jewish Historians: Essays and Addresses.* Philadelphia: Jewish Publication Society, 1964.

Barr, J. "Hebrew, Aramaic and Greek in the Hellenistic Age," in *The Cambridge History of Judaism* 2, ed. W. D. Davies and L. Finkelstein. Cambridge: Cambridge University Press, 1989.

Ben-Dov, M. *In the Shadow of the Temple: The Discovery of Ancient Jerusalem.* Jerusalem: Keter, 1985.

Bengtson, H. *History of Greece: From the Beginnings of the Byzantine Era,* trans. and updated by E. F. Bloedow. Ottawa: University of Ottawa Press, 1988.

Ben-Shalom, I. *The School of Shammai and the Zealots' Struggle against Rome.* Jerusalem: Yad Ben-Zvi, 1993 (Hebrew).

Bichler, R. *"Hellenismus": Geschichte und Problematik eines Epochenbegriffs.* Darmstadt: Wissenschaftliche Buchgesellschaft, 1983.

Bickerman, E. "On the Sanhedrin." *Zion* 3 (1938) (Hebrew).

————. "La chaîne de la tradition pharisienne." *RB* 49 (1952).

————. "The Civic Prayer of Jerusalem." *HTR* 55 (1962).

————. *From Ezra to the Last of the Maccabees.* New York: Schocken, 1962.

————. *Four Strange Books of the Bible.* New York: Schocken, 1967.

————. *The God of the Maccabees.* Leiden: Brill, 1979.

————. *The Jews in the Greek Age.* Cambridge: Harvard University Press, 1988.

Bickerman, E., and M. Smith. *The Ancient History of Western Civilization.* New York: Harper and Row, 1979.

Black, C. C., II. "The Rhetorical Form of the Hellenistic Jewish and Early Christian Sermon: A Response to Lawrence Wills." *HTR* 81 (1988).

Blidstein, G. "The Tannaim and Plastic Art: Problems and Prospects," in *Perspectives in Jewish Learning* 5, ed. B. L. Sherwin. Chicago: Spertus College of Judaica Press, 1973.

———. "Prostration and Mosaics in Talmudic Law." *Bulletin of the Institute of Jewish Studies* 2 (1974).

———. "R. Yohanan, Idolatry and Public Privilege." *JSJ* 5 (1974).

Bokser, B. *The Origins of the Seder: The Passover Rite and Early Rabbinic Judaism*. Berkeley: University of California Press, 1984.

Bowersock, G. W. *Hellenism in Late Antiquity*. Cambridge: Cambridge University Press, 1990.

Branham, J. "Vicarious Sacrality: Temple Space in Ancient Synagogues," in *Ancient Synagogues: Historical Analysis and Archaeological Discovery* 2, ed. D. Urman and P. Flesher. Leiden: Brill, 1995.

Braverman, J. *Jerome's Commentary on Daniel: A Study of Comparative Jewish and Christian Interpretations of the Hebrew Bible*. Washington, D.C.: Catholic Biblical Association, 1978.

Bright, J. *A History of Israel*. Philadelphia: Westminster, 1959.

Brooten, B. *Women Leaders in the Ancient Synagogue*. Chico: Scholars, 1982.

Broshi, M. "The Expansion of Jerusalem in the Reigns of Hezekiah and Manasseh." *IEJ* 24 (1974).

———. "Estimating the Population of Ancient Jerusalem." *BAR* 4/2 (1978).

Brown, P. *The World of Late Antiquity*. London: Harcourt Brace and Jovanovich, 1971.

———. *Society and the Holy in Late Antiquity*. Berkeley: University of California Press, 1982.

Büchler, A. *Das Synedrion in Jerusalem und das Grosse Beth-Din in der Quaderkammer des jerusalemischen Tempels*. Vienna: Israelitisch-Theologische Lehranstalt, 1902.

Byatt, A. "Josephus and Population Numbers in First Century Palestine." *PEQ* 105 (1973).

Cameron, A. *The Later Roman Empire AD 284–430*. Cambridge: Harvard University Press, 1993.

———. *The Mediterranean World in Late Antiquity*. London: Routledge, 1993.

Charlesworth, J. H. "The Origin and Subsequent History of the Authors of the Dead Sea Scrolls: Four Transitional Phases among the Qumran Essenes." *RQ* 10 (1980).

———. "Jewish Hymns, Odes, and Prayers (ca. 167 B.C.E.–135 C.E.)," in *Early Judaism and Its Modern Interpreters*, ed. R. A. Kraft and G. W. E. Nickelsburg. Atlanta: Scholars, 1986.

Chiat, M. J. "Synagogues and Churches in Byzantine Beit She'an." *JJA* 7 (1980).

Clover, F. M., and R. S. Humphreys. "Towards a Definition of Late Antiquity," in *Tradition and Innovation in Late Antiquity*, ed. F. M. Clover and R. S. Humphreys. Madison: University of Wisconsin Press, 1989.

Cohen, B. "Art in Jewish Law." *Judaism* 3 (1954).

———. *Jewish and Roman Law: A Comparative Study*. New York: Jewish Theological Seminary, 1966.

Cohen, G. D. *Studies in the Variety of Rabbinic Cultures*. New York: Jewish Publication Society, 1991.

———. "The Blessing of Assimilation," in *Great Jewish Speeches throughout History*, ed. S. Forman. North Vale, NJ: Jason Aronson, 1994.

Cohen, S. J. D. *Josephus in Galilee and Rome: His Vita and Development as a Historian*. Leiden: Brill, 1979.

———. "Patriarchs and Scholarchs." *PAAJR* 48 (1981).

———. "The Matrilineal Principle in Historical Perspective." *Judaism* 34 (1985).

———. "The Origins of the Matrilineal Principle in Rabbinic Law." *AJS Review* 10 (1985).

———. *From the Maccabees to the Mishnah*. Philadelphia: Westminster, 1987.

Collins, J. J. "Jewish Apocalyptic against Its Hellenistic Environment." *BASOR* 220 (1975).

———. *Between Athens and Jerusalem*. New York: Crossroad, 1983.

Cotton, H. M., and J. Geiger. *Masada 2: The Yigael Yadin Excavations 1963–1965, Final Reports: The Latin and Greek Documents*. Jerusalem: Israel Exploration Society and The Hebrew University, 1989.

Cotton, H. M., E. H. Cockle, and F. G. B. Millar. "The Papyrology of the Roman Near East: A Survey." *JRS* 85 (1995).

Dan, J. *The Ancient Jewish Mysticism*. Tel Aviv: Ministry of Defense, 1989 (Hebrew).

———. "Jewish Gnosticism." *JSQ* 2 (1995).

Daube, D. "Rabbinic Methods and Interpretation and Hellenistic Rhetoric." *HUCA* 22 (1949).

———. "Alexandrian Methods of Interpretation and the Rabbis," in *Festschrift Hans Lewald*. Basel: Helbing & Lichtenhahn, 1953.

———. *The New Testament and Rabbinic Judaism*. London: University of London, Athlone Press, 1956.

Davidson, I. *Otzar Hashira Vehapiyyut*. 4 vols. New York: Jewish Theological Seminary, 1924–33.

Davies, P. R. "Passover and the Dating of the Aqedah." *JJS* 30 (1979).

de Lange, N. *Origen and the Jews: Studies in Jewish-Christian Relations in Third-Century Palestine.* Cambridge: Cambridge University Press, 1976.

Dimant, D. "Use and Interpretation of Mikra in the Apocrypha and Pseudepigrapha," in *Mikra,* ed. M. J. Mulder. Assen: Van Gorcum, 1988.

Dombrowski, B. "היחד in I QS and τὸ κοινόν: An Instance of Early Greek and Jewish Synthesis." *HTR* 59 (1966).

Dothan, M. "The Figure of Sol Invictus in the Mosaic of Hammath-Tiberias," in *All the Land of Naphtali: The Twenty-Fourth Archaeological Convention, October, 1966,* ed. H. Z. Hirschberg. Jerusalem: Israel Exploration Society, 1967 (Hebrew).

―――. *Hammath Tiberias: Early Synagogues and the Hellenistic and Roman Remains.* Jerusalem: Israel Exploration Society, 1983.

Efron, J. *Studies on the Hasmonean Period.* Leiden: Brill, 1987.

Elbogen, I. *Jewish Liturgy: A Comprehensive History.* Philadelphia: Jewish Publication Society, 1993.

Epstein, J. N. *Prolegomena ad Litteras Tannaiticas.* Jerusalem: Magnes, 1957 (Hebrew).

Feldman, L. "Hengel's 'Judaism and Hellenism' in Retrospect." *JBL* 96 (1977).

―――. "How Much Hellenism in Jewish Palestine?" *HUCA* 57 (1987).

―――. *Jew and Gentile in the Ancient World: Attitudes and Interactions from Alexander to Justinian.* Princeton: Princeton University Press, 1993.

Fiensy, D. A. *Prayers Alleged to Be Jewish: An Examination of the Constitutiones Apostolorum.* Chico: Scholars, 1985.

―――. "The Composition of the Jerusalem Church," in *The Book of Acts in Its First Century Setting 4: The Book of Acts in Its Palestinian Setting,* ed. R. Bauckham. Grand Rapids: Eerdmans, 1995.

Fiensy, D. A., and D. R. Darnell. "Hellenistic Synagogal Prayers (Second to Third Century A.D.)," in *The Old Testament Pseudepigrapha* 2, ed. J. H. Charlesworth. Garden City, NY: Doubleday, 1985.

Finkelstein, L. "Maccabean Documents in the Passover Haggadah." *HTR* 30 (1943).

―――, ed. *Sifre on Deuteronomy.* Reprint. New York: Jewish Theological Seminary, 1969.

Fischel, H. "Story and History: Observations on Greco-Roman Rhetoric and Pharisaism." *American Oriental Society, Middle West Branch* (1968).

―――. "Studies in Cynicism and the Ancient Near East: The Transformation of a 'Chria,'" in *Religions in Antiquity: Essays in Memory of Erwin Ramsdell Goodenough,* ed. J. Neusner. Leiden: Brill, 1968.

―――. *Rabbinic Literature and Greco-Roman Philosophy.* Leiden: Brill, 1973.

Fishbane, M. "Use, Authority and Interpretation of Mikra at Qumran," in *Mikra*, ed. M. J. Mulder. Assen: Van Gorcum, 1988.

Fittschen, K., and G. Foerster, eds. *Judaea and the Greco-Roman World in the Time of Herod in the Light of Archaeological Evidence*. Göttingen: Vandenhoeck and Ruprecht, 1996.

Fitzmyer, J. "Languages of Palestine in the First Century A.D." *CBQ* 32 (1970).

———. *The Dead Sea Scrolls: Major Publications and Tools for Study*. Rev. ed. Atlanta: Scholars, 1989.

Fleischer, E. "Early Hebrew Liturgical Poetry in Its Cultural Setting (Comparative Experiments)," in *Moises Starosta Memorial Lectures—First Series*, ed. J. Geiger. Jerusalem: School of Graduate Studies, Hebrew University, 1993 (Hebrew).

Foerster, G. "Art and Architecture in Palestine," in *The Jewish People in the First Century* 2, ed. S. Safrai and M. Stern. Philadelphia: Fortress, 1976.

———. "Representations of the Zodiac in Ancient Synagogues and Their Iconographic Sources." *Eretz Israel* 18 (1985) (Hebrew).

———. "The Art and Architecture of the Synagogue in Its Late Roman Setting," in *The Synagogue in Late Antiquity*, ed. L. I. Levine. Philadelphia: American Schools of Oriental Research, 1987.

———. "The Zodiac in Ancient Synagogues and Its Place in Jewish Thought and Literature." *Eretz Israel* 19 (1987) (Hebrew).

———. "Allegorical and Symbolic Motifs with Christian Significance from Mosaic Pavements of Sixth-Century Palestinian Synagogues," in *Christian Archaeology in the Holy Land: New Discoveries—Essays in Honour of Virgilio F. Corbo, OFM*, ed. G. T. Bottini et al. Jerusalem: Franciscan Printing Press, 1990.

———. "The Ancient Synagogues of the Galilee," in *The Galilee in Late Antiquity*, ed. L. I. Levine. New York: Jewish Theological Seminary, 1992.

Fraade, S. "Rabbinic Views on the Practice of Targum, and Multilingualism in the Jewish Galilee of the Third–Sixth Centuries," in *The Galilee in Late Antiquity*, ed. L. I. Levine. New York: Jewish Theological Seminary, 1992.

———. "Interpretive Authority in the Studying Community at Qumran." *JJS* 54 (1993).

———. "Navigating the Anomalous: Non-Jews at the Intersection of Early Rabbinic Law and Narrative," in *The Other in Jewish Thought and History*, ed. L. Silberstein and R. Cohn. New York: New York University Press, 1994.

Fraenkel, Y. *Darchei Ha-aggadah V'hamidrash*. Givataim: Massada, 1991.

Frézouls, E. "Recherches sur les théatres de l'orient syrien." *Syria* 36 (1959); 38 (1961).

Friedländer, L. *Roman Life and Manners under the Early Empire*. Reprint. 4 vols. New York: Barnes and Noble, 1968.

Friedman, S. "The Case of the Woman with Two Husbands in Talmudic and Ancient Near Eastern Law and Literature." *Israel Law Review* 15 (1980).

Friedman, T. "Parallels: Ancient Greek and Rabbinic Culture," in *Threescore and Ten: Essays in Honor of Rabbi Seymour J. Cohen on the Occasion of His Seventieth Birthday*, ed. A. Karp, L. Jacobs, and C. Z. Dimitrovsky. Hoboken: KTAV, 1991.

Fuks, G. *Scythopolis: A Greek City in Eretz-Israel*. Jerusalem: Yad Ben-Zvi, 1983 (Hebrew).

Funkenstein, A. "Jewish History among Thorns." *Zion* 60 (1995) (Hebrew).

Gafni, I. "Concepts of Periodization and Causality in Talmudic Literature." *Jewish History* 10 (1996).

Geiger, A. *Urschrift und Übersetzungen der Bibel in ihrer Abhängigkeit von der innern Entwicklung des Judenthums*. Breslau: Hainauer, 1857.

Geiger, J. "Herod and Rome: New Aspects," in *The Jews in the Hellenistic-Roman World: Studies in Memory of Menaham Stern*, ed. I. Gafni, A. Oppenheimer, and D. Schwartz. Jerusalem: Z. Shazar Center, 1996 (Hebrew).

Geller, M. "New Sources for the Origin of the Rabbinic Ketubah." *HUCA* 49 (1978).

Goldin, J. *Studies in Midrash and Related Literature*. Philadelphia: Jewish Publication Society, 1988.

Goldschmidt, E. D. *The Passover Haggadah: Its Sources and History*. Jerusalem: Bialik, 1960 (Hebrew).

Goldschmidt, R. P. "Jerusalem in First Temple Times," in *The Jerusalem Cathedra* 2, ed. L. I. Levine. Jerusalem: Yad Ben-Zvi, 1982.

Goldstein, J. *1 Maccabees*. Anchor Bible 41. New York: Doubleday, 1976.

———. "Jewish Acceptance and Rejection of Hellenism," in *Jewish and Christian Self-Definition* 2: *Aspects of Judaism in the Graeco-Roman Period*, ed. E. P. Sanders et al. (Philadelphia: Fortress, 1981).

———. *2 Maccabees*. Anchor Bible 41A. New York: Doubleday, 1984.

Golvin, J. C. *L'Amphithéâtre romain: Essai sur la théorisation de sa forme et de ses fonctions*. 2 vols. Paris: Publications du Centre Pierre, 1988.

Goodblatt, D. *The Monarchic Principle: Studies in Jewish Self-Government in Antiquity*. Tübingen: Mohr, 1994.

Goodenough, E. *Jewish Symbols in the Greco-Roman Period*. 13 vols. New York: Pantheon, 1953–68.

Goodman, M. *The Ruling Class of Judaea: The Origins of the Jewish Revolt against Rome A.D. 66–70*. Cambridge: Cambridge University Press, 1987.

———. "Jewish Attitudes to Greek Culture in the Period of the Second Temple," in *Jewish Education and Learning*, ed. G. Abramson and T. Parfitt. Chur, Switzerland: Harwood Academic Publishers, 1994.

Gordis, R. *Koheleth: The Man and His Word*. New York: Bloch, 1955.

Grabbe, L. L. "Aquila's Translation and Rabbinic Exegesis." *JJS* 33 (1982).

———. *Judaism from Cyrus to Hadrian*. 2 vols. Minneapolis: Fortress, 1992.

———. "Hellenistic Judaism," in *Judaism in Late Antiquity: Part Two, Historical Syntheses*, ed. J. Neusner. Leiden: Brill, 1995.

Greenberg, M. "The Biblical Grounding of Human Value," in *The Samuel Friedland Lectures, 1960–1966*. New York: Jewish Theological Seminary, 1966.

———. "Mankind, Israel and the Nations in the Hebraic Heritage," in *No Man Is Alien*, ed. J. R. Nelson. Leiden: Brill, 1971. Reprinted in M. Greenberg, *Studies in the Bible and Jewish Thought*. Philadelphia: Jewish Publication Society, 1995.

Greenspahn, F., ed. *Essential Papers on Israel and the Ancient Near East*. New York: New York University Press, 1991.

Greer, R. "Alien Citizens: A Marvellous Paradox," in *Civitas: Religious Interpretations of the City*, ed. P. S. Hawkins. Atlanta: Scholars, 1986.

Griffiths, J. G. "Egypt and the Rise of the Synagogue." *JTS* 38 (1987).

Grimal, P., et al. *Hellenism and the Rise of Rome*. London: Weidenfeld and Nicolson, 1968.

Grintz, J. M. "Hebrew as the Spoken and Written Language in the Last Days of the Second Temple." *JBL* 79 (1960).

Gruenwald, I. *Apocalyptic and Merkavah Mysticism*. Leiden: Brill, 1980.

Gundry, R. H. "The Language Milieu of First-Century Palestine: Its Bearing on the Authenticity of the Gospel Tradition." *JBL* 83 (1964).

Hachlili, R. "The Zodiac in Ancient Jewish Art: Representation and Significance." *BASOR* 228 (1977).

———. "On the Mosaicists of the 'School of Gaza.'" *Eretz Israel* 19 (1987) (Hebrew).

———. *Ancient Jewish Art and Archaeology in the Land of Israel*. Leiden: Brill, 1988.

Halevi, E. *The World of Aggadah: The Aggadah in Light of Greek Sources*. Tel Aviv: Dvir, 1972 (Hebrew).

———. *Studies in Aggadah in Light of Greek Sources*. Tel Aviv: Armoni, 1973 (Hebrew).

———. *Historical-Biographical Aggadah in Light of Greek and Latin Sources*. Tel Aviv: Dvir, 1975 (Hebrew).

—————. *Aggadot of Amoraim: Biographical Aggadah of Palestinian and Babylonian Amoraim in Light of Greek and Latin Sources.* Tel Aviv: Dvir, 1976 (Hebrew).

—————. *Values in the Aggadah and Halakha in Light of Greek and Latin Sources.* 4 vols. Tel Aviv: Dvir, 1979 (Hebrew).

—————. *The Gates of Aggadah in Light of Greek and Latin Sources.* Tel Aviv: Dvir, 1982 (Hebrew).

Halperin, D. *The Faces of the Chariot: Early Jewish Responses to Ezekiel's Vision.* Tübingen: Mohr, 1988.

Hanson, R. "Jewish Apocalyptic against Its Near Eastern Environment." *RB* 78 (1971).

Harrison, R. "Hellenization in Syria-Palestine: The Case of Judea in the Third Century BCE." *BA* 57 (1994).

Hengel, M. *Judaism and Hellenism: Studies in Their Encounter in Palestine during the Early Hellenistic Period.* 2 vols. Philadelphia: Fortress, 1974.

—————. *The Son of God: The Origin of Christology and the History of Jewish-Hellenistic Religion.* Philadelphia: Fortress, 1976.

—————. *Jews, Greeks and Barbarians.* Philadelphia: Fortress, 1980.

—————. *The "Hellenization" of Judaea in the First Century after Christ.* London: SCM Press, 1989.

—————. "The Interpretation of Judaism and Hellenism in the Pre-Maccabean Period," in *The Cambridge History of Judaism* 2, ed. W. D. Davies and L. Finkelstein. Cambridge: Cambridge University Press,1989.

—————. *The Johannine Question.* London: SCM Press, 1989.

—————. *The Zealots: Investigations into the Jewish Freedom Movement in the Period from Herod I until 70 A.D.* Edinburgh: T. & T. Clark, 1989.

—————. *The Pre-Christian Paul.* London: SCM Press, 1991.

Herr, M. D. "Hellenism and Judaism in Eretz Israel." *Eshkolot,* new series 2–3 (1977–78) (Hebrew).

Heschel, S. "Abraham Geiger on the Origins of Christianity: The Political Strategies of *Wissenschaft des Judentums* in an Era of Acculturation," in *Jewish Assimilation, Acculturation and Accommodation: Past Traditions, Current Issues and Future Prospects,* ed. M. Mor. Lanham: University Press of America, 1992.

Higger, M. ed. *Masekhet Soferim.* New York: Debe'Rabban, 1937.

Hill, C. C. *Hellenists and Hebrews: Reappraising Division within the Earliest Church.* Minneapolis: Fortress, 1992.

Hirschman, M. "The Greek Fathers and the Aggada on Ecclesiastes: Formats of Exegesis in Late Antiquity." *HUCA* 59 (1988).

—————. *Mikra and Midrash: A Comparison of Rabbinics and Patristics.* Tel Aviv: Hakkibutz Hameuchad, 1992 (Hebrew).

Hoenig, S. *The Great Sanhedrin*. Philadelphia: Dropsie College, 1953.

Horovitz, H. S., and I. A. Rabin, eds. *Mechilta D'Rabbi Ismael*. Jerusalem: Bamberger & Wahrman, 1960 (Hebrew).

Humphrey, J. H. *Roman Circuses: Arenas for Chariot Racing*. London: Batsford, 1986.

Hüttenmeister, F., and G. Reeg. *Die antiken Synagogen in Israel* 1. Wiesbaden: Reichert, 1977.

Idel, M. *Kabbalah: New Perspectives*. New Haven: Yale University Press, 1988.

Isaac, B. "A Donation for Herod's Temple in Jerusalem." *IEJ* 33 (1983).

Jackson, B. S. "On the Problem of Roman Influence on the Halakah and Normative Self-Definition in Judaism," in *Jewish and Christian Self-Definition* 2: *Aspects of Judaism in the Graeco-Roman Period*, ed. E. P. Sanders et al. Philadelphia: Fortress, 1981.

Jeremias, J. "Die Einwohnerzahl Jerusalems zur Zeit Jesu." *ZDPV* 66 (1943).

Jolowicz, H. F. *Historical Introduction to the Study of Roman Law*. Cambridge: Cambridge University Press, 1961.

Jones, A. H. M. *The Greek City*. Oxford: Clarendon, 1940.

Kasher, A. "Herod and Diaspora Jewry," in *Studies on the Jewish Diaspora in the Hellenistic and Roman Periods*, ed. B. Isaac and A. Oppenheimer. Tel Aviv: Ramot, 1996 (Hebrew).

Katzoff, R. "Sperber's Dictionary of Greek and Latin Legal Terms in Rabbinic Literature: A Review-Essay." *JSJ* 20 (1989).

Kimelman, R. "Rabbi Yohanan and Origen on the Song of Songs: A Third Century Disputation." *HTR* 73 (1980).

Kloner, A. "The Necropolis of Jerusalem in the Second Temple Period." Ph.D. diss., Hebrew University of Jerusalem, 1980 (Hebrew).

Knohl, I. "The Acceptance of Sacrifices from Gentiles." *Tarbiz* 48 (1979) (Hebrew).

―――. "'A Parasha Concerned with Accepting the Kingdom of Heaven.'" *Tarbiz* 53 (1983) (Hebrew).

Kohler, K. "Über die Ursprunge und Grundformen der synagogalen Liturgie." *MGWJ* 37 (1893).

Kraabel, A. T. "The Diaspora Synagogue: Archaeological and Epigraphic Evidence since Sukenik," in *Aufstieg und Niedergang der römischen Welt* II, 19.1, ed. H. Temporini and W. Haase. Berlin: W. de Gruyter, 1979.

Kraeling, C. *The Excavations at Dura-Europos: The Synagogue*. New Haven: Yale University Press, 1956.

Krauss, S. *Griechische und Lateinische Lehnwörter im Talmud, Midrasch und Targum*. 2 vols. Berlin: Calvary, 1898–99.

Kugel, J. L., and R. Greer. *Early Biblical Interpretation*. Philadelphia: Westminster, 1986.

Kuhrt, A., and S. Sherwin-White, eds. *Hellenism in the East*. London: Duckworth, 1987.

Laistner, M. L. W. *Christianity and Pagan Culture in the Later Roman Empire*. Ithaca: Cornell University Press, 1951.

Lämmer, M. "Griechische Wettkämpfe in Jerusalem und ihre politischen Hintergrunde." *Kölner Beiträge zur Sportwissenschaft* 2: *Jahrbuch der Deutschen Sporthochschule Köln* (1973).

Landsberger, F. "The Sacred Direction in Synagogue and Church." *HUCA* 28 (1957).

Levine, D. "Public Fasts in Talmudic Tradition: Palestinian and Babylonian Contexts." *Proceedings of the Eleventh World Congress of Jewish Studies*, division C, volume I. Jerusalem: World Union of Jewish Studies, 1994 (Hebrew).

Levine, L. I. "Rabbi Abbahu of Caesarea," in *Christianity, Judaism and Other Greco-Roman Cults: Studies for Morton Smith at Sixty* 4, ed. J. Neusner. Leiden: Brill, 1975.

———. "Ancient Synagogues: A Historical Introduction," in *Ancient Synagogues Revealed*, ed. L. I. Levine. Jerusalem: Israel Exploration Society, 1981.

———. "From the Beginning of Roman Rule to the End of the Second Temple Period," in *The History of Eretz Israel* 4: *The Roman Period from the Conquest to the Ben Kozba War (63 B.C.E.–135 C.E.)*, ed. M. Stern. Jerusalem: Keter, 1984 (Hebrew).

———. "Herod, the King and His Era," in *King Herod and His Era*, ed. M. Naor. Jerusalem: Yad Ben-Zvi, 1985 (Hebrew).

———. "The Second Temple Synagogue: The Formative Years," in *The Synagogue in Late Antiquity*, ed. L. I. Levine. Philadelphia: American Schools of Oriental Research, 1987.

———. "From Community Center to 'Lesser Sanctuary': The Furnishings and Interior of the Ancient Synagogue." *Cathedra* 60 (1991) (Hebrew).

———. "Diaspora Judaism of Late Antiquity and Its Relationship to Palestine: Evidence from the Ancient Synagogue," in *Studies on the Jewish Diaspora in the Hellenistic and Roman Periods*, ed. B. Isaac and A. Oppenheimer. Tel Aviv: Ramot, 1996.

———. "The Nature and Origin of the Palestinian Synagogue Reconsidered." *JBL* 115 (1996).

———. *The Ancient Synagogue: The First Thousand Years*. New Haven: Yale University Press, forthcoming.

————, ed. *Ancient Synagogues Revealed*. Jerusalem: Israel Exploration Society, 1981.

Lieberman, S. *Hayerushalmi Kiphshuto*. Jerusalem: Darom, 1935 (Hebrew).

————. *Greek in Jewish Palestine*. New York: Jewish Theological Seminary, 1942.

————. *Tosefta Ki-Fshutah*. 10 vols. New York: Jewish Theological Seminary, 1955–88.

————. *Hellenism in Jewish Palestine*. 2d ed. New York: Jewish Theological Seminary of America, 1962.

————. "How Much Greek in Jewish Palestine?" in *Biblical and Other Studies*, ed. A. Altmann. Cambridge: Harvard University Press, 1963.

————. *Greek and Hellenism in Jewish Palestine*. 2d ed. Jerusalem: Bialik, 1984 (Hebrew).

Lieberman, S. J. "A Mesopotamian Background for the So-called *Aggadic* 'Measures' of Biblical Hermeneutics." *HUCA* 58 (1987).

Liebes, Y. "Mazmiah Qeren Yeshuʻah." *Jerusalem Studies in Jewish Thought* 3 (1983–84) (Hebrew).

Lifshitz, B. *Donateurs et fondateurs dans les synagogues juives*. Paris: Gabalda, 1967.

————. "Greek and Hellenism among the Jews of Eretz Israel." *Eshkolot* 5 (1967) (Hebrew).

Linder, A. *The Jews in Roman Imperial Legislation*. Detroit: Wayne State University Press, 1987.

MacMullen, R. "Roman Imperial Building in the Provinces." *HSCP* 64 (1959).

————. *Paganism in the Roman Empire*. New Haven: Yale University Press, 1981.

————. "The Epigraphic Habit in the Roman Empire." *American Journal of Philology* 103 (1982).

Mantel, H. *Studies in the History of the Sanhedrin*. Cambridge: Harvard University Press, 1965.

Margalioth, M. *Sepher Ha-Razim: A Newly Recovered Book of Magic from the Talmudic Period*. Jerusalem: American Academy for Jewish Research, 1966 (Hebrew).

Mason, H. J. *Greek Terms for Roman Institutions: A Lexicon and Analysis*. Toronto: Hakkert, 1974.

Mason, S. *Josephus and the New Testament*. Peabody, MA: Hendrickson, 1992.

————. "Greco-Roman, Jewish, and Christian Philosophies," in *Approaches to Ancient Judaism*, new series 4, ed. J. Neusner. Atlanta: Scholars, 1993.

Mathews, T. F. *The Early Churches of Constantinople: Architecture and Liturgy.* University Park: Pennsylvania State University Press, 1971.

Mazar, B. "The Archaeological Excavations near the Temple Mount," in *Jerusalem Revealed: Archaeology in the Holy City, 1968–1974,* ed. Y. Yadin. New Haven: Yale University Press, 1976.

———. "Jerusalem in Biblical Times," in *The Jerusalem Cathedra* 2, ed. L. I. Levine. Jerusalem: Yad Ben-Zvi, 1982.

———. "The Temple Mount," in *Biblical Archaeology Today: Proceedings of the International Congress on Biblical Archaeology, Jerusalem, April 1984.* Jerusalem: Israel Exploration Society and Israel Academy of Sciences and Humanities, 1985.

Mendels, D. "Hellenistic Utopia and the Essenes." *HTR* 72 (1979).

———. *The Rise and Fall of Jewish Nationalism.* New York: Doubleday, 1992.

Mendelson, A. *Secular Education in Philo of Alexandria.* Cincinnati: Hebrew Union College Press, 1982.

Meshorer, Y. *Ancient Jewish Coinage.* 2 vols. Dix Hills, NY: Amphora Books, 1982.

Meyer, M. "Abraham Geiger's Historical Judaism," in *New Perspectives on Abraham Geiger: An HUC-JIR Symposium.* Cincinnati: Hebrew Union College Press, 1975.

Meyers, E. M. *Jewish Ossuaries: Reburial and Rebirth.* Rome: Biblical Institute Press, 1971.

———. "Galilean Regionalism as a Factor in Historical Reconstruction." *BASOR* 221 (1976).

———. "Galilean Regionalism: A Reappraisal," in *Approaches to the Study of Ancient Judaism* 5, ed. W. S. Green. Chico: Scholars, 1985.

———. "The Challenge of Hellenism for Early Judaism and Christianity." *BA* 55 (1992).

Meyers, E. M., and J. Strange. *Archaeology, Rabbis and Early Christianity.* Nashville: Abingdon, 1981.

Millar, F. "The Background to the Maccabean Revolution: Reflections on Martin Hengel's 'Judaism and Hellenism.'" *JJS* 29 (1978).

———. "The Phoenician Cities: A Case-Study of Hellenisation," in *Proceedings of the Cambridge Philological Society* 209 (1983).

———. *The Roman East, 31 BC–AD 337.* Cambridge: Harvard University Press, 1993.

Mirsky, A. *Yosse ben Yosse: Poems.* Jerusalem: Bialik, 1977.

———. *Ha'Piyut: The Development of Post Biblical Poetry in Eretz Israel and the Diaspora.* Jerusalem: Magnes, 1990 (Hebrew).

Momigliano, A. "J. G. Droysen between Greeks and Jews." *History and*

Theory 9 (1970). Reprinted in A. Momigliano, *Essays in Ancient and Modern Historiography*. Oxford: Blackwell, 1977.

———. *Alien Wisdom: The Limits of Hellenization*. Cambridge: Cambridge University Press, 1975.

———. *On Pagans, Jews, and Christians*. Middletown, CT: Wesleyan University Press, 1987.

Murphy-O'Connor, J. "The Essenes and Their History." *RB* 81 (1974).

———. "Demetrius I and the Teacher of Righteousness." *RB* 83 (1976).

Mussies, G. "Greek in Palestine and the Diaspora," in *The Jewish People in the First Century* 2, ed. S. Safrai and M. Stern. Philadelphia: Fortress, 1976.

Narkiss, B. "Pagan, Christian, and Jewish Elements in the Art of Ancient Synagogues," in *The Synagogue in Late Antiquity*, ed. L. I. Levine. Philadelphia: American Schools of Oriental Research, 1987.

Naveh, J. "Dated Coins of Alexander Jannaeus." *IEJ* 18 (1968).

———. *On Stone and Mosaic*. Jerusalem: Israel Exploration Society, 1978 (Hebrew).

Negev, A. "The Chronology of the Seven-Branched Candelabrum." *Eretz Israel* 8 (1963) (Hebrew).

Netzer, E., and Z. Weiss. *Zippori*. Jerusalem: Israel Exploration Society, 1994.

Neusner, J. *Judaism and Its Social Metaphors: Israel in the History of Jewish Thought*. Cambridge: Cambridge University Press, 1989.

———. *The City of God in Judaism and Other Comparative and Methodological Studies*. Atlanta: Scholars, 1991.

———. *Judaism in the Matrix of Christianity*. Atlanta: Scholars, 1991.

Nilsson, M. P. "Pagan Divine Service in Late Paganism." *HTR* 38 (1945).

Nock, A. D. *Essays on Religion and the Ancient World*. 2 vols. Oxford: Clarendon, 1972.

Nock, A. D., T. S. Skeat, and C. Roberts. "The Gild of Zeus Hypsistos." *HTR* 29 (1936).

Novak, D. *The Image of the Non-Jew in Judaism: An Historical and Constructive Study of the Noahide Laws*. Lewiston: Mellen Press, 1983.

Ovadiah, A. "Art of the Ancient Synagogues in Israel," in *Ancient Synagogues: Historical Analysis and Archaeological Discovery* 2, ed. D. Urman and P. Flesher. Leiden: Brill, 1995.

———. "The Mosaic Workshop of Gaza in Christian Antiquity," in *Ancient Synagogues: Historical Analysis and Archaeological Discovery* 2, ed. D. Urman and P. Flesher. Leiden: Brill, 1995.

Perkins, A. *The Art of Dura-Europos*. Oxford: Clarendon, 1973.

Porton, G. G. *Goyim, Gentiles and Israelites in Mishnah and Tosefta*. Atlanta: Scholars, 1988.

Price, J. J. *Jerusalem under Siege: The Collapse of the Jewish State 66–70 C.E.* Leiden: Brill, 1992.

Purvis, J. D. *Jerusalem the Holy City*. 2 vols. Metuchen, NJ: Scarecrow, 1988.

Rabin, C. "Hebrew and Aramaic in the First Century," in *The Jewish People in the First Century* 2, ed. S. Safrai and M. Stern. Philadelphia: Fortress, 1976.

Rabinowitz, Z. M. *Halakha and Aggada in the Liturgical Poetry of Yannai*. Tel Aviv: A. Kohut Foundation, 1965 (Hebrew).

Rahmani, L. Y. "Jason's Tomb." *IEJ* 17 (1967).

———. "Ancient Jerusalem's Funerary Customs and Tombs I–IV." *BA* 44 (1981); 45 (1981); 45 (1982).

———. *A Catalogue of Jewish Ossuaries in the Collections of the State of Israel*. Jerusalem: Israel Antiquities Authority and Israel Academy of Sciences and Humanities, 1994.

———. "Ossuaries and Ossilegium (Bone-Gathering) in the Late Second Temple Period," in *Ancient Jerusalem Revealed*, ed. H. Geva. Jerusalem: Israel Exploration Society, 1994.

Rajak, T. *Josephus: The Historian and His Society*. Philadelphia: Fortress, 1984.

———. "The Hasmoneans and the Uses of Hellenism," in *A Tribute to Geza Vermes: Essays on Jewish and Christian Literature*, ed. P. R. Davies and R. T. White. Sheffield: Sheffield Academic Press, 1990.

———. "The Location of Cultures in Second Temple Palestine: The Evidence of Josephus," in *The Book of Acts in Its First Century Setting* 4: *The Book of Acts in Its Palestinian Setting*, ed. R. Bauckham. Grand Rapids: Eerdmans, 1995.

Rappaport, U. "On the Hellenization of the Hasmoneans." *Tarbiz* 60 (1991) (Hebrew).

———. "Hellenization of the Hasmoneans," in *Jewish Assimilation, Acculturation and Accommodation: Past Traditions, Current Issues and Future Prospects*, ed. M. Mor. Lanham: University Press of America, 1992.

Reinhardt, W. "The Population Size of Jerusalem and the Numerical Growth of the Jerusalem Church," in *The Book of Acts in Its First Century Setting* 4: *The Book of Acts in Its Palestinian Setting*, ed. R. Bauckham. Grand Rapids: Eerdmans, 1995.

Rofé, A. "Jerusalem: The City Chosen by God," in *Jerusalem in the First Temple Period*, ed. D. Amit and R. Gonen. Jerusalem: Yad Ben-Zvi, 1991 (Hebrew).

Rosén, H. B. *Hebrew at the Crossroads of Cultures: From Outgoing Antiquity to the Middle Ages*. Leuven: Peeters, 1995.

Roth-Gerson, L. *The Greek Inscriptions from the Synagogues in Eretz-Israel*. Jerusalem: Yad Ben-Zvi, 1987 (Hebrew).

Roussin, L. "The Beit Leontis Mosaic: An Eschatological Interpretation." *JJA* 8 (1981).

Rozlaar, M. "The Song of Songs in Light of Hellenistic Erotic Poetry." *Eshkolot* 1 (1954) (Hebrew).

Rubenstein, J. L. *The History of Sukkot in the Second Temple and Rabbinic Periods*. Atlanta: Scholars, 1995.

Rubin, N. "Secondary Burials in the Mishnaic and Talmudic Periods: A Proposed Model of the Relationship of Social Structure to Burial Practice," in *Graves and Burial Practices in Israel in the Ancient Period*, ed. I. Singer. Jerusalem: Yad Ben-Zvi, 1994 (Hebrew).

Rutgers, L. V. *The Jews in Late Ancient Rome: Evidence of Cultural Interaction in the Roman Diaspora*. Leiden: Brill, 1995.

Safrai, S. "Was There a Women's Section in the Ancient Synagogue?" *Tarbiz* 32 (1964) (Hebrew).

———. "Religion in Everyday Life," in *The Jewish People in the First Century* 2, ed. S. Safrai and M. Stern. Philadelphia: Fortress, 1976.

———. "The Temple," in *The Jewish People in the First Century* 2, ed. S. Safrai and M. Stern. Philadelphia: Fortress, 1976.

———. *In Times of Temple and Mishnah: Studies in Jewish History*. 2d ed. 2 vols. Jerusalem: Magnes, 1996 (Hebrew).

Safrai, Z. "*Dukhan, Aron* and *Teva*: How Was the Ancient Synagogue Furnished?" in *Ancient Synagogues in Israel*, ed. R. Hachlili. BAR International Series 499. Oxford: B.A.R., 1989.

Sanders, J. T. *Ben Sira and Demotic Wisdom*. Chico: Scholars, 1983.

Sandmel, S. "Parallelomania." *JBL* 81 (1962).

———. "Hellenism and Judaism," in *Great Confrontations in Jewish History*, ed. S. M. Wagner and A. D. Breck. Denver: University of Denver Press, 1977.

Sarna, N. *Understanding Genesis*. New York: Jewish Theological Seminary, 1966.

———. *Exploring Exodus: The Heritage of Biblical Israel*. New York: Schocken, 1986.

Schalit, A. *King Herod*. Jerusalem: Bialik, 1960 (Hebrew).

Schatzman, I. *The Armies of the Hasmoneans and Herod: From Hellenistic to Roman Framework*. Tübingen: Mohr, 1991.

Schiffman, L. *Reclaiming the Dead Sea Scrolls: The History of Judaism, the*

Bibliography

Background of Christianity, the Lost Library of Qumran. Philadelphia: Jewish Publication Society, 1994.

Scholem, G. *Jewish Gnosticism, Merkavah Mysticism, and Talmudic Tradition.* New York: Jewish Theological Seminary, 1960.

Schorsch, I. "Ideology and History," in H. Graetz, *The Structure of Jewish History and Other Essays,* trans. and ed. I. Schorsch. New York: Jewish Theological Seminary, 1975.

Schulz, F. *History of Roman Legal Science.* Oxford: Clarendon Press, 1946.

Schürer, E. *The History of the Jewish People in the Age of Jesus Christ (175 B.C.–A.D. 135).* Rev. ed. 3 vols. Edinburgh: T. & T. Clark, 1973–87.

Schwartz, S. "Language, Power and Identity in Ancient Palestine." *Past and Present* 148 (1995).

Schweid, E. *Judaism and Mysticism According to Gershom Scholem: A Critical Analysis and Programmatic Discussion.* Atlanta: Scholars, 1985.

Seager, A., and A. T. Kraabel. "The Synagogue and the Jewish Community," in *Sardis from Prehistoric to Roman Times,* ed. G. M. A. Hanfmann. Cambridge: Harvard University Press, 1983.

Segal, A. F. *Rebecca's Children: Judaism and Christianity in the Roman World.* Cambridge: Harvard University Press, 1986.

Segal, A. "Theatres in Ancient Palestine during the Roman Byzantine Period (An Historical-Archaeological Survey)." *SCI* 8–9 (1989).

Sevenster, J. N. *Do You Know Greek? How Much Greek Could the First Jewish Christians Have Known?* Leiden: Brill, 1968.

Shaked, S. "Qumran and Iran." *Israel Oriental Studies* 2 (1972).

———. "Iranian Influence on Judaism: First Century B.C.E. to Second Century C.E.," in *Cambridge History of Judaism* 1, ed. W. D. Davies and L. Finkelstein. Cambridge: Cambridge University Press, 1984.

Shanks, H., ed. *Christianity and Rabbinic Judaism: A Parallel History of Their Origins and Early Development.* Washington, D.C.: Biblical Archaeology Society, 1992.

Shinan, A. "Hebrew and Aramaic in Synagogue Literature," in *Tura— Studies in Jewish Thought: Simon Greenberg Jubilee Volume.* Tel Aviv: Hakibbutz Hameuchad, 1989 (Hebrew).

Sjøqvist, E. "Kaisareion." *OR* 1 (1954).

Smith, G. E. *A Guide to the Roman Amphitheatre.* Los Angeles: Westland, 1984.

Smith, M. "Palestinian Judaism in the First Century," in *Israel: Its Role in Civilization,* ed. M. Davis. New York: Jewish Theological Seminary, 1956.

———. "The Image of God: Notes on the Hellenization of Judaism, with

Especial Reference to Goodenough's Work on Jewish Symbols." *Bulletin of the John Ryland's Library* 40 (1958).

———. "Goodenough's 'Jewish Symbols' in Retrospect." *JBL* 86 (1967).

———. *Palestinian Parties and Politics That Shaped the Old Testament.* New York: Columbia University Press, 1971.

———. "On the *Yoṣer* and Related Texts," in *The Synagogue in Late Antiquity*, ed. L. I. Levine. Philadelphia: American Schools of Oriental Research, 1987.

Sokoloff, M., and J. Yahalom. "Aramaic Piyyutim for the Byzantine Period." *JQR* 75 (1985).

Stegemann, H. *Die Entstehung der Qumrangemeinde.* Bonn: Rheinische Friedrich-Wilhelms-Universität, 1971.

Stein, S. "The Influence of Symposia Literature on the Literary Form of the Pesah Haggadah." *JJS* 8 (1957).

Steinberg, A. *The Zodiac of Tiberias.* Tiberias: Ot, 1972 (Hebrew).

Stern, E., ed. *New Encyclopedia of Archaeological Excavations in the Holy Land.* 4 vols. Jerusalem: Carta, 1993.

Stern, M. "The Jewish Diaspora," in *The Jewish People in the First Century* 1, ed. S. Safrai and M. Stern. Philadelphia: Fortress, 1974.

———. *Greek and Latin Authors on Jews and Judaism.* 3 vols. Jerusalem: Israel Academy of Sciences and Humanities, 1974–84.

———. "Social and Political Realignments in Herodian Judaea," in *The Jerusalem Cathedra* 2, ed. L. I. Levine. Jerusalem: Yad Ben-Zvi, 1982.

———. *Studies in Jewish History: The Second Temple Period.* Jerusalem: Yad Ben-Zvi, 1991 (Hebrew).

———. *The Kingdom of Herod.* Tel Aviv: Ministry of Defense, 1992 (Hebrew).

Stern, S. *Jewish Identity in Early Rabbinic Writings.* Leiden: Brill, 1994.

———. "Synagogue Art and Rabbinic Halakhah." *Le'ela* 38 (1994).

———. "Figurative Art and *Halakhah* in the Mishnaic-Talmudic Period." *Zion* 61 (1996) (Hebrew).

Stone, N. "Notes on the Shellal Mosaic ('Ein ha-Besor) and the Mosaic Workshops at Gaza," in *Jews, Samaritans and Christians in Byzantine Palestine*, ed. D. Jacoby and Y. Tsafrir. Jerusalem: Yad Ben-Zvi, 1988 (Hebrew).

Tabory, J. "The Passover Eve Ceremony: An Historical Outline." *Immanuel* 12 (1981).

———. *The Passover Ritual throughout the Generations.* Tel Aviv: Hakibbutz Hameuchad, 1996 (Hebrew).

Taft, R. "Liturgy of the Great Church: An Initial Synthesis of Structure and

Interpretation on the Eve of Iconoclasm." *Dumbarton Oaks Papers* 34–35 (1980–81).

Tchalenko, G. *Villages antiques de la Syrie du Nord.* 3 vols. Paris: Guethner, 1953–58.

Tcherikover, V. *Hellenistic Civilization and the Jews.* Philadelphia: Jewish Publication Society, 1961.

———. "Was Jerusalem a 'Polis'?" *IEJ* 14 (1964).

Tcherikover, V., A. Fuks, and M. Stern. *Corpus Papyrorum Judaicarum.* 3 vols. Cambridge: Harvard University Press, 1957–64.

Tellegen-Couperus, O. *A Short History of Roman Law.* London: Routledge, 1993.

Tov, E. *Textual Criticism of the Hebrew Bible.* Minneapolis: Fortress, 1992.

Towner, W. D. "Hermeneutical Systems of Hillel and the Tannaim: A Fresh Look." *HUCA* 53 (1982).

Trebilco, P. *Jewish Communities in Asia Minor.* Cambridge: Cambridge University Press, 1991.

Treu, K. "Die Bedeutung des Griechischen für die Juden im römischen Reich." *Kairos* 15 (1973).

Tsafrir, Y. *Eretz Israel from the Destruction of the Second Temple to the Muslim Conquest 2: Archaeology and Art.* Jerusalem: Yad Ben-Zvi, 1984 (Hebrew).

———. "The Byzantine Setting and Its Influence on Ancient Synagogues," in *The Synagogue in Late Antiquity,* ed. L. I. Levine. Philadelphia: American Schools of Oriental Research, 1987.

Turner, V. *From Temple to Meeting House.* The Hague: Mouton, 1979.

Urbach, E. E. "The Rabbinical Laws of Idolatry in the Second and Third Centuries in the Light of Archaeological and Historical Facts." *IEJ* 9 (1959).

———. "The Homiletical Interpretations of the Sages and the Expositions of Origen on Canticles, and the Jewish-Christian Disputation." *SH* 22 (1971).

———. *The Sages: Their Concepts and Beliefs.* 2 vols. Jerusalem: Magnes, 1979.

———. "Humanistic Aspects of Jewish Law." *Immanuel* 18 (1984).

———. *The World of the Sages: Collected Studies.* Jerusalem: Magnes, 1988 (Hebrew).

van der Horst, P. W. *Ancient Jewish Epitaphs.* Kampen: Pharos, 1991.

Visotzky, B. *Fathers of the World: Essays in Rabbinic and Patristic Literatures.* Tübingen: Mohr, 1995.

Wacholder, B. Z. *Eupolemus: A Study of Judaeo-Greek Literature*. Cincinnati: Hebrew Union College, Jewish Institute of Religion, 1974.

Waldman, N. M. *The Recent Study of Hebrew: A Survey of the Literature with Selected Bibliography*. Cincinnati: Hebrew Union College Press, 1989.

Walker, P. W. L. *Holy City, Holy Places?* Oxford: Clarendon, 1990.

Walter, N. "The Apocrypha and Pseudepigrapha of the Hellenistic Period," in *Cambridge History of Judaism* 2, ed. W. D. Davies and L. Finkelstein. Cambridge: Cambridge University Press, 1989.

———. "Jewish-Greek Literature of the Greek Period," in *Cambridge History of Judaism* 2, ed. W. D. Davies and L. Finkelstein. Cambridge: Cambridge University Press, 1989.

Ward-Perkins, J. B. "The Caesareum at Cyrene." *PBSR* 26 (1958).

Wasserstein, A. "Rabban Gamaliel and Proclus the Philosopher (Mishna Aboda Zara 3, 4)." *Zion* 45 (1980) (Hebrew).

Weinert, F. D. "A Note on 4Q159 and a New Theory of Essene Origins." *RQ* 9 (1977).

Weinfeld, M. *The Organizational Pattern and the Penal Code of the Qumran Sect*. Fribourg: Éditions Universitaires, 1986.

———. "From Tribe to Kingdom," in *Jerusalem in the First Temple Period*, ed. D. Amit and R. Gonen. Jerusalem: Yad Ben-Zvi, 1991 (Hebrew).

———. *Deuteronomy and the Deuteronomic School*. Reprint. Winona Lake, IN: Eisenbrauns, 1992.

Weiss, I. H., ed. *Sifra d'be rav*. Reprint. New York: Om, 1947 (Hebrew).

Weiss, Z., and E. Netzer. *Promise and Redemption: A Synagogue Mosaic from Sepphoris*. Jerusalem: Israel Museum, 1996.

Weiss Halivni, D. *Midrash, Mishnah, and Gemara: The Jewish Predilection for Justified Law*. Cambridge: Harvard University Press, 1986.

White, L. M. *Building God's House in the Roman World*. Baltimore: Johns Hopkins University Press, 1990.

Wilken, R. L. *John Chrysostom and the Jews*. Berkeley: University of California Press, 1983.

———. *The Land Called Holy: Palestine in Christian History and Thought*. New Haven: Yale University Press, 1992.

Wilkinson, J. "Ancient Jerusalem: Its Water Supply and Population." *PEQ* 106 (1974).

Wills, L. "The Form of the Sermon in Hellenistic Judaism and Early Christianity." *HTR* 77 (1984).

Wilson, R. "The City in the Old Testament," in *Civitas: Religious Interpretations of the City*, ed. P. S. Hawkins. Atlanta: Scholars, 1986.

Winston, D. "Iranian Components in the Bible, Apocrypha and Qumran." *History of Religion* 5 (1966).

Wolfson, H. A. *Philo: Foundations of Religious Philosophy in Judaism, Christianity, and Islam.* 2 vols. Cambridge: Harvard University Press, 1948.

Yahalom, J. "*Piyyut* as Poetry," in *The Synagogue in Late Antiquity*, ed. L. I. Levine. Philadelphia: American Schools of Oriental Research, 1987.

Yuval, I. J. "The Haggadah of Passover and Easter." *Tarbiz* 65 (1995) (Hebrew).

Zakovitch, Y. "Biblical Traditions Regarding the Sanctification of Jerusalem," in *Jerusalem in the First Temple Period*, ed. D. Amit and R. Gonen. Jerusalem: Yad Ben-Zvi, 1991 (Hebrew).

———. *The Song of Songs: Introduction and Commentary.* Tel Aviv: Am Oved, 1992 (Hebrew).

Zlotnick, D., ed. *The Tractate "Mourning."* New Haven: Yale University Press, 1966.

Zucker, H. *Studien zur jüdischen Selbstverwaltung im Altertum.* Berlin: Schocken, 1936.

Zunz, L. *Die Namen der Juden: Eine Geschichtliche Untersuchung.* Leipzig: L. Fort, 1837.

———. *Literaturgeschichte der syngogalen Poesie.* Berlin: Gerschel, 1865.

Source Index

Source Index

NEW TESTAMENT

Matthew	27:46, *81*
Mark	5:41, *81*; 14–15, *89*; 15:43, *84*
Luke	4:20–21, *167*
Acts	2:9–11, *52*; 5, *89*; 6:1, *74*; 6:9, *55*; 7, *89*; 13:15, *167*; 21:37, *78*; 21:40, *75*, *81*; 22:2, *75*, *81*; 22–23, *89*
Hebrews	12, *37*
Revelation	21–22, *37*

MISHNAH

Shevi'it	10:4, *76*
Bikkurim	3:3, *71*
Shabbat	1:4, *105*
Pesaḥim	10:8, *122*
Sheqalim	3:2, *80*
Yoma	3:10, *54*
Megillah	1:8, *127*
Ketubot	4:7–12, *83*; 4:12, *67*, *118*
Nazir	3:6, *54*
Sotah	7:1, *127*, *161*; 7:2, *127*; 9:14, *80*, *125*
Sanhedrin	4:5, *102*
'Avodah Zarah	3:1, *159*; 3:4, *107*
Avot	1:3, *40*; 1:13, *74*; 2:6, *74*; 3:14, *102*
Middot	1:4, *54*; 2:3, *54*; 2:6, *54*; 4:6, *71*
Parah	3:5, *94*
Yadaim	4:6, *80*

TOSEFTA

Shabbat	1:16–22, *105*; 13:2, *82*
Megillah	2:17, *54*; 3:11, *176*; 3:13, *161*
Ketubot	4:9, *113*
Sotah	7:7, *161*
Sanhedrin	2:6, *83*
'Avodah Zarah	2:5–7, *126*

JERUSALEM TALMUD

Berakhot	5.9d, *176*
Peah	1.1.15c, *129*
Shevi'it	8.11.38b–c, *109*
Terumot	5.3.43c, *130*
Shabbat	1.4.3c, *126*; 1.4.3c–d, *105*; 6.1.7d, *127*
Yoma	1.38c, *84*

Source Index

Antiquities	1.121, *29*; 12.138–44, *34*; 13.260, *40*; 13.364, *84*; 14.90–91, *88*; 14.146, *40*; 14.175, *88*; 14.411, *40*; 15.173, *88*; 15.267–79, *55, 58*; 15.273–74, *58*; 15.280, *60*; 15.280–91, *60*; 15.371, *110*; 16.137, *59*; 16.357, *88*; 17.46, *88*; 17.93, *88*; 17.193–94, *59*; 20.11, *84*; 20.49–55, *54*; 20.194, *84*; 20.200, *88*; 20.216, *88–89*; 20.216–18, *88–89*; 20.263–64, *78–79*
Life	12, *110*; 12.64, *84*
Against Apion	1.180–81, *xi*

JUSTINIAN

Novella	146, *160–161*

MARCELLUS

De Medicamentis	*129*

PAUSANIAS

Description of Greece	7.16.4–5, *62–63*

PHILO

Embassy	281–82, *52*
Hypothetica	7.13, *167*
On Moses	2.215, *167*; 2.216, *30*

TACITUS

Histories	5.5.4, *44*

Subject Index

A

R. Abbahu: and figural art in synagogue, 130–31; Greek education, 128, 129; Hellenistic proclivities, 129–31

Absalom's tomb, 62, 63, 64

R. Abun: and figural art, 159

Ackroyd, P. R., 100

Additions to Book of Esther: contact between Alexandria and Hasmonean Judaea, 118; highlights differences between Jews and Greeks, 45; Greek linguistic and stylistic techniques, 45; translated by Lysimachus in Jerusalem, 79–80

Adoraim, 25

Aegina: synagogue art, 172

afikoman: at symposium and seder, 122–23

Agrippa II: and *sanhedrin*, 88, 89

R. Aha, 130

Albeck, C., 123

'*Alenu* prayer, 136

Alexander, P., 12–13, 134, 135

Alexander Jannaeus, 41, 116; Aramaic on coins, 82; Greek on coins, 42–43; persecution of Pharisees, 118

Alexander the Great: conquest of Palestine, xi, 6, 28, 96; death of, 11; assimilation of Persian customs, 19

Alexandria, 10, 17, 19, 21, 79–80; burial practices from, 41; Jewish community, 25, 78; Hellenistic rhetorical circles, 113; Hellenization of, 25; and Hillel, 113; Pharisees in, 118–19; ties with Hasmonean Judaea, 118

Alon, G., 18, 120; critique of S. Lieberman, 14

R. Ami, 130

'*Amidah*: civic prayer for Jerusalem, 166; Hellenistic model, 166; language of prayer, 127

Ananus (high priest): and *sanhedrin*, 88

Antigonus, 41

Antigonus of Socho, 40

Antioch, 10, 17, 19

Antiochus III: edict on behalf of Jews, 34

Antiochus IV: persecutions, 6–7, 11–12, 39, 44

Antonia (fortress), 47, 73, 91

Apamaea: synagogue art, 172

apocalyptic literature: Hellenistic influences, 110–11

apocryphal-pseudepigraphal literature, 26, 182; in Aramaic, 82; written in Jerusalem, 75

R. 'Aqiva, 135

Aquilas: Greek translation of Bible, 80; and Yavnean sages, 126–27

Aramaic, 10–11, 171; in catacomb inscriptions in Rome, 73–74, 180; on

Q

R